Nonprofit Accounting

for

Volunteers, Treasurers, and Bookkeepers

Lisa London, CPA

Deep River Press, Inc.
Sanford, North Carolina

Nonprofit Accounting for Volunteers, Treasurers, and Bookkeepers

ISBN 978-1-945561-15-3

Library of Congress Control Number: 2020907692

Published by Deep River Press, Inc. May 2020

Graphics by Rachel Stahl

Edited by Anatasia Christilles

Books by Lisa London

The Accountant Beside You series

BANISH Your Bookkeeping Nightmares

Using QuickBooks® for Nonprofit Organizations, Associations, & Clubs

QuickBooks® for Churches and Other Religious Organizations

QuickBooks® para Iglesias y Otras Organizaciones Religiosas

Church Accounting—The How-To Guide for Small & Growing Churches

Contents

1. Proper Procedures & Internal Accounting Controls 1
   - A. The Need for Strong Internal Controls 2
   - B. Governing Body's Responsibility 3
   - C. Separation of Duties 4
   - D. Basic Controls for Receiving Cash & Donations 5
   - E. Cash Out And Controls for Paying Bills 11
   - F. Summary 18
2. What is Special About Nonprofit Accounting? 19
   - A. Nonprofit Accounting Terminology 20
   - B. Accounting 101 23
   - C. Cash vs. Accrual Accounting Methods 24
   - D. Chart of Accounts 25
   - E. Basic Bookkeeping 27
   - F. Nonprofit Reporting Differences 28
   - G. Summary 32
3. How Do I Select an Accounting System? 33
   - A. Time Vs. Money 33
   - B. Spreadsheets 34
   - C. Off-The-Shelf Accounting Software 36
   - D. Online Nonprofit-Specific Accounting Packages 36
   - E. Summary 37
4. Administrative Issues 39
   - A. Basic Steps to Start a New Nonprofit Organization 39
   - B. Organization Bylaws 40
   - C. Record Retention 42
   - D. Summary 44
5. Donations, Part I: Receiving and Recording 45
   - A. Internal Controls and Written Policies 45
   - B. Counting Money Received In Person 46
   - C. Making the Deposits 47
   - D. Recording Donors' Contributions 48
   - E. Recording Credit Card Donations 49
   - F. Summary 51

6. Donations, Part II: Acknowledgement 52
A. Cash Contributions 52
B. Stock Donations 55
C. Noncash Contributions 56
D. Donated Labor/Services 60
E. Impact of the TCJA (2017 Tax Law) 61
F. Quid Pro Quo Donations 62
G. Gifts of Autos, Boats, and Airplanes 65
H. When You Do Not Need Disclosure Statements 69
I. Summary 72
7. Donations, Part 3: Other Topics 73
A. Gifts to Specific Individuals 73
B. Discounts As Donations 75
C. Checks Written to Another Charity 75
D. Summary 76
8. Rules For Helping Local Families And Individuals 77
A. Requirements 78
B. Types of Benevolence Funds 79
C. Disbursement Procedures 81
D. Written Benevolence Policy Example 82
E. Summary 82
9. Paying the Bills 84
A. Terminology 84
B. Approving & Paying the Bills 85
C. Scams 85
D. Insurance & Contracts 87
E. Entering Data 88
F. Allocation of Expenses 89
G. Bills Drafted Out of the Bank Account 90
H. Credit Card Payments 90
I. Petty Cash Replenishment 91
J. Summary 92
10. Reimbursement Policies and Procedures 93
A. Setting Up a Reimbursement Policy 94
B. Example of a Reimbursement Policy Resolution 94
C. Employee Business Expenses To Include 94
D. Examples of Proper Reimbursement Items 95
E. Examples of Improper Reimbursement Items 96
F. Standard Mileage Rates 97

G. Reimbursing the Expense 98
H. Volunteer Mileage 100
I. Timing 101
J. Advance Payments 101
K. Ticketless Airline Expenses 102
L. Ramifications of Not Following the Policy 102
M. Inability To Reimburse a Valid Expense 103
N. Summary 103

11. Payroll, Part I: Basic Steps 104
A. Terminology 104
B. Forms & Publications 106
C. Setting Up the Payroll 107
D. Wages Vs. Salaries 112
E. Determining the Pay Period 112
F. Employee Forms 112
G. Establish Your Payroll Records 115
H. Summary 116

12. Payroll, Part II: Calculating & Filing 117
A. Wage Bracket Method 118
B. Percentage Method 120
C. State Tax Withholding 123
D. FICA—Social Security & Medicare Taxes 123
E. The Employee's Payroll Check 124
F. Posting the Payroll Expense 125
G. Other Taxes 126
H. Payroll Tax Deposits 127
I. Payroll Tax Filings With Form 941 128
J. Year-End Filings 133
K. Ordering IRS Forms 136
L. Summary 137

13. Budgeting For Nonprofit Organizations 138
A. The Budget Process 138
B. Example Budget Spreadsheet 141
C. Monthly Budgeting 142
D. Forecasts 144
E. Cash Flow Analysis 147
F. Summary 148

14. Month-End Financial Requirements....149
A. Monthly Processes For Complete Financials....149
B. Bank Reconciliation....150
C. Investment Account Reconciliations....153
D. Generate Reports....153
E. Summary....157
15. Year-End....158
A. Forms W-2 (Wages) and W-3 (Taxes)....158
B. Form 944 (Employer's Annual Federal Tax Return)....158
C. Form 1099 (Independent Contractors)....159
D. Form 1096 (Transmittal of U.S. Information Returns). 161
E. Year-End Donor Acknowledgements....162
F. State Filings....163
G. Other IRS Requirements....163
H. Audit Needs....163
I. Summary....166
16. Unrelated Business Income Taxes (UBIT)....167
A. What is Unrelated Business Income?....167
B. "Trade or Business"....168
C. "Regularly Conducted"....169
D. "Not Substantially Related" To The Mission....170
E. Excluded Trade/Business Activities....172
F. Examples....175
G. Miscellaneous Excluded Revenues....178
H. 990-T (Exempt Organization Business Income Tax)....179
I. Summary....187
17. Form 990 (Annual Filings for Exempt Organizations)...... 188
A. Types of 990s....188
B. IRS Summary of Forms to File....190
C. Completing Form 990-N (e-Postcard)....191
D. Completing Form 990-EZ (Short Form Return)....198
E. Schedule A (Public Charity Status & Public Support)...212
F. Schedule B (Schedule of Contributors)....219
G. Summary....223
18. Appendix....224
A. Month-End Check List....2245
B. Simplified UCOA (Unified Chart of Accounts)....2246

Introduction

Have you suddenly found yourself thrown into being treasurer or bookkeeper of a small nonprofit or club? You know it is a crucial job for an organization, but you may feel unsure or even unqualified to be in the role.

Don't worry. I'm Lisa London, a CPA with decades of experience helping organizations, nonprofits, and businesses of various sizes with their accounting systems, and I'm here to guide you through this important, but often frustrating, process.

Together, we'll go through the processes, procedures, and steps for your organization to have an efficient and effective accounting system. I will explain it in a way you will not need an accounting degree to understand. You will also learn how to handle different types of contributions (including designated funds or grants), how to establish controls so the money is safe and employees and volunteers can stay above suspicion if something does go wrong. You will also learn how to read the financial statements to help the staff and the board work towards their mission.

I know this is a lot to cover, but remember, I'm here to help just like I am **The Accountant Beside You**.

Lisa London, CPA

1. Proper Procedures & Internal Accounting Controls

Nonprofits receive special privileges in the tax law. With any privilege comes responsibility. An organization must be extra careful with the accounting and internal controls or risk losing their tax-exempt status. The process often seems difficult for small organizations that rely on volunteer labor or overworked directors.

Directors and volunteers are typically good, caring people with strong interpersonal skills. These skills do not necessarily translate to understanding accounting rules, tax laws, and internal accounting controls. The lack of understanding can lead to the loss of donors' tax benefits, monetary penalties for the organization, or even prison time.

In 2010, pastors in Charlotte, NC were sentenced to prison for conspiracy and tax evasion.

The organization did not have adequate documentation for expenses, no internal controls over contributions were established, bank deposits frequently did not match count sheets, and board minutes were missing.

The pastors were informed as early as 2001 that their systems were out of compliance but were worried about the energy it would take to "get it right."

Forbes magazine ran an article about the case entitled: "Tax Fraud—If You Are Not Going to Listen to Advice, Better You Don't Ask."

In the previous example, the organization had to file for bankruptcy to avoid a foreclosure sale as the succeeding pastor and the congregation struggled to keep the organization alive. As with any case, there is more to the story than can be summarized here. The lesson to be learned is:

Strong, appropriate accounting processes and controls are required for any organization, including nonprofits.

In this chapter, we will discuss:

- The need for strong internal controls.
- The governing body's responsibilities.
- How to deal with the separation of duties with a small staff.
- Detailed procedures for handling the money coming in and leaving the organization.

A. The Need for Strong Internal Controls

During my experience as an auditor, I saw firsthand what a difference robust internal controls could make to an organization.

Many people assume that if someone works for a nonprofit, that person would never steal. Unfortunately, this is not the case—just do an Internet search on "stealing money from a nonprofit." Over 12 million results should refute that notion. People are human, and money does get stolen, even by the volunteers. Setting up proper controls will help stem that possibility.

"But we are too small to have controls!" If I had a dollar for every time I heard that, I'd be living on the beach in the Caribbean. Yes, the smaller the organization, the harder it is to have separate people in the required positions to maintain strong controls. Don't worry; this book will highlight control options for an organization of any size. Additionally, *you* know that *you* wouldn't steal from the organization, but having controls in place provides reassurance that no one else will either.

People often think internal controls are there to keep employees from stealing. Internal controls are not only in place to protect against fraud but also to prevent errors from occurring and to make it easier to catch when they do.

> *A good bookkeeper will require strong internal controls to keep themselves above suspicion if something goes wrong.*

The most basic start for establishing internal controls begins at the governing body level (whether a board or advisory council). A solid governing body with transparency, stewardship, and accountability sets the tone and is the first defense against fraud.

B. Governing Body's Responsibility

The governing body (such as a board) has a crucial role to play in setting the tone for financial management. The board members serve as counsel for the director and offer direction for the organization's mission and goals. The members of the board are also responsible for the assets of the organization.

Here is a list of the MINIMUM standards the board should require:

- **Financial statements** should be reviewed by the board on a regular basis (monthly or quarterly).
- **Annual budgets** should be prepared, and variances reported.
- The **designated treasurer** should NOT be the bookkeeper.
- Any **notices from the IRS** should be handed unopened to someone who is not the bookkeeper.*
- **A conflict of interest policy** should be established to limit the level of related party transactions. The policy will determine steps to ensure an appropriate price is paid for services, etc. These rules do not mean members or volunteers can't do business with the organization.
- **An annual audit must be performed.** If the organization cannot afford an outside auditor, designate an audit committee composed of members not associated with the accounting part of the organization.

---

* A far-too-common occurrence is for the bookkeeper to steal the federal or state withholding from employees' payroll and not pay the IRS. If the same bookkeeper receives the notices from the IRS, he can stall the discovery of the fraud for years.

C. Separation of Duties

Separation of duties should be used for each area of the accounting system. As you read through keep in mind this basic rule:

The person with access to the records MUST NOT have access to the money!

The person entering the data in the accounting system or tracking donor contributions should NOT have access to the checking account or donations. I realize this may seem counter-intuitive, but with the next examples, consider the rule above.

A donor hands the bookkeeper a check to be deposited. He deposits the check into a dummy account that he controls and sends a false donor acknowledgment to the donor. The donor assumes the organization has received it. The charity never receives it or knows of the donation.

To prevent this from happening, the check should be given to a *separate* person to deposit, and then a *copy* of the check or deposit is given to the bookkeeper. The bookkeeper should record the deposit in the financial statements and send out the donor acknowledgment.

A donor hands staff money, but the donor does not receive an acknowledgment from your organization.

The latter scenario is more likely to be discovered if confirmations are routinely sent out. With either situation, you need controls to prevent these mistakes from happening at all. In the accounting world, this is referred to as a **separation of duties**. It will not stop all fraud and error but makes it more likely to be discovered.

In a small nonprofit, the treasurer and bookkeeper are often the same person. Sometimes this person is even the director.

> *A small staff is no excuse not to have controls.*

A director can be the treasurer OR the bookkeeper, but NOT both. If they receive the bills and know which program should be charged, it's okay for them to enter bills, write checks, and enter donations, but designate someone from the governing body to sign the checks.

Don't worry. Even if you have minimal staff, I will give you the tools to implement the necessary controls. I promise you; you are never too small to have the controls required to protect your staff and assets.

> *Consider having the people handling the cash for the organization bonded. This is an insurance policy against theft.*

If there is a volunteer or part-time assistant in the office, you can train him to enter the bills and donations and allow the director to be the treasurer/check signer.

If the director has at least one other person to call, access to the funds can be separated from the access to the records.

D. Basic Controls for Receiving Cash & Donations

1. Money Received In Person

If you have members who pay dues or collect money at events, you will need to establish controls for these collections. In other words, make sure related persons (i.e., husband and wife) do not handle the money until it is counted and deposited. This policy will decrease the likelihood of collusion (two or more people working together to steal) if the counters are unrelated.

Any collection of money should be in the sight of two unrelated people.

Before you repeat the "we don't have enough people" argument, remember, if you have at least two unrelated people in your group, they can count the money together.

Any donor or member who gives the organization *cash* must receive a receipt. If you have a computer set up, one person can enter the donation into the system and print out the receipt while the second person handles the money. You can also use a duplicating receipt book to fill them out by hand.

Once the meeting or event is over, have the two people count the cash and checks and fill out a summary form or count sheet showing the amounts and any special donor notations for the cash collection (i.e., for a specific program or to be applied to pledge). If possible, copies should be made of any checks, so check notations or additional information can be seen by the bookkeeper later.

The summary form is reconciled to the total in the receipt book (or a donation report from the computer system) by the counters. Each counter will then sign the count sheet.

For a free, downloadable version of a count sheet, go to https://accountantbesideyou.com/collections/freebies.

A deposit slip is then filled out and copied, and the deposit is driven to the bank and put in the deposit (or night deposit). It is acceptable to have only one of the counters make the deposit as there is a record of the receipts at the organization.

When the bookkeeper is ready to enter the data, use the copy of the deposit to input the donations into each member's contribution account. We will cover this concept in more detail later in the book.

Any donor restrictions on the donations (desired program, special use requests) need to be noted so they can be correctly recorded and so appropriate acknowledgments can be sent.

If your organization receives a large number of *checks*, ask your bank about a **Remote Imaging Device (RID)** scanner. Banks usually charge a fee for RID scanners, but the time, savings, and control features are often worth the additional expense. The RID scanner allows you to quickly scan the checks and print out a report for your files. The scanned data is automatically sent to the bank, so the deposit can be made immediately rather than waiting on a volunteer to drive to the bank. Once the bank has the scanned image, it does not need the physical check. The scanner will not let you send the same check twice. Beware, though, if you accidentally try to deposit the scanned checks at the bank, a deposit correction fee may be charged. To keep this from happening, mark the original checks with a highlighter to show they were scanned. File the marked copies for future reference.

By scanning the checks immediately after the meeting, there is less likelihood of someone taking them and depositing them into their account. The scanner is also less likely to make math errors.

It is now easy to have the ability to swipe a *credit card* at a meeting or an event. The convenience is wonderful, but you must also be sure the money is being deposited to the correct bank account. If you are using a mobile phone app with a plug-in device, the app needs to be registered to the organization.

Have a second person assist in assuring that the gift is being deposited in the organization's account and not a personal account. Just like cash, you don't want only one person in control of the donations being received.

When a donation is made, have the second person log the donor and amount on a summary form. At the end of the day or event, give the count sheet to the bookkeeper. She will reconcile it with the cash deposited in the bank.

2. Money Received Through the Mail

Often members/donors prefer to mail in their dues/donations rather than bringing them to the organization, so it's a good idea to have a post office box. The P.O. box keeps anyone from stealing the checks out of the organization's mailbox.

The bookkeeper should NOT pick up the mail. Theoretically, anyone with access to the accounting system could steal checks and make the member's account look like it was received. Designate someone without access to the accounting system to pick up and receive mail, as well as open envelopes in front of a second person.

Each check should be recorded, and the summary signed by the two who opened the mail. If you have an RID scanner, the checks should be scanned immediately, and the deposit report and the marked checks given to the bookkeeper.

3. Electronic Payments Received Through the Website

If you have not added a donation button to your website, I highly recommend it. You should make it as easy as possible for donors to give you money. The button can be activated through many different services. If you are using a donor management system, such as Donor Perfect or Method:Donor, it is essential that it works with your payment system.

> *The most crucial thing to do with electronic payments is to safeguard the link to the bank account.*

Many online credit card processors will require signed corporate resolutions stating you are a legal organization, and the check signers have authorized the funds to go to that account. Others, like PayPal®, simply use an email/password combination. This is potentially a problem as the person who has the password could reroute the appointed deposit bank account to their personal account number.

To keep any of these problems from occurring with your organization, I would recommend the account be linked to an email address administered by your organization (e.g., admin@yourorganization.org) and assigned to someone who has no access to the members' records. This person would have the authorization to change the bank deposit account number and permit transfers from the payment system to the bank. As they could change the bank account number to their personal account, they must NOT have access to the member records.

A real-world example was given to me by a PayPal® employee. They told me of a woman associated with a small nonprofit who had set up its PayPal account. She had a falling out with the organization and refused to tell them the password to collect the money.

PayPal does allow for a secondary user with limited rights that can only see reports, not change bank account numbers. This person can verify the amounts received in PayPal were recorded in the organization's accounting records. You will want this to be your bookkeeper so that he can reconcile the receipts PayPal is reporting to the cash posted into the bank. Any discrepancies should be investigated immediately.

4. Donor Acknowledgments

A donor acknowledgment statement typically gives a summary of all their donations and the number of pledges still outstanding. It is a powerful tool to thank your donors and also remind them of any unpaid balance (if pledged, but not received yet).

Acknowledgments are an efficient control to ensure all of the money donors have given has been recorded in your accounting records.

At a minimum, this should be done at year-end for the donor's tax purposes. Still, if you get recurring monthly donations, I recommend doing it quarterly, or at least semiannually.

Send donor acknowledgment letters summarizing the donor's gifts on a regular basis.

To use the acknowledgment as an accounting control, add a sentence near the bottom, encouraging the donor to contact the treasurer with any questions or differences from the statement. (This assumes the treasurer is not the bookkeeper. If she is, have the questions go to the director.) If you have an office administrator, make sure they know not to give these calls to the bookkeeper. Any discrepancies between the donor's records and the organizations should be investigated by someone besides the bookkeeper. Usually, the differences will be recording errors, which can be reviewed with the bookkeeper, but be aware of the possibility of theft.

5. Fundraisers and Controls

Various groups within the organization may need to hold fundraisers to support their activities. People involved in the fundraisers need to be given specific instructions on how to handle any cash received.

If there are raffle or admission tickets, have them printed with numbers. If there is more than one person selling tickets, track ticket numbers by each person selling the tickets. After sales are completed, each seller should return the unused tickets plus cash equal to the tickets not returned. See the example in the shadow box on the next page.

For example, Mary takes raffle tickets 101-200 with a ticket value of $1 each. Sue logs Mary's name and the ticket numbers she has taken. At the end of the event, Mary turns in ticket stubs for ticket numbers 101-125 with the purchaser's name and $25. She also turns in tickets numbered 126-200. Sue logs the numbers sold and the numbers returned for Mary and all sellers.

With another person present, Sue counts the money at the end of the event, compares it to the log of money received, investigates any differences, signs it to acknowledge the amount, and deposits the money in the bank. The log and deposit slip are left at the organization for the bookkeeper to record.

If a carnival-style fundraiser is being held, consider selling food/game tickets at a single booth to be used throughout the carnival. The volunteers at each booth will not have to handle and track cash. The booth receiving money should always have two unrelated people and have pre-numbered tickets.

For other types of fundraisers, ask yourself, "What is the best way to be certain the money donated is deposited in the organization account?" The procedures and controls can be designed around the answer to that question.

We have covered some necessary steps to protect your people and your money in the most common ways donations are received. Now, make a list of all the other ways money is received. Ask yourself—for each case:

- How can you get it to the bank?
- How can you record it in the financial statements?
- How can you provide good stewardship of your gifts?
- How can you protect your volunteers and employees?

These are the minimum steps to take to safeguard cash.

If your organization already has more complete procedures, please follow them.

E. Cash Out And Controls for Paying Bills

Fraud, theft, and mistakes are as much of a concern with the money going out as they are with the money coming in.

Procedures and controls need to be in place to keep phantom employees or fake vendor invoices from being paid. To ensure proper stewardship over your organization's money, you will need strong accounting controls in place as it relates to the money paid out. The next few sections will cover some basics for the outgoing controls.

> *Remember the basic rule. If someone has access to the money, he should not have access to the financial records.*

1. Check Signers

The bookkeeper must NOT be an authorized check signer. I know this sounds nearly impossible for a small organization, but here again, you may need to utilize the members of the governing body or other volunteers.

No one should ever sign a check made out to himself. If the director is a check signer and needs to be reimbursed, the treasurer or another check signer should sign the check.

You need at least two check signers in case one is on vacation or leaves the organization. I recommend three just to be safe. Stay away from too many signers as a fraudulent bookkeeper could use this to his advantage by submitting the same invoice to be paid twice and pocketing the second payment.

Large purchases should require two signers. The definition of "large" is determined by the size of your organization. If it is common for your organization to pay $500 invoices, perhaps the limit should be $1000 for two signers. *For the dual signatures to work, the dollar limit must be printed on the check.* Keep in mind; however, banks do most things electronically and no longer look for the two signatures.

It is probably a good idea to have printed on your checks, "Not Valid after 90 Days." This keeps you from having to incur stop payment charges on checks people may have lost.

2. Paying Bills

Bills should not be entered into the system without documentation and approval from someone other than the bookkeeper. Approvals are often made by the director or treasurer. The documentation is usually an invoice from a vendor or an expense report with the receipts attached. If the expense is to be charged to more than one program, the approver should also notate this.

The approval process should not be taken lightly. If the director or treasurer is not familiar with the vendor, the bill should be questioned.

Most importantly, all bills to be paid must be approved. Invoices to be paid should be approved before they are entered into the system and checks cut.

The bookkeeper will enter and code the bills into the correct expense categories and programs or grants, print the checks, match them up with the approved documentation, and give them to an authorized check signer.

Even with frequently used vendors, large dollar purchases or repairs need to be discussed beforehand with the governing body.

The check signer should ensure that the payee, address, and amounts agree with the approved documentation before signing the checks. The invoices should be marked paid to keep from issuing a duplicate check.

I recommend you use a voucher-style check. It is a multi-part check that allows a space for the payee to see what invoice was paid. A three-part voucher check is also available, which enables the bookkeeper to staple the third section to the approved invoice.

The checks can then be mailed or given to the vendor, and the documentation filed or scanned. I recommend filing by vendor name. Set up a file for each letter of the alphabet and place infrequently paid vendors invoice in its appropriate folder. Saving them as electronic scans is fine as long as the related check number is notated, and the scans are adequately backed up offsite. Also, set up a naming and filing protocol for scanned files for ease of retrieving the data.

3. Electronic Bill Pay & Automatic Drafts

Using the "Bill Pay" option through the bank and automatic drafts are convenient and efficient ways to streamline the bill payments, and I highly recommend using them. However, it is just as essential to set up controls and review them for reasonableness as it is for any other bill.

The check signer who has access to the online bill pay should verify all bills have been documented and approved before submitting them for payment, then give the documentation to the bookkeeper for entry into the accounting system. If it is an automated system, the bookkeeper can set up standard rules, so when a vendor is paid, the bank feed with that payment will automatically post, saving data entry time. The bookkeeper must review these payments and verify there are documentation and approval for the charge. If the documentation is in an electronic format, many systems allow you to attach the scanned or electronic file to the payment.

For automatic drafts, most vendors send an email or mail a bill stating the date and amount. These are reviewed, approval noted by the treasurer, and held in a pending file until the bank account is reconciled.

4. Petty Cash

Often volunteers or employees of the organization may need to make a quick run for supplies or other small-dollar items. If the bookkeeper and check signers are not always available, it may make sense to have a petty cash fund. The fund is often called an **imprest fund**, which means the fixed fund is only replenished after the money is spent.

Assuming an organization has a petty cash fund of $100, cash can be given to a person to buy supplies. If $20.00 is given, the person is required to bring back a receipt for the amount spent and any change from the $20.00. At the end of the month, the drawer or envelope holding the petty cash should have receipts and cash totaling $100. The receipts are then used as support for the replenishment check.

For example, Your Organization has $100 in their petty cash fund. Throughout the month, various volunteers used the money and brought back the following receipts:

$9.95 for donuts for a meeting

$44.37 for gas to take members to a Habitat for Humanity house

$15.68 for copier paper for the office

The receipts total $70.00. There should be $30.00 of cash left in the drawer. A check for $70.00 should be made out to Your Organization (never Cash, as the check is for the organization, not whoever is cashing it) with the receipts as the support for the check signer to review. The check can then be cashed, and the drawer replenished.

Petty cash can be tracked using a simple spreadsheet:

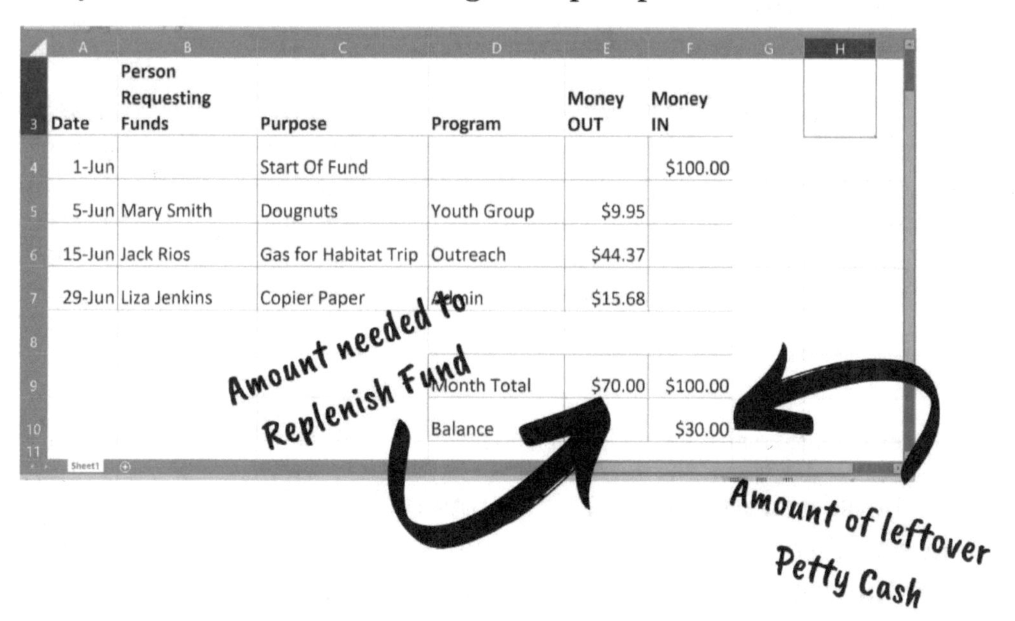

Date	Person Requesting Funds	Purpose	Program	Money OUT	Money IN
1-Jun		Start Of Fund			$100.00
5-Jun	Mary Smith	Dougnuts	Youth Group	$9.95	
15-Jun	Jack Rios	Gas for Habitat Trip	Outreach	$44.37	
29-Jun	Liza Jenkins	Copier Paper	Admin	$15.68	
			Month Total	$70.00	$100.00
			Balance		$30.00

The person responsible for the petty cash fund should be the one in the organization's office the most. The monthly count needs to be performed by someone else.

5. Gift Cards or Prepaid Store Cards

Some organizations find it easier to use prepaid store cards or gift cards instead of a petty cash fund. If so, the same basic procedures should be followed. A log of persons holding the gift cards and the amounts must be maintained. Those persons must be able to show at any time that the receipts plus the balance of the card equal the purchase price of the card.

6. Credit Cards

If your nonprofit uses a credit card for purchases, procedures need to be documented and taught to volunteers and employees. The procedures will lay out how and when the card can be used, who reviews receipts, as well as how often you would like the receipts brought in.

VISA Credit Card Receipts

Your Name ____________ **Approved by:** ____________

Date	Vendor	Purpose	Program	Amount
6/5/2020	Staples	Printer Paper Resupply	Main Office	$27.49
6/12/2020	Exxon	Gas	Recruiting	$45.11
6/12/2020	Avis	Car Rental	Recruiting	$350.00
6/12/2020	Panera	Lunch	Recruiting	$12.35
6/21/2020	USPS	Stamps	Main Office	$9.20
*All Receipts must be attached to this document			Total	$444.15

Some bookkeepers prefer the receipts be brought to them as soon as possible so that cash requirements can be monitored. Others prefer the user to fill out a form once a month before the bill is due with all the receipts attached. Either way, the receipts need to be approved by the reviewer before the credit card bill is paid.

Personal expenses should <u>NOT</u> be allowed to be charged to the organization's card. Any personal charges that are inadvertently charged to the card should be repaid immediately.

7. Payroll

For many organizations, payroll is the most significant expense. Payroll can be processed through an outside service, by the bookkeeper, or by a combination of the two. Regardless of the way it is paid, the nonprofit must maintain some basic controls.

The best control for payroll is to require employees to use direct deposit. Direct deposit ensures the check goes directly to the employee's bank account and cannot be taken before they have a chance to get to the bank.

If timesheets are used, these must be approved by the employee's manager and given to the bookkeeper. The bookkeeper should prepare the payroll and review it with the director or treasurer before submitting to the payroll service or cutting the checks. Every employee should be known by the person approving unless you have a very large organization.

If a payroll service is used, the executive director or treasurer should be the point person to authorize additions of new employees, not the bookkeeper.

The treasurer or director must also be sure that all withholding and taxes are submitted to the government. Look for electronic payments or checks monthly or quarterly. Ask your accountant or payroll provider for the rules for your specific organization. Not paying withholding is a common way to steal money from an organization.

> *All letters from the IRS must be given unopened to the treasurer or executive director, NOT the bookkeeper.*

8. Other Payment Controls to Consider

Another way money can be stolen from a nonprofit is to issue payments for legitimate bills twice and then deposit the extra check into a dummy account. One way to guard against this is for the treasurer or someone who is NOT the bookkeeper to review checks' images on the bank's website to see if they were appropriately endorsed and not duplicated. Additionally, the treasurer will need to review the check register regularly, looking for duplicate payments or unknown vendors.

> *Any money leaving the nonprofit needs to be approved by someone other than the person requesting the money.*

F. **Summary**

Strong internal controls are necessary to keep the organization's assets, employees, and volunteers safe. Remember, no organization is too small for strong controls!

In this chapter, we went over the basic rules and controls.

- The person with access to the accounting records (i.e., the bookkeeper) may not have access to the bank account or cash.
- No one is left alone with the cash.
- All expenditures must be approved before payment.
- Notices from the IRS and calls from donors should be handled by someone other than the bookkeeper.
- Someone other than the bookkeeper must review the financial statements on a regular (preferably monthly) basis.

You now have a blueprint for designing the procedures and controls for your organization. This next section will explain how the accounting works in a nonprofit environment.

2. What is Special About Nonprofit Accounting?

You may have some experience with bookkeeping or accounting for a business or your personal finances and are wondering, "How can nonprofit accounting be any different?"

The big difference is that a nonprofit is not concerned with net income or how much money it makes. A not-for-profit organization will receive donations for many different areas, such as:

- general support of the organization
- money to an outreach program
- capital campaign and
- an endowment.

Often the money given is considered unrestricted. It is assumed the organization will use this money as needed, and the donor has not requested any particular use of the funds.

Other times, the money will be received for a particular purpose—an outreach program or a capital campaign, or for a specific time (say next year's donation). Then the money is considered "with donor restrictions," which means it can only be used for the purpose or time period the donor has specified.

In this chapter, I'll explain:

- Accounting terms and processes,
- The difference between cash and accrual basis of accounting,
- What a chart of accounts is and how to design one,
- The basic steps in bookkeeping, and
- How nonprofit accounting is *different* from business accounting to give you the background you need to handle your organization's basic bookkeeping.

Your organization must be certain the money it raises is spent as the donors intended.

A. Nonprofit Accounting Terminology

When speaking with an accountant, you often hear terms like "FASB" and "GAAP" as they explain the need to track something a certain way. You don't need to remember these specifically. Still, familiarity with these acronyms allows you to nod your head intelligently when your accountant mentions one of these, often confusing, terms to you.

FASB stands for the Financial Accounting Standards Board.

GAAP is the Generally Accepted Accounting Principles that stem from the FASB rules.

SFAS is the Statement of Financial Accounting Standards.

ASU are Accounting Standard Updates to existing rules.

Nonprofit organizations' reporting is governed by SFAS numbers 95, 116, 117, and 124 and ASU 2016-14, which describe how nonprofits should account for contributions, present their financial statements, and account for certain investments.

Also, as most small organizations do not need to report to outside agencies, they do not have to follow all the specifics of various SFAS. If you are required to have an external audit by a donor, bank, or other organization, you will need to work with your outside accountants to determine how to make your financial statements GAAP-compliant.

In this book, we will focus on designing the accounting system to give the nonprofit management the precise information they need to support the mission of the organization and be good stewards of its assets. The system will not be completely GAAP-compliant, but close enough that the organization's auditors can make the appropriate adjustments if GAAP financials are required.

This system is referred to as a modified form of **fund accounting**.

A **fund** is defined as a discrete accounting entity with its own set of accounts that must balance the cash and other assets against the liabilities and reserves of the organization. In other words, each significant donation (given for a particular purpose) should be tracked separately.

> *A fund is NOT an asset account. It is NOT a checking or savings account. It is the nonprofit equivalent of an owner's equity or a retained earnings account.*

Most organizations don't keep separate bank accounts for each fund. To stay compliant, funds can be combined by the restrictions placed on them. This approach makes a bit easier to track your funds. This system is called **net assets**.

Net assets are the components of equity in the organization. Net assets are what is left over after the liabilities (what is owed) are subtracted from the assets (what the organization owns). In the business world, this would be the accumulated profit or loss of the company and is called "retained earnings."

Net assets are divided into two categories:

Net Assets without Donor Restrictions—These come from donations given to the organization to be used for any purpose. Regular contributions and gifts are usually unrestricted and go first toward the operating expenses of the organization. Older terms for this category were "General Fund" and "Unrestricted *Net* Assets."

Net Assets with Donor Restrictions—These are restricted by the donor based on purpose or time, but the restrictions are not permanent. Older terms for this category were "Temporarily Restricted" and "Permanently Restricted Net Assets."

The other type of restriction is a **board restriction**. If the board of directors decides to put aside some money in an investment account to be used at a later date, this would be recorded as a Net

Asset *without* Donor Restrictions but should be specified in the notes to the financial statements.

> *An example is when money is given to support the building of a new community center. The money cannot be used for anything but the costs to build the building. If the building is not built, the donor must be contacted to see if the money must be returned or if the donor will authorize its use for another project. As the building is built, the restriction is released, so the money can be given to the vendors.*

Some nonprofit treasurers or finance administrators may think you need to open a separate checking account for each fund. A separate account is not required, as it requires a lot more paperwork. It also makes it more difficult for your volunteers and staff to keep the books accurate.

I am not saying you can't open multiple bank accounts. Having a specific bank account for a donor-restricted fund such as building can be beneficial.

Evaluate whether the extra effort is worth the benefit of opening the account. I have seen some organizations with just two or three funds, and I've seen some with 20 or more. Try to combine as many as you can; however, if the project or program has its own income coming in and expenses going out—set it up as a fund.

The three primary reasons a nonprofit uses a fund accounting method are:

1. *Accountability* is measured instead of *profitability*.
2. Financial reports are directed toward contributors, organization members, or the nonprofit's governing board. These members are more concerned with having adequate fund balances to carry on services provided rather than seeking a profit on investments as investors do.
3. Funds are set up to provide reporting of expenditures for designated purposes.

You should set up and use an accounting system that can detail expenditures and revenues for multiple funds. Each fund should have a dedicated **general ledger**. The general ledger is the complete record of the financial transactions for a fund or organization and often referred to as the GL.

With a GL, you will be able to produce reports that detail each fund's income and expenses as well as summarize and total all the organization's funds.

B. Accounting 101

We have gone over how nonprofit accounting is different than business accounting, but now it is time to cover how to do basic accounting. If you are already familiar with debits, credits, assets, and liabilities, go ahead and skip to the next section. If not, I'll try to walk you through as painlessly as possible.

Assets are things the organization owns or is owed and includes the bank and investment accounts, donations receivable, buildings, furniture, and equipment. It can also cover expenses you've paid for but not yet used, like prepaid insurance or prepaid postage.

Liabilities are what the organization owes. The mortgage to the bank, the credit card bill, payroll due to employees, and payroll taxes due to the government are all liabilities.

Net assets are what is left. They are separated into "With donor restrictions" or Without donor restrictions," as we discussed previously.

> *Think of accounting as a balanced equation.*
>
> *Assets = Liabilities + Net Assets.*

Additionally, you will have income and expenses.

Poppy Davis, CPA, sums up the accounting terms wonderfully in her *Small Business QuickBooks Primer*. I've changed the wording slightly to relate more to organizations.

Assets stick around; expenses go away. If you buy a stove, it sticks around, so it is an asset. If you hire a repairman to fix the stove, he goes away, so the repair cost is an expense.

Income is yours; liabilities belong to others. If you receive a donation to feed others, it is income, but if you borrow money from the bank to build a new kitchen, it is a liability.

Net Assets are what is left over for your organization.

C. Cash vs. Accrual Accounting Methods

There are two methods to track expenses and revenues in the accounting world—Cash and Accrual.

The **cash method** is the simplest. The cash is recorded in the financial statements when it is physically received and when the checks are written. The cash method gives you a better idea of when the money has come in or gone out. Most smaller organizations use the cash method or a modified cash method, which reflects current amounts due to vendors.

The **accrual method** requires dating the transaction when the income was earned (i.e., when the grant was awarded) or the expense item was ordered, not when cash changed hands, or the check was written. The accrual method gives you the most accurate financial picture of your organization, showing the money you have earned and the expenses you have incurred.

For example, assume you receive an invoice from a contractor who did repairs on July 31, but you didn't write him a check until August 15. If you are using the accrual method, enter the invoice with a date of July 31. Your financial reports for July would show the expense and its offset in accounts payable. If you wanted your reports to reflect the cash method, you would record the expense when it was paid in August.

For businesses that pay taxes or are publicly held, the difference between these two methods is significant. Nonprofits can use either depending on your governing boards or donor requirements.

D. Chart of Accounts

To keep track of the assets, liabilities, income, and expenses, we use accounts. Accounts define the transactions that occur within your small business. There are no set rules as to what accounts are required, but I am going to explain the basics.

The list of all accounts is called the **Chart of Accounts**. It consists of a combination of numbers and words that can help categorize your accounts and allow an account to be easily located within your ledger. I am a firm believer in using a limited chart of accounts and then tracking things by programs.

Depending on the accounting system you are using, you will want to group similar accounts using account numbers, as shown below. Notice the "Ask My Accountant" account. It is a placeholder to record transactions when you are not sure where they should go. It should be cleared out each month once you've verified the correct location with your accountant.

1000s—Assets: bank accounts, receivables, computers, buildings, etc.

2000s—Liabilities: accounts payable, due to other organizations, payroll, loans, etc.

3000s—Net Assets: without donor restrictions, with donor restrictions.

4000s—Operating Revenues: pledges, donations, book sales.

5000s—Non-operating Revenues: bequests, capital campaigns, endowments, sale of equipment, etc.

6000s—Operating Expenses: facilities, salaries, program costs, etc.

7000s—Non-operating Expenses: extraordinary repairs, depreciation, etc.

8000—Ask My Accountant.

Within this structure, I recommend using the following for the balance sheet asset accounts:

1101-1299	Cash and investments,
1301-1399	Receivables—amounts owed to you,
1401-1499	Prepaid assets—this can be insurance, postage, etc.,
1501-1699	Available for **current assets** categories in the future,
1701-1799	Buildings, real estate, equipment, and depreciation,
1801-1899	Available for future **long-term assets** categories,
1901-1999	Other long-term assets.

*A **current asset** or **liability** is due or used within a year.*

*A **long-term asset** or **liability** is available or due in more than a year.*

For example, a pledge made for the next year is a current asset, but a capital campaign contribution due in five years is a long-term asset.

As you can see, this chart gives you 99 accounts under each of the categories. There is an example of a simplified uniform chart of accounts (UCOA) in Appendix A. It and other charts of accounts designed for different types of small nonprofits are available at AccountantBesideYou.com. Use this numbering scheme for the liability, equity, revenue, and expense accounts.

Within these ranges, you may also have sub-ranges, especially in the expense categories. For example, the facility costs may be in 6000-6399, personnel expenses in 6400-6599, and program expenses from 6600-6999. As you need to add accounts within a range, consider adding them by 10s so you will have space between accounts.

Once you have figured out your numbering system, you need to determine how you are going to name the accounts. It may sound basic, but if you aren't careful, you may have accounts called "Postage and Mailing," "Postage," etc., which should be combined. If you already have a naming protocol, use it. If not, keep things simple. Have a policy that significant words are written out with no punctuation marks, and to save space use ampersands (&) instead of the word "and."

E. Basic Bookkeeping

Bookkeeping is the process of recording monetary transactions to prepare useful financial reports reflecting the financial health of your organization. In the beginning, an organization may start out with a simple checkbook and a spreadsheet showing where the money came from and where it is going to.

A spreadsheet is an adequate way to keep track of the money coming in and going out if there are very few transactions. Once you start to issue more checks and have more donations brought in for specific things, you will want to have a **double-entry accounting system**.

Your Organization
Basic Check Register

DATE	Check/Deposit #	Payee/Payor	Purpose	Cash In	Cash Out	Balance	Revenues Donations	Mission	Expenses Postage
01-Jun	1	Joe Wilson	donation	200.00		200.00	200.00		
04-Jun	101	USPS	Roll of Stamps		37.00	163.00			37
04-Jun	2	Mary Smith	gift	100.00		263.00	100.00		
						263.00			
						263.00			
						263.00			
						263.00			
						263.00			
						263.00			
Total				$ 300.00	$ 37.00		$ 300.00	$ -	$ 37.00

Put simply, every transaction has two sides. A double-entry system records both sides. Accountants refer to these sides as **debits** and **credits**. They are not good or bad; they are simply opposite sides of an equation.

The check register example above would use a double-entry even if you didn't realize it. Cash deposited from a donation increased the cash (debited) and increased the revenues (credited) by the same amount. The roll of stamps decreased cash (credited) and increased expenses (debited) by the same amount.

Debits and credits affect each type of account in a particular way. As the chart on the next page shows, cash is an asset. Any increases to cash will be recorded as a debit and any decreases as a credit. If we receive a donation, we debit *Cash* (because it increased) and need to credit another account, *Revenue (Donations)*.

Impact of Debits & Credits on Account Types		
Account	**Debit**	**Credit**
Assets	Increases	Decreases
Liabilities	Decreases	Increases
Equity	Decreases	Increases
Income	Decreases	Increases
Expense	Increases	Decreases

Revenue is an income account, and, from the chart above, we see that we need to credit it to increase the income. If you were to write this out as a journal entry, it would look like this:

Date		Ref #	Debit	Credit
04/15/2020	Cash	xxxxx	100.00	
	Donations (revenue)	xxxxx		100.00

The total amount of the debits **must** equal the credits.

Don't worry if you feel your eyes glazing over at this point. The good news is most accounting programs do both sides of the entry for you. You rarely have to record actual journal entries.

F. Nonprofit Reporting Differences

Now that you have the basics of what the accounts are, you need to understand how they are pulled together to help make informed decisions with **financial reports**. Financial reports compile and summarize activity within the individual accounts you track. Financial statements for nonprofits also have different names than those for most businesses. Here is a table showing the terminology differences.

By recording the money properly, you can judge the health of your nonprofit.

Description	Nonprofit Terminology	Business Terminology
Your organization	Club, association, organization, foundation, etc.	Company
People or organizations you receive money from	Members, donors, etc.	Customers
People you pay money to	Vendors, suppliers, or people you reimburse	Vendors
People who are employed to work at the nonprofit	Employees (payroll)	Employees (payroll)
Report to show money in versus money out (track income and expenses)	Statement of Activities	Income Statement or Profit & Loss
Report to show assets and liabilities to track the accumulated net wealth	Statement of Financial Position	Balance Sheet
Accumulated net wealth/profit	Net Assets	Net Worth
Grants necessary to track related expenses	Grants	Jobs

For example, if you are using an accounting program like QuickBooks, the people or granting agencies you receive money from will be designated as "Customers," grants received will be tracked as "Jobs," and designated monies and programs will be referred to as "Classes."

The "Income Statement" or "Profit & Loss Statement" that tracks income and expenses will be called a **Statement of Activities** for your organization. The Statement of Activities allows the governing board to see how much money has been donated or received and how the money is being used. Below is a basic example showing the activity of all the funds.

Note <u>*only*</u> income and expense accounts are detailed.

Sample Statement of Activity Per Month/ Year to Date

		General Fund	Restricted Funds	Plant Funds	Endowment Funds	All Total Funds
Revenue	Contributions	$309,027.00	$5,472.00	$16,575.00		$331,074.00
	Interest Income	$6,132.00	$3,655.00	$640.00	$5,130.00	$15,557.00
	Workshop/ Events	$733.00				$733.00
	Bequests				$10,000.00	$10,000.00
	Total	**$315,892.00**	**$9,127.00**	**$17,215.00**	**$15,130.00**	**$357,364.00**
Expenses by Program	Worship	$98,541.00	$2,435.00		$5,000.00	$105,976.00
	Education	$10,205.00	$750.00			$10,955.00
	Care/Fellowship	$9,876.00	$219.00			$10,095.00
	Evangelism	$9,545.00				$9,545.00
	Resources	$46,723.00				$46,723.00
	Community Relief	$3,000.00	$1,934.00			$4,934.00
	Youth	$3,025.00				$3,025.00
	Administration	$123,786.00		$11,000.00		$134,786.00
	Total	**$304,701.00**	**$5,338.00**	**$11,000.00**	**$5,000.00**	**$326,039.00**
Change in Net Assets		**$11,191.00**	**$3,789.00**	**$6,215.00**	**$10,130.00**	**$31,325.00**
Beginning Net Assets		**$41,730.00**	**$72,158.00**	**$446,995.00**	**$55,370.00**	**$616,253.00**
End Net Assets		**$52,921.00**	**$75,947.00**	**$453,210.00**	**$65,500.00**	**$647,578.00**

Assets, liabilities, and equity are tracked by companies in a "Balance Sheet." A nonprofit organization calls this a **Statement of Financial Position.**

Management can refer to the Statement of Financial Position to see how much cash is in the bank, how much is owed to the organization, and how much the nonprofit owes to others. It also separates the unrestricted funds from the restricted funds.

You will likely also need to adapt your terms to fit within the accounting program you are using so that the accounting software can tag information accurately, and reports can be run.

Church Sample Statement of Financial Position for Month/ Year-to-Date

		General Fund	Restrcted Fund	Plant Fund	Endowment Fund	Total
Assets	Cash and Cash Equivalents	$62,533.00	$32,947.00	$16,210.00	$8,500.00	$120,190.00
	Account Recivables	$1,768.00				$1,768.00
	Pledges Receivabes			$72,000.00		$72,000.00
	Other Current Assets	$4,765.00				$4,765.00
	Land, Buildings, & Equipment			$525,000.00		$525,000.00
	Investments	$10,000.00	$43,000.00		$62,000.00	$115,000.00
	Total	**$79,066.00**	**$75,947.00**	**$613,210.00**	**$70,500.00**	**$838,723.00**
Liabilities	Account Payable	$3,621.00			$5,000.00	$8,621.00
	Payroll Withholdings	$524.00				$524.00
	Deferred Revenue	$22,000.00				$22,000.00
	Current Position Long-Term Debt			$10,000.00		$10,000.00
	Long-Term Debt			$150,000.00		$150,000.00
	Total	**$26,145.00**	**$0.00**	**$160,000.00**	**$5,000.00**	**$191,145.00**
Fund Balances	Without Donor Restriction	$52,921.00				$52,921.00
	With Donor Restriction		$75,947.00		$65,500.00	$141,447.00
	Net Investments in Plant			$453,210.00		$453,210.00
	Total	**$52,921.00**	**$75,947.00**	**$453,210.00**	**$65,500.00**	**$647,578.00**

G. Summary

Accounting for nonprofits is different than accounting used by for-profit companies. In this chapter, you learned not only terminology but significant differences such as:

- How net assets are used instead of equity accounts,
- How net assets are tracked With Donor Restrictions or Without Donor Restrictions,
- How the donations and expenses are recorded in the general ledger through the chart of accounts,
- Why most smaller nonprofits use the cash basis method of accounting, which records the transactions when cash is received or spent, not when promised or ordered,
- How transactions are recorded and summarized in the Statement of Financial Position (Balance Sheet) and the Statement of Activities (Income Statement).

You now have the basic terminology to use for your bookkeeping, as well as tools to track your business.

Next, we will discuss selecting an accounting system.

3. How Do I Select an Accounting System?

If you have simply been keeping track of things with a checkbook, it's time to start thinking about how to set up an accounting system to give you the management reports you need.

In this chapter, I'll go over the following:

- Time vs. money,
- Spreadsheets
- Low-cost options, and
- Over-the-counter options.

A. Time Vs. Money

We must be good stewards of the gifts given to our organization, so I recommend looking at any free or inexpensive options first. But we also must not be penny wise and pound foolish.

One of the ways to determine if you can afford a new program is to understand what your current program is actually costing you. If you are paying someone $15 per hour to spend 20 hours per month manipulating spreadsheets, that "free" program is costing you $300 per month.

If converting to an automated accounting program will save 5 hours per month, the new program may pay for itself in 5 months.

$300 program /(5 hours x $15 per hour)=5 months

I will cover some of the more affordable options before analyzing the more expensive, but more robust, commercial programs.

B. Spreadsheets

The simplest and cheapest option is to design a spreadsheet with a few accounts to track simply. I've included a couple of screenshots to give you an idea of how the spreadsheet can be laid out.

Account # / Date	Item Description	Ck#	Debit *(Expenses)*	Credit *(Income)*	Balance
					0.00
1001	Plate Offering / Tithe /				
	Beginning Balance				0.00
					-
					-
					-
					-
					-
	Total		-	-	
1002	Covenant Missions				
	Beginning Balance				-
					-
					-
					-
					-
	Total		-	-	
1003	Marco Missions Support				
	Beginning Balance				-
					-
					-
					-
					-
	Total		-	-	
1004	Presbytery Support				
	Beginning Balance				-
					-
					-
					-
					-
	Total		-	-	
1005	Not Assigned				
	Beginning Balance				-
					-
					-

This sheet is where the data is entered and linked to a summary Profit & Loss Statement (or Statement of Activities).

		Bank 1 - Savings		0
		Bank 1 - Checking		0
Cash Beginning of Period		Bank 2		0
				$ -
Revenue Accounts				
1001	Plate Offering / Tithe /	$	500.00	
1002	Covenant Missions	$	-	
1003	Marco Missions Support	$	-	
1004	Presbytery Support	$	-	
1005	Not Assigned	$	-	
1006	External Support / Fundraising & Unkno	$	-	
1007	Support - Covenant Members	$	-	
1008	Transfer - into Bank 1 from Bank 2	$	-	
1009	Transfer - out of Bank 2 to Bank 1	$	-	
	Total Revenue:			$ 500.00
Expenses:				
2001	Pastor Salary	$	350.00	
2002	Pastor Housing	$	-	
2003	Pastor's Ministry & Continuing Educatio	$	-	
2004	Travel & Travel Allowance	$	-	
2005	Music & Worship Program & Materials	$	-	
2006	Christian Education Materials & Supplie	$	-	
2007	Pulpit Supply	$	-	
2008	Audio Visual and other Equipment	$	-	
2009	Ministry Support	$	-	
2011	Special Events and Projects	$	-	
2012	Intern Program	$	-	
2013	Missions & Presbytery	$	-	
2014	Outside Services, Accounting, Legal, etc	$	-	
2021	Office Supplies, stationary, postage, mi	$	-	
2022	Computer costs and supplies	$	-	
2023	Communications - Internet & Telephone	$	-	
2024	Unassigned	$	-	
2031	Janitorial Supplies and Services	$	-	
2032	Repair and Maintenance - (Non-Covena	$	-	
2033	Insurance - Liability	$	-	
2034	Use Agreement (Utilities & Maint. Reser	$	-	
2035	Unassigned	$	-	
2041	Food & Beverages	$	-	
2042	Other Hospitality Related - Incl. Busines	$	-	
2043	Unassigned	$	-	
2051	Van Maintenance & Gasoline	$	-	
2052	Van Insurance	$	-	
2061	Overdraft Charges	$	-	
	Total Expenses:			$ 350.00
Net : Income Gain / (Loss)				$ 150.00
Cash End of Period				$ 150.00

INTRO / Chart of Accounts / Budget vs. Actual 1 / Summary by Month / GL-

At AccountantBesideYou.com, I offer a more complex worksheet that allows for up to five funds. It also includes individual donor worksheets, bank reconciliation worksheets, and much more.

Whether you design your own or download mine, these are very cost-effective and useful ways for a small organization to track their finances. As your organization grows and has more restricted donations and transactions, you will probably want to research more robust, automated accounting programs.

C. Off-The-Shelf Accounting Software

The next price level of options is off-the-shelf software used by businesses. QuickBooks® and Sage® are two of the most common seen at local office supply stores. They usually run between $300 and $600 and are more than adequate for most small nonprofits needs. Many people use these programs to help avoid a long learning curve when switching bookkeepers. The downside to these programs is that they were designed for businesses, not nonprofits. Specific "tweaking" is required to record the fund accounting accurately, as I have described in my book, *QuickBooks® for Nonprofits & Churches- A Step-by-Step Guide to the Pro, Premier, & Nonprofit Versions* and *QuickBooks Online® for Nonprofits & Churches.*

D. Online Nonprofit-Specific Accounting Packages

Several companies are now offering an online accounting option. Aplos Accounting® is known for its ease of use and lower cost than some other online options. Web-based accounting packages offer the convenience of getting information without having to go to the office. They also allow numerous users to see the same information without copying or emailing.

I have three major concerns with online systems: security, reliability of the Internet connection, and ongoing cost.

If you decide to use an online program, research their controls against hackers. A significant amount of confidential data may be included in your financial information.

If you are not completely satisfied with your Internet reliability, using an online program can be very unproductive. If your Internet connection is lost, you can't access your data. As someone who lives in a rural area, I know how frustrating this can be.

Another consideration is the ongoing cost. With a desktop package, once purchased, you do not need to spend any more money until you are ready to upgrade. Web-based programs charge a monthly fee for as long as you use the program.

E. Summary

One of the biggest mistakes you can make selecting an accounting package is to go with the first one you hear about. Research, ask other nonprofit bookkeepers, request a demo copy, and play around with the software. On the next page is a table summarizing the options.

The bottom line is there is no perfect accounting package. You need to evaluate the options based on the following:

- What is your budget?
- What are the ongoing costs (technical support, program updates, monthly fees)?
- How intuitive is the software? Is the learning time significant?
- Is your current computer sufficient for the program?
- Is multi-user capability important?
- Does it do the reporting you need?

In the next chapter, I'll explain some of the essential administrative steps to start a new nonprofit and rules for how long to keep your accounting records.

This book explains the accounting concepts no matter what system you are using. If you would like detailed instructions on how to use QuickBooks in a nonprofit environment, I (shamelessly) recommend my book, QuickBooks® for Nonprofits & Churches-A Step-by-Step Guide to the Pro, Premier & Nonprofit versions, available at Amazon.com, www.accountantbesideyou.com, and other retailers. If you are using QuickBooks Online, please consider reading QuickBooks Online for Nonprofits & Churches.

Type	Pros	Cons
Spreadsheet	Inexpensive, relatively easy to set up	Prone to errors, time-intensive, limited reporting
Off the Shelf	Relatively inexpensive, experienced bookkeepers easy to find, easy bank reconciliations, substantial reporting	Requires careful setup and recording to make fund accounting work, limited donor management options
Nonprofit Specific	Geared towards nonprofit management, robust donor database	Expensive, significant learning curve, often requires continued licensing fees or technical support fees
Online	Convenience of working from anywhere, ease of sharing data, automatically upgraded as systems are improved	Must pay monthly for as long as the system is in use If the Internet is not working, reports and transactions cannot be accessed Online data security risks

4. Administrative Issues

Hopefully, you are feeling more comfortable with the accounting requirements of a nonprofit, but there are always administrative items you may need to be concerned with. In this chapter, we'll go over:

- The basic steps required to start a nonprofit and
- Record retention policy recommendations.

A. Basic Steps to Start a New Nonprofit Organization

If you are interested in starting a new organization, there are some initial steps you will need to follow. Do NOT consider this legal advice as every state and locality is different. You will need to find a local attorney with knowledge of the requirements for your specific location.

Starting points include:

1. Pick a name. Though this seems obvious, you can't fill out any of the necessary forms without a name.
2. Have an address. A post office box may make sense if you will be using temporary quarters or haven't yet found a location. P.O. boxes are inexpensive and will save you from changing stationary and change of address forms if you don't have a permanent address.
3. Find out the rules for incorporating in your state. An experienced nonprofit attorney will be invaluable. To be incorporated as a nonprofit, specific wording is necessary for the bylaws, a board of directors may be needed, and there may be annual filing requirements. Inquire as to the risk to your volunteers and board members individually if your Nonprofit is not incorporated.
4. Develop bylaws even if they are not required in your state. (In the next section, we'll discuss the guidelines for writing bylaws).

5. Apply for a Federal Employer Identification Number (EIN). The EIN is necessary to submit the payroll filings, and most banks now require it before you can open an account.
6. Apply for a State Identification Number, if applicable. Some states simply use the Federal EIN, but others have their state IDs.
7. Once you have the EIN, you should open a checking account. It is CRUCIAL to keep the organization's funds separate from any personal funds. Most banks waive the service charges for nonprofits. If your bank charges a monthly fee, shop around to other banks.
8. Request a sales tax exemption from your state. This can save a substantial amount of money. Be sure to understand and follow the rules of when you can use the exemption. Instead of exempting nonprofit organizations, some states refund the sales tax after it has been paid. Either way, you will need to request exempt status from your state agency.
9. Determine if the executive director should be treated as an employee or independent contractor. Document the director's compensation package.
10. Determine who will take care of the financial information and how it will be handled. *Remember, the person handling the money should NOT have access to the records.*
11. Apply to the IRS for Exemption Status by electronically filing Form 1023-EZ if you have not had revenue of more than $50,000 in any of the last three years and don't expect to have more than $50,000 in any of the next three years and you have total assets valued at less than $250,000. Go to https://pay.gov/public/form/start/62759871 to start the application process. If you expect to exceed those amounts, you will file a Form 1023 online.

B. Organization Bylaws

Define the guidelines and procedures to operate your nonprofit with your bylaws. They can be very detailed or more general.

Meet with the board to decide your bylaws and determine the focus of your organization. The secretary of the board should take minutes for the bylaw meeting.

Please note that each state has a nonprofit corporation statute that may require the bylaws to be modified to meet that state's requirements.

Here are some initial steps and considerations for writing your bylaws:

1. Include the organization's official name, bank documents, bills, bank accounts, and other pertinent documentation.
2. Define the organization's purpose, what you plan to address through your ministries, and your legal status.
3. Is your organization a registered tax-exempt nonprofit organization, or do you have another tax status? How you will operate in terms of donations, as only nonprofit organizations can accept tax-deductible contributions, is determined by your status.
4. Discuss any associated charities. If your group belongs to a national association, you must mention this in your bylaws.
5. Develop your mission statement and outline how the leaders plan to achieve its purpose and goals. What is your organization's focus?
6. Discuss the requirements for membership, if applicable, including the process of becoming a member, and each member's rights and responsibilities. Include whether members will have voting rights or if the voting rights are held solely by the board.
7. Define how board members are chosen or elected, their responsibilities, and the length of their terms. Clearly outline how the choosing or election process will work.
8. Include the rules for board meetings, including who has the right to vote, how the meetings will be regulated, and how often financial updates should occur.
9. Define the departments within your charity.
10. Discuss the organization's ability to own land and have assets and under whose name they will be listed.
11. Explain how to amend the bylaws and if a majority vote is required. As the organization grows, revisions may be

necessary. If members have voting rights, be careful not to make the percentage voting so high future boards will not be able to change the bylaws as needed.

12. Plan in case the organization is dissolved and how the assets will be distributed.
13. Have an experienced nonprofit lawyer, accountant, or another professional review the bylaws to save a lot of time and trouble in the long run.
14. Hold a vote to approve the bylaws. If a majority of the board members endorse it, this will be a legally binding document to guide the organization.

C. Record Retention

Once the year is closed out, and all the quarterly and annual filings are completed, it is time to review your record retention policy. Put simply, how long do you need to store all relevant tax documents? The IRS rules are to keep most records three years after the return is filed and all employment tax records at least four years after the date the tax is paid. If your organization requests an extension, you will need to keep the records closer to four years. If the IRS finds fraud, they can go back seven years for an audit.

1. Records to Keep Forever

There are a few things that should be kept as long as the organization is functioning. These include:

- Incorporation papers
- Bylaws
- Titles to property
- Any legal documents
- Vital records (baptisms, weddings, etc.)
- Permanent restricted funds documents
- Retirement and pension records.

If you think it is crucial, save it. Essential documents should be kept in a fire-proof safe or safety deposit box.

To play it safe, keep your financial records for seven years.

2. Records to Keep for an Extended Period

Some documents need to be retained for an extended period as they pertain to long-term assets. Property records (i.e., mortgage documents) and equipment and other property purchase records should be kept for at least three years after you dispose of the property or pay off the loans. Check with your bank or insurer as they may have other guidelines.

3. Records to Keep for 7 Years

Any financial information the IRS may require during an audit should be kept for seven years. Only three years is mandatory, but if fraud is discovered, the IRS can go back seven years, so be prepared. As a whole, IRS agents are trained to differentiate fraud from "stupid" mistakes, but, as fraud is still a possibility, it is a good idea to keep the financial data for a full seven years. Financial data includes invoices, bank statements, canceled checks or scans, employee reimbursements, and audit reports.

Employment records should be kept for at least seven years after the employee leaves and MUST be kept in a locked, secure location. Your employment files should include:

- Applications for employment
- W-4 forms for each employee
- Personnel files
- Performance appraisal and evaluation forms
- Employee handbook
- Immigration I-9 form

Electronic information needs to be backed up and protected. If you have elected to have your bills and bank statements sent electronically, you do not have to print them out to save them, but you do have to be sure you can access them and that there is adequate backup. I recommend backing up the financial system and all electronic statements to a flash drive after the end of each year. Mark the flash drive with the contents and store in a fire-proof safe or safety deposit box for at least three years.

If you are using a cloud service to back up, copy data to a flash drive at least once a year.

> *Do NOT store the backup files on the same computer as the original documents. Computers crash, get upgraded, or sometimes simply disappear.*

4. Keep the Historical Data Organized

It doesn't do any good to have saved all the necessary information if you can't find it. Carefully label each box with the contents and mark a "Destroy By" date on it. Within the containers, have the materials well labeled and filed alphabetically or in some rational fashion.

D. Summary

We've covered a lot in this section. I hope you have a good understanding of:

- Necessary steps for setting up a new nonprofit,
- How to get a start on saving your nonprofit from headaches and money loss,
- Considerations for bylaws,
- What records to keep and for how long, and
- Best safety controls for your documentation.

In the next chapter, we'll get into the details of receiving and acknowledging donations.

5. Donations, Part I: Receiving and Recording

Donations are the financial lifeblood of your nonprofit. Keeping accurate records of these contributions is imperative for the organization and the donors.

In this section, we will cover how to:

- Handle contributions from the moment they are received until they are recorded in the donor's contribution records and an acknowledgment is sent,
- Classify donations,
- How to record various kinds of donations, and
- Accept and acknowledge the contributions of automobiles, boats, and airplanes.

A. Internal Controls and Written Policies

In the first chapter, I explained the need for separation of duties and the necessary controls for receiving cash. Please go back and re-familiarize yourself with these concepts as they are critical.

Take the recommendations I made and put them in a written policy for your nonprofit. A written policy is necessary for the protection of your volunteers and employees as well as the company. This policy should layout your nonprofit's internal controls. Having documented procedures helps guard against mistakes as well as fraud. You should also share your written policies with your volunteers; this will help to keep everyone above suspicion. There is a handbook available at www.accountantbesideyou.com to help with the documentation.

On top of a written policy, you should review with any person handling the donations the importance of confidentiality. Donors may or may not want their gifts publicized as this is the donor's decision, not that of some volunteer who happens to see a check and wants to talk about it. Gossiping about the amounts people donate is a sure-fire way to lose donors.

B. Counting Money Received In Person

Incoming money from meetings or events needs to be collected following the written procedures of your organization. The counters will need to count the money, record who it came from, and notate any donor restrictions.

There is an example sheet.

NAME
COLLECTION COUNT SHEET

Date: ____________

☐ Dues ☐ Event____________

Cash Received:	Bills	Qty	Amount	Total
	100.00	____	____	
	50.00	____	____	
	20.00	____	____	
	10.00	____	____	
	5.00	____	____	
	1.00	____	____	
	Total Bills Received:			$____
	Total Coin Received:			$____

Checks Received:

Check No.	Contributor	Amount
____	____	____
____	____	____
____	____	____
____	____	____

Total Checks: ____

Total Collections: ____

Income from other donations included in the deposit:

Amount	Purpose

Counted By:

1- ____

2- ____

3- ____

Notice there is an area for both counters to sign, showing their agreement with the total. You will want your counters to do the following:

Pay attention to anything written on the memo section of the checks and envelopes received. If a donor notates the money should be used for a particular purpose, the counters should record it on the summary sheet.

Examine the date of each check. Some donors may give their check early but not want you to deposit it until their next payday. If a check is post-dated, set it aside in a secure location to be deposited on the appropriate date.

Be sure the "Payee" section of the check is filled in correctly. It is safe to assume the organization is the intended recipient, but the name of the charity needs to be filled in as soon as possible.

Double-check the amount written out is the same amount in the $ blank. If there is a difference, the bank assumes the written-out amount is the correct one. Your deposit should reflect the written value. If it is not apparent to the counters that the written amount is the donor's wish, they should contact the donor and ask for clarification.

Make sure the signature line is signed. Sometimes people are in a hurry and just forget. The bank will most likely send any unsigned checks back, and the organization may incur a change in deposit fee. If the check is unsigned, contact the donor to come by and sign it or send a new one.

C. Making the Deposits

After the donations are checked, tallied, and totaled, the counters are ready to deposit the money.

Money must be deposited intact, meaning cash should not be taken out of it for the reimbursement of expenses.

Before the deposit, all checks must be stamped with a "For Deposit Only" stamp with the organization's legal name. Then the tallied cash and checks should be deposited in the bank with a copy of the deposit slip and any notes from the donors for the bookkeeper. These deposits can then be taken to the night drop or, if necessary, locked in a secure location.

If you have a RID scanner, you do not need to drop the checks at the bank. The stamped checks should be scanned, then marked with a highlighter to ensure they are not scanned twice, and a deposit detail report is printed from the scanner. Attach the scanned checks to the back of the report along with any notes from the donor. The bookkeeper will enter the data in the donor records.

D. Recording Donors' Contributions

The money has been deposited, but the process is not complete. You need to record the contributions in the financial statements and give the correct donor credit for the donation. From the tally sheet or deposit report, the bookkeeper or administrator can record the donor's contributions. You should use the date the organization received the payment unless the offering comes in near January 1.

The IRS has stringent rules regarding year-end donations and receipts:

- If the organization receives a contribution in the mail in early January, it should be recorded in the new year, no matter when the check is dated, unless the envelope is postmarked in the previous year.
- If the postmark is dated 12/31 or prior, the contribution should be included in the donor's previous year statement; otherwise, it is included in the current year regardless of the date on the check.
- Every contribution should be recorded in your donors' records regardless of whether you plan on sending an annual statement to them.

Sometimes it can be challenging to know how to record the contribution to a donor, so we have some general guidelines. These can be modified for your organization's needs but are a good starting point.

When recording a check from a joint account:

If a husband and wife's names are on the check and they both attend your organization, record in the husband's name.

If just the wife attends, record in her name even if the checking account is both names.

If the wife has her own checking account and uses that account to give contributions, record in her name only unless told differently.

If there are two unrelated names on the contribution check, record the name of the person who signed the check.

If the contribution check is from a business, it must be recorded as the business's name unless an individual's name appears with the business name.

E. Recording Credit Card Donations

More nonprofit organizations have websites than ever before. The site is a perfect location to allow members and others to donate money through credit cards or PayPal links. Nonprofits encouraging their members to enroll in an automatically recurring donation program have seen a significant increase in the number of contributions received and consistency.

For example, if Mr. Smith donates $100 per month but goes out of town for the summer and forgets to send in payments, the organization would only receive $900 instead of the expected $1200. Usually, the additional cost of processing the credit card transactions are more than offset by the increased revenue.

In Chapter 1, we discussed how to set up the controls for online payments. Now we will review how to record the donation and the related fees.

When a donor uses a credit card to donate, the nonprofit is charged a **discount fee**. The discount fee is the percentage the processor bills the organization for processing the payment. The fee is handled differently based on the processor, but the two main ways it is charged are discussed here.

- The full amount of the donations is added to the organizations' checking account, but the discount and service fees are charged against it or
- The contribution is discounted by the discount amount, and the net is deposited into the checking account.

The first scenario is the easiest. Your processor should have a report detailing the persons making donations. You will input the amounts donated into each donor's account in your accounting system. Don't forget to send them a thank you or acknowledgment as appropriate. The discount and service fees are entered into your general ledger in the Service Charge Expense or Bank Fees Expense account.

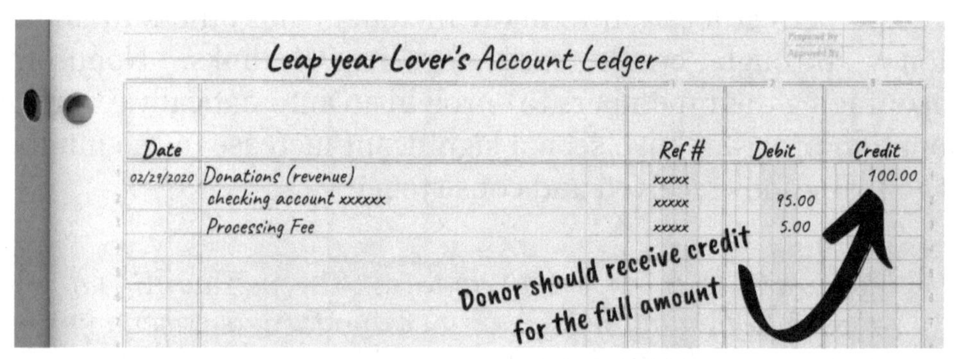

In the second scenario, the total amount of the donation does not show up in the checking account. Instead, the amount deposited is the gift less the fees. For the donor to get full credit for his donation, you will need to record the total contribution under the donor's name and the fees under expenses. The net should be the amount transferred to the checking account.

If you are using an automated bank feed, I recommend setting up a rule that will automatically record the fees when they are downloaded from the bank to save time.

The donor record should always reflect the amount donated, not the net amount received.

F. Summary

Keep in mind, anytime money is being handled, two unrelated people should be involved. The person in charge of the donor records should NOT be managing the money. In this chapter, you learned how to:

- set up controls for receiving donations,
- record the donations in your accounting records, and
- handle credit card fees on donations.

Now that you understand how to receive and record cash and credit card donations, let's review the acknowledging and reporting requirements for all donations.

6. Donations, Part II: Acknowledgement

There are definite IRS rules regarding the tax-deductibility of contributions based on amounts and type of nonprofit. Additionally, each state has specific laws.

> *As rules can change, be sure to review tax law changes with your local CPA or tax specialist on an annual basis.*

In this section, we will discuss the four primary types of contribution categories—*cash*, *noncash*, *gifts*, and *donated labor and services*—and when to issue a contribution acknowledgment.

Additionally, we will go over:

- Impact of the TCJA (2017 Tax Law),
- Quid pro quo donations (when you receive something for your donation),
- Reporting requirements for contributions of property,
- Gifts of vehicles, and
- When acknowledgments are needed and when they are not.

A. Cash Contributions

Most of your donations will probably be cash and stock (which is treated as cash for these purposes). According to IRS Pub 1771, the donor is responsible for obtaining a written acknowledgment from a charity for any single contribution of $250 or more before the donor can claim a charitable contribution on his/her federal income tax return.

1. Required Information

According to IRS rules, a contributor may only deduct a donation by cash or check if the contributor has a receipt issued by the nonprofit or a bank record of the contribution. The bank record for this requirement includes bank or credit union statements, canceled checks, or credit card statements.

For every acknowledgment, the record must show the date paid or posted, name of the charity, and amount of the payment.

Your issued receipt must include:

- Organization's name,
- Donor's name,
- Date of the contribution,
- Date the receipt was issued,
- Amount of the cash contribution, and
- Statement saying whether the organization provided any goods or services in exchange for the gift contribution.

> *Most importantly, the receipt must include a statement along the lines of*
>
> *"The donor did not receive goods or services in exchange for their donation."*

If something <u>IS</u> exchanged for the donation, it is considered a *quid pro* quo gift. Refer to the quid pro quo section of this chapter for instructions and wording. A religious organization would add "other than intangible religious benefits."

If you are using an automated system to send donor acknowledgments, you should have the "The donor did not receive goods or services in exchange for their donation" statement as a permanent line along the bottom.

Here is an example of an annual contribution statement. Besides providing a required tax document, a well-written acknowledgment letter also serves as an excellent donor management tool.

Note in this template, the donor is being thanked for her support, reminded of the good works the donation funded, and told how much it is appreciated. You want your donor to feel good about herself and your organization when she reads this.

Dear [Donor],

Thank you for your generous donations to [Your Nonprofit's Name] throughout the year. Your continued support helps us continue to do the good work our community needs and appreciates.

Because of your generosity, we have been able to continue to grow and maintain our outreach programs [provide examples of what you have done this year].

Attached [or "Here" if it is a short list... just list below] is an itemized statement of your contributions for [Year], according to our records. If you have any concerns about the accuracy of this information, please let us know.

For income tax purposes, it is important for us to state here that you did not receive any goods or services in return for any of these contributions other than intangible benefits. You made these out of your own generosity and commitments to our Non-Profit.

Once again, thank you for your commitment to our cause,

Sincerely,

[Your Name]

[NPO Title]

[Date]

Do NOT ask for additional money when sending an acknowledgment. The acknowledgment is to thank the donor, not to hit them up again.

2. Timing

At a minimum, annual contribution statements need to be mailed out after the end of the year. These should be received by the donor no later than January 31 for your donors to have the tax information they need on a timely basis.

I recommend sending acknowledgments out more frequently. Any significant or non-pledged gift should be acknowledged promptly (and graciously) upon receipt. Thanking them ensures the donor that the money was received by the organization and thus allowed you to thank them.

Regular contributions should be acknowledged quarterly or semi-annually. Besides the benefit of communicating with your supporters, this allows additional controls to ensure donations are received and recorded correctly.

Don't forget to add a line on the statement letting the donor know who to call if there are any discrepancies. That contact must not be the bookkeeper. Have someone else research the difference!

B. Stock Donations

For the most part, contributions of publicly traded stock are treated the same as a cash donation. I highly recommend the nonprofit have an investment account available for donors to transfer gifts of stock as there is a tax benefit for the donor who transfers stock instead of selling the stock and donating cash.

Assume a donor has sold stock valued at $5000 and given the money to the organization. If the stock's value has appreciated since the donor acquired it, the donor must pay taxes on the difference between the sales price and the purchase price. However, if he were to transfer the equivalent of $5000 stock to the nonprofit instead of selling it, he could deduct the same amount as a charitable contribution but not have to pay the tax on the gain.

Instruct your donors to speak to their tax specialist to see if this would be beneficial to them.

C. Noncash Contributions

Frequently, generous members of your organization may wish to donate by giving computers, supplies, food, and other useful items. They sometimes also want to donate things the nonprofit does not need. In the attics of many organizations are collections of noncash contributions the administration didn't know how to refuse. Every organization should have a written policy stating they will only accept gifts that can be used by the organization, or, if not needed, they can be sold.

> *A written policy gives the executive director a graceful way to tell a donor "no thank you."*

1. Requirements

For noncash donations the nonprofit is willing to receive, a written receipt is required. The organization is NOT required to establish the value of the item, and no value should be included on the receipt. The following items, however, must be included:

- donor's name,
- description of the property (but not the value)
- a statement declaring if any goods or services were provided to the donor in exchange for the contribution,
- a statement regarding the usefulness of the donated property to further the nonprofit's tax-exempt purpose,
- the date and location of the donation, and
- the date the contribution receipt was issued.

Donors should also be made aware that IRS regulations require all donors who make noncash contributions valued by the donor at $250 to $500 to obtain a contemporaneous written acknowledgment from the charitable organization.

"Contemporaneous" means the taxpayer must have the receipt in their possession at the time they claimed the tax deduction on a timely-filed tax return. Along with the noncash contribution receipt, records the donor should keep include notation of how much they claimed as a deduction, the fair market value of the property at the time it was donated, and the calculation of the fair market value of the property. Extra documentation from your organization is required for donations of vehicles and will be covered in a later section.

2. Contributions of Property Over $500

If donors give your organization items valued over $500, there is a bit more paperwork involved for both you and the donor.

Your donors should be aware that for contributions of property valued at more than $500 but less than $5,000, the IRS requires a written acknowledgment as described above, plus the donor's records must include:

- How the donated property was acquired (by purchase, gift, inheritance, exchange, etc.),
- When the donor acquired the property (approximately), and
- The cost and any adjustments to the cost basis of donated property held less than 12 months (Does not apply to publicly traded securities)

Part of Form 8283 must be completed and attached to Form 1040 by donors whose total deductions for noncash contributions in a calendar year are over $500. Many organizations will advise their donors of this obligation and provide Form 8283 as a courtesy with the donor's noncash contribution receipts.

3. Contributions of Property Over $5000

If your organization is fortunate enough to receive donations of property other than money and publicly traded securities with a reported value over $5,000, the donor must obtain a qualified appraisal and attach an appraisal summary to the return on which the deduction is claimed. There is an exception for non-publicly traded stock. If the declared value of the stock does not exceed $10,000 but is greater than $5,000, the donor does not have to obtain an appraisal by a qualified appraiser.

The appraisal summary (for anything over $5000) must be on Form 8283, signed and dated by the charity and the appraiser, and attached to the donor's tax return. The signature by the nonprofit does not represent agreement in the appraised value of the contributed property.

> *Your organization should advise your donors of their responsibility and provide them with Form 8283 as a courtesy.*

It is the DONOR's responsibility to file a Form 8283 if required. Your organization is under no obligation to ensure the donor files this form or that it is accurately completed. However, it is good practice to advise them to do so.

4. Reporting For Donated Personal Property:

Organizations receiving donated property valued at over $5,000 by the donor have two requirements:

1. The donor must be given a written noncash acknowledgment containing the information stated under "Requirements."
2. A representative of the organization must complete and sign Part IV of Section B of the donor's Form 8283 appraisal summary. Your signature does not represent agreement in the appraised value of the contributed property.

Additionally, your organization may be required to file a Form 8282, Donee Information Return, with the IRS if all three of the following conditions occur:

1. The nonprofit receives a noncash contribution of personal property valued at more than $5,000 by the donor,
2. The donor presents your organization with a qualified appraisal summary (Form 8283, Section B, Part IV) for signature, and
3. The donated property is sold, exchanged, or disposed of by the organization within three years after the date of the contribution.

Form 8282 must be filed within 125 days of the date the donated property was sold, exchanged, or otherwise disposed of. Usually, an organization that receives a charitable contribution valued at more than $5,000 from a corporation does not have to complete Form 8283.

Any time you receive property valued over $5000, I'd recommend consulting your local accountant to ensure everything is completed and filed correctly.

Important note: Form 8282 provides detailed information on the contribution and the disposal of the property. A copy of Form 8282 must be provided to the donor and retained by the organization.

5. Example of Property Donation Acknowledgment

Dear [Donor Name],

Thank you for your contribution of a Lenovo G510 laptop computer in good condition. The laptop is just what is needed for our Youth Center and we will be setting it up for use immediately.

You did not receive any goods or services in connection with this contribution other than intangible benefits.

As you know, we are a qualified 501 (c)(3) organization, so if you plan on claiming a tax deduction for this contribution you are responsible for establishing the value of the donated item. Under section 1709(f)(8)(b) of the Internal Revenue Code, we at [Nonprofit Name] are prohibited from estimating the fair market value of your donated personal property.

For your information, if the value of the item exceeds $500, you will be required to file Form 8283. If the value exceeds $5,000, you may be required to obtain a certified appraisal. Consult your tax preparer for additional details.

Once again, thank you for the much-needed donation. Help us keep up the good work!

Sincerely,

[Organizatin's Treasurer]

[Date]

Retain for Tax Purposes

To help visualize the acknowledgment, here is an example. Note that the donor has been thanked, the property donated described (but not valued), and the letter explains how the contribution will be used by the nonprofit. Additionally, the letter tells the donor what he needs to do to make the donation deductible.

D. Donated Labor/Services

Most organizations have volunteers who use their professional talents to help. It is not uncommon to be asked: "Can I get a receipt for donated labor or services?"

Sadly, the answer to that question is, "No." The IRS does not permit a tax deduction for donated labor or services. The rule applies to CPAs, attorneys, and other much-appreciated individuals that may generously donate their talent and services to helping a nonprofit.

> *A nonprofit is NOT ALLOWED to issue a contribution receipt for donated labor or services, no matter how valuable that individual's time is.*

You can, however, track the value of these services as an **in-kind donation**. In-kind donations can be thought of as a service or good directly given, instead of a donation to pay for the same service or good.

Accounting rules do allow you to record the fair market value of professional services, like attorneys and accountants, in an in-kind donation account in the revenue section of the statement of activities. Nonprofit organizations that need to show potential donors the strength of their total donations are more likely to record in-kind donations of services.

For in-kind work, a contribution receipt may be issued for donated materials and other out-of-pocket expenses, but not the donated labor.

Un-reimbursed expenses that volunteers incur while performing their volunteer services can generally be deducted from their personal tax return if they itemize on their tax return. Examples of deductible items include mileage at the current federal standard mileage rate, travel, and lodging, and meals incurred during travel, which require an overnight stay.

For example, a repairman voluntarily came and fixed your organization's air conditioner. He usually charges $75 per hour for his labor and he spent $50 for parts. You can issue him a NONCASH contribution receipt for the parts that can be used in his deduction; however, his labor is a generous non-deductible gift. The repairman can also deduct his mileage to the job and back if he itemizes deductions on his tax return.

If a volunteer claims a deduction for unreimbursed expenses exceeding $250, they should receive a letter from your organization indicating the type of services they provided. The letter should not include the value of the volunteer's expenses. The burden is upon the *volunteer* to prove their expenses.

E. Impact of the TCJA (2017 Tax Law)

In the Tax Cuts and Jobs Act (TCJA), the standard deduction was increased significantly for individuals. Unfortunately for nonprofits, donations to charities were not separated. If the donor had fewer donations than the standard deduction amount ($12,200 for single filers and $24,400 for joint filers), they would not see any additional tax benefit for their charitable contribution. If you have donors who give a significant amount, you may want to recommend "donation stacking."

Donation stacking involves grouping donations together in a fiscal year to meet the required threshold.

In order to do this, your contributers would give two years of their normal support in one year, allowing them to get above the standard deduction amount and take the additional deduction.

In the second year, they don't donate at all and take the standard deductions. Then in the third year, they give the two year rate again.

If you see donors doing this, remember to budget accordingly. For cash flow purposes, you could even request one payment on January 1 and a second on December 31st of the same year.

F. Quid Pro Quo Donations

In some situations, a donor may receive more than "intangible benefits" with their donation. Perhaps your organization held an auction or a dinner to raise money for a program. Anytime something tangible or of monetary value is received by the donor when he contributes, it is considered a *quid pro quo* contribution.

1. Requirements

Nonprofits are required to provide a receipt for all transactions of $75 or more where a donor makes a payment and receives goods or services in return. The gifts are not cumulative; you would only be required to issue a quid pro quo receipt for single payments of more than $75.

The receipt must:

- Inform the donor he may only deduct the excess of any money given over the fair market value of goods or services provided by your organization. In other words, the donor must subtract the value of the products or services received from your organization from the total they donated. If property was given instead of cash, only the value of the property above the fair market value of goods or services would be deducted.
- Provide the donor with a good-faith estimate of the fair market value of the goods or services that the donor received.
- Furnish a disclosure statement in connection with either the solicitation or the receipt of the quid pro quo contribution. The acknowledgment must be in writing and must be likely to come to the attention of the donor. For example, a disclosure in small print within a larger document might not meet this requirement (*ref: IRS Pub 1771: Charitable Contributions*).

Though your receipt needs to explain to the donor how much of the donation is tax deductible, it is the actual amount paid by the donor that triggers a requirement for a quid pro quo receipt, not the deductible amount. For example, a donor buys an $80 ticket to a gala with a fair market value of $40. A receipt is required, as more than $75 was received by the organization.

2. Example Letter

If a nonprofit organization held an event in which a donation was required to attend, your acknowledgment letter might say something like this:

> *"Thank you for your participation in the Cystic Fibrosis Night with Chefs. This letter is a formal acknowledgment for federal tax purposes of the gift you made of $____. You received goods and services in exchange for this gift valued at $____ (the value of the dinner). Federal tax law permits you to deduct as a charitable contribution only the excess (if any) of your gift over the value of items you received in exchange."*

3. Determining Value

One of the more challenging aspects of a quid pro quo donation is determining the value of the good or service received. Some goods and services can have a fair market value of $0, or some can make up a substantial percentage of your donor's deductible amount.

> *In short, quid pro quo value is calculated by comparing what you would pay for a similar item or service in the same circumstances.*

Next are some examples that may help with value determination.

From the sample excerpt in the last section, if the dinner was semiformal, and a local restaurant would charge $30 for a similar meal, that is the nondeductible amount.

If there is an auction where a member purchased a pie for $50.00 and the local baker sells pies for $10.00, $10 is the nondeductible amount. The donor can deduct the remaining $40.00.

The IRS gives the following example in the article "Charitable Contributions - Quid Pro Quo Contributions" on their site:

> *"For a payment of $1,000, a charity provides an evening tour of a museum conducted by a well-known artist. The artist does not provide tours on a commercial basis. Tours of the museum are normally free to the public. A good faith estimate of the FMV of the evening museum tour is $0 even though the artist conducts it."*

The donor in the above example could deduct the full $1,000 because the FMV of the item or service received was $0. If tours of the museum were usually $50, only $950 would be considered deductible.

Let's suppose local merchants donated items to your company raffle. Even though the items raffled off were donated and did not cost the organization anything, the fair market value would be the cost of the goods if they were bought at full price from those merchants. Your donors could only deduct the difference between the price given to your organization and the amount they would have paid at the store.

> *Do your best to locate the retail or fair market value and make certain the donors are made aware of the amount.*

4. Acknowledgment Possibilities

If you aren't sending formal letters after the event, print up the invitation or admission tickets with the required information on it.

The ticket may include a line like the one circled in this example.

G. Gifts of Autos, Boats, and Airplanes

Sometimes there may be a tax benefit to your donor if they give your organization a vehicle instead of selling it themselves and then donating the money. For this reason, nonprofits often receive gifts of automobiles, boats, or even airplanes.

Before you accept a donation of an automobile, boat, or even an airplane, it is imperative that you understand all the regulations that guide the acceptance of these types of vehicles. The last thing you want is an upset donor who did not receive his tax deduction because the nonprofit did not follow the rules! You should make sure your donors understand the regulations as well.

> *Give vehicle donors a copy of IRS Publication 4303, A Donor's Guide to Vehicle Donations.*

If your nonprofit has decided to accept the gift, all the regulations relating to gifts discussed previously apply.

IRS Form 1098-C can be used as your written acknowledgment to the donor. Your organization must provide additional information to the donor, including your intended use of the vehicle, within 30 days of the contribution or the sale of the vehicle.

It is important to note that if you sell the donated car or other qualified vehicles before you put them to any significant use, the donor's deduction is limited to the gross proceeds of the sale, NOT the fair market value.

The value of the vehicle determines what reporting is required.

1. Vehicles Donations With Claimed Value of Over $500

Nonprofits are required to provide contemporaneous written acknowledgment for any gift of a car or other qualified vehicle with a claimed value of at least $250. If the declared value is less than $500, that written acknowledgment MUST include the following information:

- Donor's name,
- Description of the property (but not the value)
- A statement declaring if any goods or services were provided to the donor in exchange for the contribution, and
- A statement that goods or services provided by the charity consisted entirely of intangible religious benefits if that was the case.

If your organization sells the car without significantly using or improving it and for less than $500, your donor can claim a tax deduction equal to or less than the fair market value of the car. The donor is responsible for substantiating the declared value.

2. Vehicle Donations With Claimed Value of Over $500:

If your organization receives a donation of a qualified vehicle with a claimed value of $500 or more, the organization must provide the donor with a written acknowledgment (detailed in the next two sections) within 30 days of the sale of the donated property. If your charity plans on keeping and using the vehicle to further its tax-exempt purpose, there is a whole other set of regulations we will examine after we look at the regulations regarding sold vehicles.

3. Sold Donated Vehicles

The written acknowledgment for sold donated vehicles must include the following:

- Name and taxpayer identification number of the donor,
- Vehicle, boat, or airplane identification number or similar number,
- Date of contribution,
- Date of sale,
- Gross proceeds from the sale,
- Certification that the property was sold in an arm's length transaction (the buyer and seller act independently and have no personal relationship between them),
- A statement that the deductible amount may not exceed the amount of the gross proceeds,
- A statement declaring if any goods or services were provided to the donor in exchange for the contribution, and
- A statement that goods or services provided by the charity consisted entirely of intangible religious benefits if that was the case.

Your organization can provide all this information to the donor using IRS form 1098-C. You can order this form from the IRS by calling 800- TAX-FORM or searching IRS.gov. The organization will then need to submit Form 1098-C to the IRS by February 28th of the following year.

In some circumstances, a car may be sold for quite a bit lower than the fair market value or even given to a person in need. In that case, the written acknowledgment must include all the information detailed above plus certification that the organization will sell the car at a price significantly below fair market or gratuitously transfer the property to a person in need. The sale or transfer will be related to the organization's charitable purpose of relieving the poor and distressed or the underprivileged who are in need of a means of transportation.

See IRS Publication 4302, *A Charity's Guide to Car Donations*, for more details and how to handle improvements done on the donated vehicle.

Donors can lose their deductions if you do not acknowledge the gifts correctly.

4. Vehicles Not Sold

Your nonprofit may plan to significantly use or materially improve a donated auto, boat, or airplane before or instead of selling the property. In such circumstances, your organization would not include a dollar amount in the written acknowledgment.

One of the best ways for a donor to obtain fair market value is with a used vehicle pricing guide such as Kelly Blue Book.

Instead, the written acknowledgment, sent within 30 days of the contribution of the vehicle to be considered contemporaneous (i.e., timely), would include the following information:

- Name and taxpayer identification number of the donor,
- Vehicle, boat, or airplane identification number or similar number,
- Date of contribution,
- A statement declaring if any goods or services were provided to the donor in exchange for the contribution,
- A statement that goods or services provided by the charity consisted entirely of intangible benefits if that was the case,
- Certification and description of the intended use or material improvement of the property and the intended duration of the use, and
- Certification that the property will not be transferred in exchange for money, other property, or services before completion of such use or improvement.

As with the sold vehicles, Form 1098-C may be used as the acknowledgment. Your organization will be required to submit Form 1098-C to the IRS by February 28th of the following year. The donor will use the fair market value of their donated vehicle for their tax deduction, not a higher dealer retail price.

As a courtesy to your donors, inform them that:

The amount of their charitable contribution deduction is limited to the gross proceeds from the sale of their donated vehicle.

No deduction is allowed unless the donor itemizes his deductions on his annual returns rather than using the standard deduction.

The donor will be required to attach IRS Form 8283 and a written acknowledgment or completed Form 1098-C to their tax return.

An appraisal is not required if the donor's deduction is limited to the gross proceeds of the sale.

H. When You Do Not Need Disclosure Statements

We have covered instances in which reports are needed and when acknowledgments are required for the donors' tax purposes. Disclosures need not be given in the following circumstances.

1. Insubstantial Or *De Minimis* Value

If your organization is giving out key chains and T-shirts with the organization logo, no disclosure of these gifts is required. These types of things are considered goods or services of insubstantial or ***de minimis*** value. Examples are the small giveaways an organization may offer that are treated as having no value for disclosure purposes, like pencils, company mailings, etc. In general, the IRS puts a price cap on these "fringe benefits" of $100.

For tax deduction purposes, the IRS calculates *de minimis* benefits by comparing the fair market value of a benefit received to the amount of the contribution. Currently, if the value of the benefit is no more than 2% of the contribution or $102[†] (whichever is greater), the donor can usually take a full deduction. For example, if you are having a fundraising event and give each donor a photograph of the organization with any donations of $100 or more, you don't have to worry about disclosures as the photograph's value is less than $102.

2. Provided Goods or Services at Fair Market Value

Any paid services or products offered such as books, DVDs, hall rentals, etc. are all considered provided goods or services and are not deductible; therefore, they should not be included on a contribution acknowledgment.

If the nonprofit has a preschool, money received for the tuition is not considered a donation but payment for a service. Likewise, if a donor offers a check for the use of your building for a party, it is not deductible, since a service was provided, even if marked as a "donation,"

3. Examples of the Quid Pro Quo Rules

Often your organization may have fundraisers or events. Here are some cases on how the quid pro quo rules apply.

Bake Sales: Payments for items sold at bake sales and bazaars are not usually tax-deductible to donors since the purchase price generally equals the fair market value of the item.

Admission to Events: Most of the time, donors receive a benefit equal to the contribution they gave to attend a nonprofit-sponsored event, such as a concert, and no charitable deduction is generated. However, if the contribution is higher than the fair market value, a quid pro quo receipt may be required.

Auctions: In the eyes of the IRS, there is usually no charitable contribution generated when a bidder purchases an item at a charitable auction. The IRS generally takes the position that the fair market value of an object is set by the bidders with the purchase price.

[†] The IRS changes the amount annually for inflation.. Check the IRS website for the current level.

Example 1: Your organization sponsors a banquet to raise money for a new sign charging $35 per person to attend. The meal costs the nonprofit $10 per person. There is no disclosure requirement since the amount charged was less than $75. However, the amount deductible by each donor is only $25.

Example 2: Your organization invites members to attend a banquet without charge. At the end of the dinner, the members are asked to donate to the organization fund. Those contributions would probably not require quid pro quo receipts or disclosure even if the amount given is $75 or more because there is not a direct relationship between the meal and the donation.

However, some tax professionals will advise you that when the purchase price exceeds the fair market value of the items, the amount that exceeds the FMV is deductible as a charitable contribution.

If your organization takes this position, the quid pro quo rules addressed in section D will apply. To comply with those rules, some organizations will set the value of every object sold and provide receipts to buyers. A penalty can be imposed on an organization that does not make the required written disclosure in connection with a quid pro quo contribution of more than $75. The penalty can be up to $10 per contribution.

4. Donors & the Good Faith Estimate

To determine fair market value, the organization must sometimes use their best guess based on the information they have. This best guess is called the **good faith estimate**. A good faith estimate is based on the fair market value of the goods or services received, but sometimes there is room for disagreement. You may have a donor who believes your good faith estimate is wrong. There are two ways a donor may be able to increase the deductible amount above the organization's good-faith estimate.

1. A donor may disagree with an organization's good-faith estimate of the deductible amount. If the donor can justify why he feels the estimate is inaccurate, he may ignore it. The

donor must keep any documentation supporting his choice to ignore the value for review by the IRS if audited.

2. A full deduction can be claimed by the donor if they refuse the goods or services provided by your organization at the time the contribution is made.

For example, if a donor purchases tickets to a charity banquet but decides a week later not to go, they still must deduct the value of the tickets from their contribution before claiming a deduction. If he buys the tickets as support for the function but tells the coordinator he is not coming at the time of purchase, the full amount of the ticket is deductible.

If this is a common situation in your organization, consider providing a form with a refusal box the donor can check at the time of his donation to indicate he did not accept the banquet tickets. Perhaps, "If you cannot attend, please consider a donation of $____."

I. Summary

You want your donors to be happy and continue to support your mission. To keep them happy, you must do everything you can to ensure their donation is tax-deductible. In this chapter, you learned how to:

- Use the correct language to acknowledge simple donations,
- Handle stock donations,
- Recognize a quid pro quo donation,
- Determine the value of and acknowledge a quid pro quo donation,
- Evaluate if a disclosure statement is needed,
- Handle noncash contributions, and
- How to accept, record, and acknowledge gifted vehicles

You can never be too careful. Penalties apply to charities that knowingly furnish a false or fraudulent acknowledgment or fail to furnish an acknowledgment in accordance with the time and content requirements.

7. Donations, Part 3: Other Topics

Most of the time, the contributions your organization receives are relatively standard. From time to time, contributions of a more personal nature may come up. In this chapter, we'll cover how to handle:

- Gifts designated to specific individuals,
- Discounts received from vendors, and
- Checks received but written to another charity.

A. Gifts to Specific Individuals

The donors to your organization are probably very generous and caring individuals. If they hear of a family in need, they may wish to "pass the hat" and give a donation directly to the family.

Your donors or members need to be aware that any gifts designated to a particular person or family are considered a "conduit transaction" or "pass-through transaction" and is not deductible by the donor. Collected monies can be given to the family. Still, as the family is not a nonprofit organization, the donation is not deductible by the donor, nor should it be included in their contribution summary.

> *If contributions to the fund are earmarked by the donor for a particular individual, they are treated, in effect, as being gifts to the designated individual and are not deductible. However, a deduction is allowable if the gift is intended by a donor for the use of the organization and not as a gift to an individual. The test in each case is whether the organization has full control of the donated funds, and discretion as to their use, to ensure that they will be used to carry out its functions and purposes. IRS, Revenue Ruling, 62-113.*

If a donor makes a gift to the hurricane relief fund, it is an appropriate restriction and therefore deductible. If the donor requests it be given to a specific family, it is not deductible as the IRS would consider it a gift to the individual.

1. Before Accepting a Gift For a Specified Individual

There are two options to consider before accepting a gift earmarked for a specified individual:

- The first option is to refuse to accept the donation. Per IRS publication 3833, donors cannot earmark contributions to a charitable organization for a specific individual or family. You would inform him that his thoughtful gift is very much appreciated. Still, he needs to give it directly to the designated family or individual as the organization does not handle pass-through contributions.
- The second option would be to accept the check and stamp "NONDEDUCTIBLE" in red ink on the front of the check. That action would let the donor know that he could not use that check as a tax deduction with his itemized deductions in his personal income tax forms. Any local office supply store can usually make such a stamp for your organization.

If you accept the donation, do not include the nondeductible contribution to the donor's annual contribution statement. If it is included, there should be a notation indicating that the gift is not tax-deductible and was not included in their deductible total.

> *If the donor has written a person's name on the check, you should NOT include that check in the annual donor acknowledgment report.*

2. Exception For Missionaries

There is an exception to the nondeductible issue when it pertains to offerings taken up for missionaries. If an organization initiates and controls an offering taken up for a specific missionary, the contribution is tax-deductible for the donor. It should be included in the donor's contribution receipts as the missionary falls within the prevue of your Nonprofit.

Remember: it all boils down to the organization having complete control of funds and using those funds to further its tax-exempt purpose.

B. Discounts As Donations

Local businesses will often give a nonprofit a substantial discount on goods or services. Unfortunately, a discount in any form is not considered a qualified charitable contribution for a tax deduction. Your organization is not allowed to issue a contribution receipt for a discount.

It may make more sense for the landlord or merchant to charge the fair market value and then donate the amount that would be discounted. In this situation, the nonprofit would issue a contribution receipt for the donation money.

C. Checks Written to Another Charity

It is not uncommon for a nonprofit to take up an offering for another organization. Donors may write the check made out to your nonprofit with a designation for the other charity, or they may write out the check in the other charity's name.

For checks made out to your organization, record them in the donors' records and include the amount on their contribution statements. The nonprofit should also set up an accounts payable account for the charity. If any of the checks were written payable to the other organization, you would not record it in your organization's records. The check should be delivered to the other charity, not deposited into your bank account.

In this situation, your nonprofit would not issue a receipt for that contribution. The other organization would need to issue the acknowledgment to entitle the donor to claim the gift as a charitable contribution.

Also, be aware that donations by U.S. taxpayers to a foreign charity are not eligible for a tax deduction.

D. Summary

This chapter highlighted some other types of contributions a nonprofit may receive, which are deductible to the donor, and what not to acknowledge on donor reports.

In this chapter, you learned how to:

- Handle designated gifts for specified for individuals or families (unless it is for a missionary),
- Record donated supplies and out-of-pocket expenses, but not acknowledge donated labor/services,
- Receive discounted donations from vendors, and
- Manage checks written to other charities.

In the next section, I'll review the different types of expenditures and how to record them accurately.

8. Rules For Helping Local Families And Individuals

As we discussed in Chapter 7, the IRS has definite rules relating to raising money for a specific individual. Without these rules, unethical people could request a tax deduction for a gift to a relative regardless of their need. This becomes particularly important if your nonprofit's mission is to help care for individuals in its community.

To avoid potential issues with your community outreach, your nonprofit should set up a **benevolence policy**. A benevolence policy is simply a fund set up to assist those in need. These often assist with basic needs, such as help with food or utility payments.

Your nonprofit must have a benevolence policy set up to ensure your donors can take advantage of tax benefits for those in need and that the recipients are not taxed on the gift. To receive these tax-free advantages, an organization needs a policy that meets specific criteria, is approved by the board, and is followed closely.

Let's say Mary Jones makes a donation to your nonprofit and either verbally tells you or writes on her check that this contribution is for Joe Smith. Joe Smith may very well be in need of help from your organization, but the donation would be considered a pass-thru contribution (no donor benefits, receiver may be taxed).

IRS publication 3833 *states, "Donors cannot earmark contributions to a charitable organization for a particular individual or family."*

Keep the above in mind, even when your organization has a benevolence policy in place. It is unwise to take up a special offering for a specific person. Instead, encourage your members to give to the benevolence fund regularly. Then, the contributions solicited are tax-deductible to the donor.

To promote the fund, your executive director *can* give examples of families who have already benefited, or could benefit, from the fund but cannot promise to give the funds to a particular person.

In this chapter, we'll review:

- The requirements for a benevolence fund,
- How to handle a discretionary fund,
- Benevolence for employees,
- Disbursement procedures, and
- An example of a benevolence policy.

A. Requirements

Individuals will often seek out charities when they are in need. The most common requests for benevolence include utilities, rent, lodging, food, medical expenses, transportation, and funerals. For your organization to properly help these individuals, it is imperative for you to have a board-approved written policy in place.

Your benevolence policy should include requirements that the nonprofit must document in writing that all benevolent expenditures meet at least two requirements: **need** and **lack of recipient resources**.

Need is defined as something necessary or a necessity. It is up to the nonprofit to define "need" in their policy. When deciding your criteria for need, make sure you consider the specific purpose of your nonprofit.

The second requirement, **lack of resources**, should be defined by your nonprofit as well. It could be a specific threshold or a general need.

Both of these requirements should be backed up by documentation from the recipient, and the documentation should be kept by your organization.

Types of documentation the individual can share with the organization to show *need* include:

- a cutoff notice from the electric company,
- a medical bill, or

- a written memo by a staff employee who has called and verified the need.

A recipient's *lack of resources* could be satisfied by reviewing:

- a paycheck stub,
- a tax return, or
- a bank statement.

You may also wish to have the recipient sign a statement detailing their lack of resources to pay for their need.

Your policy may also have other requirements; I recommend these include *what* kinds of needs are eligible for benevolence payments and *who* will decide as to what needs the organization may or may not assist.

Clearly defining requirements and practices for this policy is necessary not only to protect donors and recipients but also to protect your nonprofit.

As much as I hate to bring this up, remember there are unscrupulous people and con artists out there. Nonprofit organizations that do not have the resources to verify the need requirements should encourage those requesting help to go directly to a more appropriate nonprofit that is set up to assist persons of need. If a person unknown to the executive director comes to the organization requesting funds, he can send them to the better-equipped charity to be adequately vetted and helped as appropriate.

B. Types of Benevolence Funds

Benevolence funds are distributed in one of these three categories:

- **Discretionary**, in which a designated person or committee responds to requests as they occur from persons of need,
- **Employee benevolence** for instances when an employee is having an issue and needs additional help, and
- **Earmarked by a donor** for the organization to give the money to a specific person.

Each of these has different considerations.

1. Discretionary Benevolence Funds

Benevolence funds may be administered via a committee or set up as a **discretionary benevolence account**. A discretionary benevolence account is administered by the executive director only and has the advantage of allowing the executive to meet an individual's needs privately.

There are special precautions you need to set up to avoid all amounts coming into the fund becoming taxable income to the executive:

- The director must account for the expenditures. Whether it is a checkbook register, spreadsheet, or another system, it should be reconciled on a timely basis.
- Written documentation must be required.
- A review of the expenditures needs to be included in your annual audit of the charity financials.

2. Benevolence for Employees

When the individual in need is an employee, the nonprofit's gift to them is taxable in most situations. Even though benevolence payments are generally not taxable to the person of need, payments made to employees are not tax-free. The Internal Revenue Code requires all benevolence payments provided to employees to be considered taxable income and included on the employee's W-2. Furthermore, if the employee is not a director, you should even withhold all applicable payroll taxes as if the payment were wages.

The same rule applies to expenses paid on behalf of the employee, such as a medical bill. Benevolence to family members of employees can also be considered income to that employee. If this situation arises, be sure to read Internal Revenue Code Section 102 or talk to a tax specialist.

However, there is an exception to this rule. If an employee suffers losses due to a natural or civil disaster, the benevolence payments are tax-free, as long as they are for qualifying expenses. The requirements for that exception are quite lengthy, so see Section 139 of the Internal Revenue Code. IRS Publication 3833 is available to explain how these requirements work. Please refer to it if your employees are affected.

3. Earmarked Benevolence Contributions

Remember, even with a benevolence fund set up, contributions to specified individuals are not tax-deductible.

> *The only way the contribution can be considered tax-deductible is for the company to have full control over the destination of that gift.*

In a nutshell, this means your donor cannot tell you who should receive his funds. Written names on checks or verbal requests where donors become the decision maker concerning who receives charity are not tax-deductible.

As we discussed in Chapter 7, the organization has the option to decline the donation or to mark it as nondeductible and not include it on the contribution summary.

C. Disbursement Procedures

Whether your benevolence fund is run by a committee or is a discretionary fund managed by the executive director, formal disbursement controls and policies are required. These controls should include reviewing and storing the written documentation discussed in Chapter 1.

Your organization may also wish to have a formal request for assistance application to ensure the consistency of the information gathered. The application should be reviewed and collaborated by a designated representative.

The committee or executive reviews the requests and comes to a decision. If approved, the request is signed by the person authorizing the payment. Checks are then written through the normal process and disbursed. Where possible, the checks should be made payable to vendors, utility companies, hospitals, etc. instead of the individual.

> *Remember: donors may NOT specify a particular individual or family either on their check or verbally. The organization must have full control over the funds.*

D. Written Benevolence Policy Example

You understand what a benevolence fund is and the importance of having a standard benevolence policy. Next, let's examine what the written policy should include.

At a minimum, your policy should address the purpose of the fund, the type of assistance it will provide and what it CANNOT provide, how the assistance will be provided, who is eligible, and how eligibility will be determined and by whom

A sample benevolence policy is shown on the next page.

E. Summary

The use of a benevolence fund is fundamental to meet some nonprofit organizations' missions. For the donations to the fund to be deductible, the following are crucial:

- A written policy is approved by the board.
- Documentation of need is obtained and kept.
- Donors are not allowed to direct where benevolence money is disbursed.
- Employees should not be given benevolence payments without including it in their taxable wages unless it falls within the natural disaster rules.

With a few simple steps, the nonprofit can ensure donors their contributions are tax-deductible, and individuals can be helped as needed.

In the next chapter, I'll go over the appropriate controls and what you need to know to get the bills paid.

THE SLIPPERS
FOR KIDS FOUNDATION

Making the world a better place one pair of slippers at a time

Benevolence Fund Policy

In the exercise of its charitable purposes, The Slippers for Kids Foundation has established a benevolence fund to help individuals in need. Our members are welcome to suggest individuals that they think would be good candidates for our benevolence fund. Donors may contribute to the fund at any time. However, donors may not specify that their contributions should go to a certain individual. Suggestions can only be just that—suggestions—not requirements of their contributions.

The Slippers for Kids Foundation has full control of administrating its benevolence fund.

A benevolence team is appointed by the board and requests are approved by the team. (*Your policy should also spell out who exactly will make the final determination on which applicants will receive payments.*)

The purpose of The Slippers for Kids Foundation's benevolence fund is to meet qualifying individuals' basic needs. (*You will need to spell out exactly what kind of assistance your group provides and what it CANNOT provide, when it can be provided, and how the assistance should be provided.*)

Any check for the fund should be made payable to "The Slippers for Kids Foundation" with a notation that the funds are to be placed in the organization's benevolence fund.

The Slippers for kids Foundation

123 Anywhere St., Any City,
State, Country 12345
123-456-789

hello@reallygreatsite.com
www.reallygreatsite.com

9. Paying the Bills

So far, we have covered how to handle the various types of contributions and other money coming in. Now we need to review the systems necessary to pay the bills.

In this chapter, we'll cover how to:

- Approve and pay the bills,
- Allocate the expenses across programs and funds,
- Account for automatic drafts from the checking account and credit card payments, and
- Replenish the petty cash fund.

A. Terminology

I'd like to review some terminology for a moment here just to make sure we are all thinking about the same thing.

Accountants like to use the term **vendor** to encompass anyone we owe money to for a good or service. Our employees and donors can also be vendors if we need to reimburse them for an expense. As I refer to vendors throughout this chapter, I could be talking about the electric company, the landlord, a supply company, or even a nonprofit the organization raised money for.

The term **invoice** is used both with vendors and with donors (or customers). If someone owes the charity for a summer day camp, we may send them an invoice asking for the money. When the organization buys something from someone else (i.e., a vendor), the vendor will send the organization an invoice. For this chapter, when I mention invoices, I mean the bills.

Another term you will find me using is **allocations**. Your organization probably has several different programs, funds, and projects. Each of these may have specific expenses related to them, like copying or postage. As you are paying the bills, you may need to allocate (i.e., distribute or assign) the expenses to these different areas.

B. Approving & Paying the Bills

In Chapter 2, we spent some time discussing the chart of accounts. The chart of accounts is the list of items we use to summarize our financial system. As we are paying the bills, we need to be sure we are coding the expenses to the right area for our financial system to be correct and to produce detailed reports.

When a bill comes into the organization, it should be given to the person who purchased the items for approval. This person should review the bill for accuracy and sign it with a notation explaining the purpose and related program or project. General organization bills (utilities, copier lease, etc.) should be reviewed by the nonprofit administrator or the executive and signed. Once the invoices are approved, they can be given to the bookkeeper to issue the checks.

Bills should not be entered before they are approved. I understand sometimes people aren't always available. It might be tempting to go ahead and print out the checks with the thought, "I'll remind him to approve the invoice when he signs the check," but the invoices are often not as well scrutinized when there is a stack of checks waiting to be signed. Additionally, if any corrections need to be made to the bills, the check must be voided and reissued.

To help combat these issues, select one day a week or two specific days a month that checks will be printed. Let all the staff and volunteers know that if they want a bill paid, they need to have it approved and on the bookkeeper's desk by the designated days.

It may take a week or two to train the staff (and expect some complaining), but if you stick to your guns, bill paying will go much smoother regularly.

C. Scams

Scams are becoming more and more sophisticated. Even the most intelligent people can get caught in scams, and nonprofit organizations are becoming a prime target. Beware of scams!

Other common scams are to send bills that look like regular businesses. For example, a bill might be received for office supplies from a familiar-sounding company. If no one can verify they received the supplies, do NOT pay the bill. Bills need to be approved before checks are distributed. Charges for copier maintenance and phone line maintenance are also standard. Even if you have been paying these recurring charges, check with your vendor that you are receiving the service, and for how much.

Lynne Albert, a North Carolina attorney, warned me about the increase in calls she has been recieving from nonprofits caught in scams. One of the most egregious scams involved a company calling to ask for permission to run a free yellow page ad and would record their conversation. The nonprofit would then be billed for an ad, and when they disputed the bill, the recording was doctored to sound as if it was approved. A credit card was requested to give the charity a "break" on the price.

Scammers may also set up dummy collection agencies to scare you if you don't pay. Tell them you will be contacting the Federal Trade Commission's Bureau of Consumer Protection (http://www.ftc.gov/bureaus/bureau-consumer-protection), and I doubt they will bother you again. In fact, anytime I receive calls that sound suspicious at home or through work, I tell the person on the line, "This sounds like a scam." You won't believe how quickly they hang up.

If someone is asking for money, verify the expenditure. Do not be intimidated into giving them information.

If they are legitimate, you should be able to verify what they have told you independently. Do not rely on the information given to you. Some legitimate calls will give you a phone number and additional data for you to research the claim. Regardless, do NOT give them a credit card number or confidential data. As much as I hate to say this, BE CYNICAL!

> *Do not ever give banking or credit card information to someone who has called you!*

D. Insurance & Contracts

It is the responsibility of the administration of the nonprofit to ensure that risks to the organization are minimized. Failure to do so can significantly damage your reputation or end the viability of your nonprofit. Two areas to familiarize yourself with are insurance and contracts.

Many companies carry insurance. Be sure you understand what is and what is not covered under the insurance. The insurance can affect day to day operations or one-time circumstances.

Do you have a van to transport members or goods? If so, is the insurance sufficient to cover accidents or day-to-day wear? Do you need waivers signed by the riders? Are nonprofit-sponsored mission trips to another state covered? What about trips to a third world country? Anytime you will be doing something "out of the ordinary" for your organization, contact your insurance company.

Another area I'd like to address is contracts. With any luck, you may have an attorney in your organization. If so, ask her to review ANY contracts before approval. If you do not have a council, you may incur some legal fees, but a review by legal counsel is essential. Contracts are legally binding documents. They bind whoever signs the contract.

Even if your nonprofit is not incorporated, the contract still needs to be in the organization's name signed by the person and his title.

> *If your nonprofit is incorporated, the contract must be signed in the name of the corporation with the name of the authorized agent and their title.*

The title is important because if you sign it "John Doe" and not "John Doe, Director of Your Organization, Inc.," you may be personally liable. Check with local legal counsel to determine the personal liability in your state.

E. Entering Data

Accuracy is vital when entering data. The more details you can record, the easier it will be if you need to return to a particular bill or allocation, but don't put in unnecessary detail that will slow you down. If you are using a simple spreadsheet as we discussed in the first section, enter the amount of the invoice under the appropriate expense category of the general ledger tabs and key in the check number used to pay the bill.

	A	B	C	D	E	F
1	**Date**	**Payee**	**Invoice #**	**Check #**	**Amount**	**Balance**
2			Outside Services, Accounting, Legal, etc.			
3					**Beginning Balance**	$ 100.00
4	6/13/2020	Kinkos	12212	103	$ 23.00	$ 77.00
5	6/20/2020	Hannaford	52B2	105	$ 25.00	$ 52.00
6						
7					**Remaining Balance**	$ 52.00
8			Office Supplies, Stationary, Postage, Misc.			
9					**Beginning Balance**	$ 100.00
10	6/19/2020	USPS	1234567	104	$ 12.00	$ 88.00
11	6/23/2020	Office Max	1245	106	$ 54.00	$ 34.00
12						
13					**Remaining Balance**	$ 34.00

If you are using a computerized accounting program (like QuickBooks), there will be an area to enter invoices from vendors. You will need to set up the vendor and then designate which accounts to record the expenses.

The computerized program may also allow you to designate the program by assigning a class. Once the checks are written, look at your cash balance and be sure there is enough money left in the checking account to cover the checks.

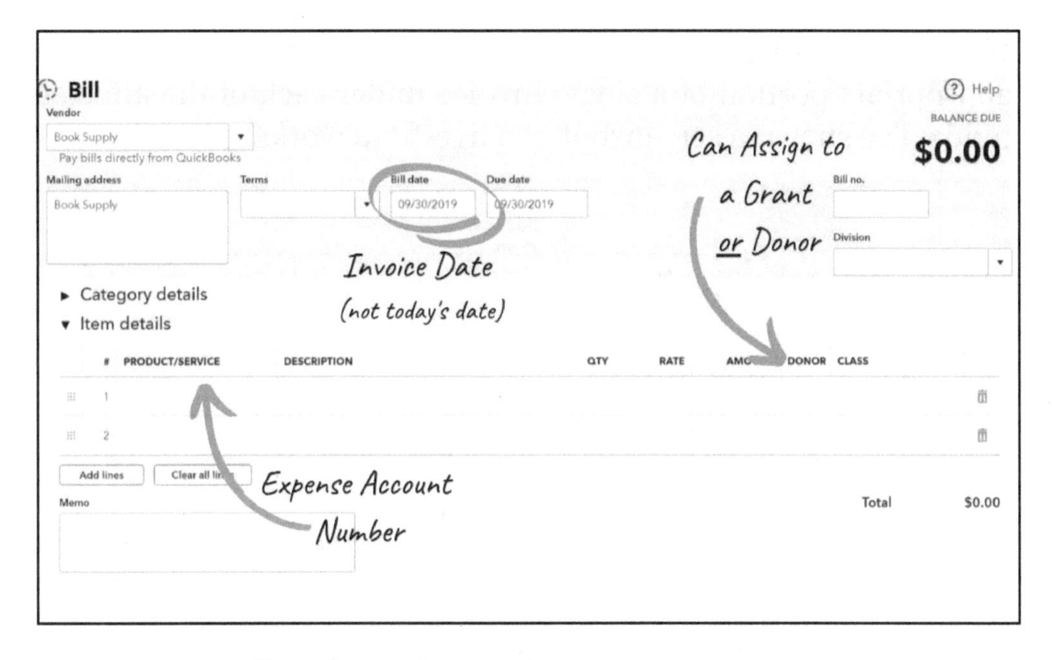

F. Allocation of Expenses

If your charity would like to track expenses by program, grant, or fund, you have an extra step or two to take.

First, decide if the **overhead expenses** will be allocated to the programs. Overhead is the facilities and administrative costs of running the organization. The related costs can be allocated based on the square footage of the building used by the program, payroll dollars associated with the program, or a myriad of other ways.

Unless you have a grant that covers some overhead costs, or the data that will help your governing board run the organization, I wouldn't go to the trouble of allocating the overhead. For individual bills like supplies or postage, you can allocate them based on actual usage, i.e., the development director printed a newsletter and mailed it to potential donors. In this type of situation, I would recommend allocating, so have a real understanding of the costs to run a program.

If you have an off-the-shelf or specialized accounting program, this is quickly done on the invoice entry screen. Refer to the manual of your specific program for directions, or my *QuickBooks for Nonprofits & Churches* if you are using QuickBooks.

If you are using a spreadsheet, you will need to enter the appropriate portion of a single invoice under each of the affected funds. I've shown a screenshot of a five-fund worksheet.

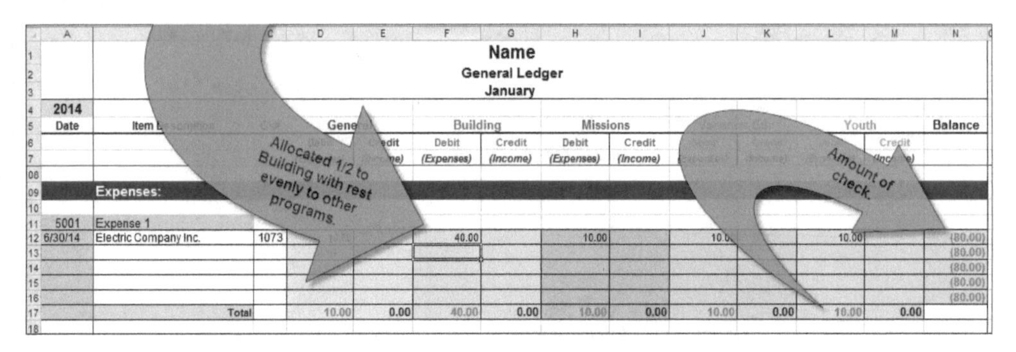

G. Bills Drafted Out of the Bank Account

It is often convenient to have regular, recurring bills drafted out of the nonprofit bank account. These usually are things like utility and phone bills that must be paid monthly for the organization to stay open. Always check the bills for any irregularities. You need to keep on top of any changes to these bills, as they may affect your future budgeting. You will also record these just like you would a check, but instead of inputting a check number, you will indicate it is a draft. I often use the date of the draft as part of the number.

The draft amounts should be entered into your general ledger or check register as soon as you know the amounts, so you always have an accurate balance in your checking account. They are also necessary to enter so the bank statement reconciles.

H. Credit Card Payments

In the first chapter, I explained the need to have the credit card receipts tracked by the user and brought to the bookkeeper before the credit card payment is due. The receipts may be brought to the bookkeeper throughout the month, so he has an idea of how much cash will be required, or they can be all brought in after the statement is received.

Either way, the receipts should be compiled together, documented as to the purpose and the program, and the summary approved by the appropriate charity representative.

Receipts Must be attached before approval

The Philanthropic Peaches

Credit Card Receipts **Approved By:**

Month:

Date	Vendor	Purpose	Program	Amount
3/15/2020	Home Depot	Tree Fertilizer	Garden	$3,222.99
3/21/2020	Staples	New Toner	Office	$65.30
3/22/2020	Exxon	Gas for Tractors	Garden	$120.56
			Total*	$3,408.85

*This must agree to credit card bill

The total must agree with the credit card bill. The individual line items can be entered by fund or program, and then the check can be issued.

I. Petty Cash Replenishment

As we discussed in the first chapter, Petty Cash is an *imprest* fund, which means the fixed fund is only replenished after the money is spent.

The example from Chapter 1 is repeated here. Your Charity has $100 in their petty cash fund. Throughout the month, various volunteers used the money and brought back the following receipts:

- $9.95 for donuts for the youth group meeting
- $44.37 for gas to take members to the Habitat for Humanity house
- $15.68 for copier paper for the office

The receipts total $70.00. There should be $30.00 of cash also in the drawer. A check for $70.00 should be made out to Your Charity with the receipts as the support for the check signer to review. The check can then be cashed, and the drawer replenished.

A simple spreadsheet should be maintained. Here is an example:

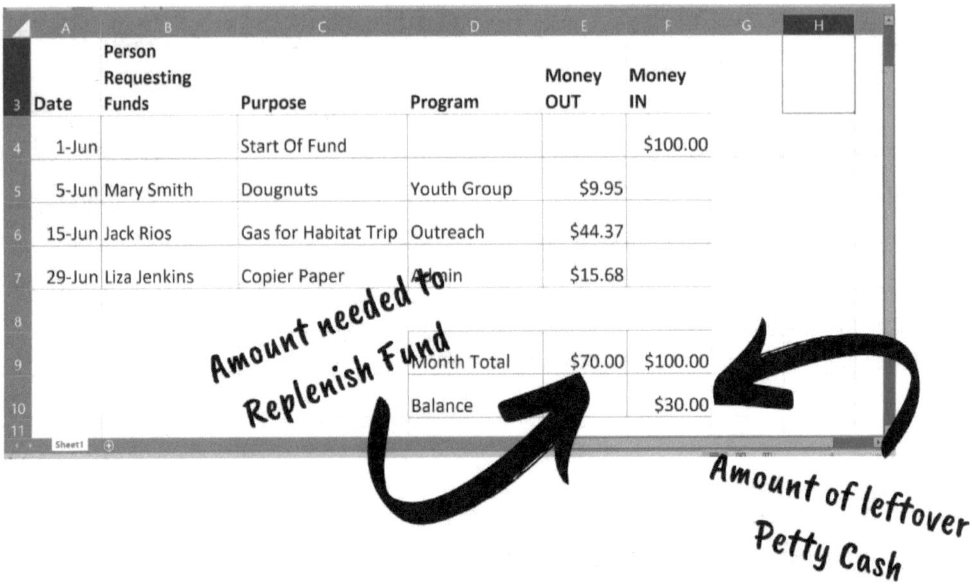

Date	Person Requesting Funds	Purpose	Program	Money OUT	Money IN
1-Jun		Start Of Fund			$100.00
5-Jun	Mary Smith	Dougnuts	Youth Group	$9.95	
15-Jun	Jack Rios	Gas for Habitat Trip	Outreach	$44.37	
29-Jun	Liza Jenkins	Copier Paper	Admin	$15.68	
			Month Total	$70.00	$100.00
			Balance		$30.00

Amount needed to Replenish Fund

Amount of leftover Petty Cash

The check should be written for the amount of the receipts and each of the line items charged to the correct account and program.

J. Summary

A crucial element of paying the bills is to have an approval process for expenditures. Besides guarding against fraud and waste, approvals allow the administrators of the organization to stay on top of activities and cash needs. Bills should be approved before the checks are cut and only approved if someone can verify the expenditure. Contracts need to be in the charity's name and signed by an authorized agent with his title. Insurance should be reviewed regularly, especially with the introduction of new programs or projects.

In this chapter, I have explained:

- the basics of recording regular and recurring bills,
- allocating the expenses across different programs,
- recording credit card charges, and
- replenishing the petty cash fund.

Next, we will go over expense reimbursement policies and procedures.

10. Reimbursement Policies and Procedures

During the day-to-day operations, your executive director or other employees and volunteers probably run to the post office or retail store to pick up necessary items. They may drive to a local hospital to visit a sick member or buy books to help plan their programs. Theoretically, you would have them purchase through a vendor who would send an invoice to the organization for payment.

It is far more common for an employee or volunteer to make a purchase and then ask for reimbursement from the charity. An **accountable reimbursement policy** is a method for claiming and reimbursing professional or business expenses. The IRS refers to these as **accountable reimbursement plans**. This written policy is imperative to keep misunderstandings low and to ensure tax laws are being followed.

> *The rules for employee expense reimbursements are the same for nonprofits as they are for all other businesses.*

This chapter will explain:

- How to set up a reimbursement policy,
- Give an example of a reimbursement policy resolution,
- Which expenses can be included, and which cannot,
- How to reimburse the expense, and
- How to handle advance payments.

A. Setting Up a Reimbursement Policy

To be accountable, a strong reimbursement policy should:

- Be written. It can be a simple, short paragraph in the form of a resolution, or an extended, detailed plan as needed depending on your organization.
- Be adopted by a resolution of the nonprofit board.
- Provide payment for only legitimate expenses with a business purpose, incurred solely for the benefit of the paying entity.
- Require proper substantiation of the expense, including a written record made at or near the time of the expenditure, plus documentary evidence, such as receipts.
- Require that the substantiation be submitted to a third party (usually the treasurer), within a reasonable period.

B. Example of a Reimbursement Policy Resolution

On the following page is an example of a short reimbursement policy resolution. Each organization should establish its policy based on its unique needs. All that is necessary for the establishment of a policy is a simple resolution.

If you would like a more tailored resolution for your company, consider addendums to the resolution. Your organization may wish to designate certain items that it elects to have covered by this policy, such as travel, continuing education, attendance at an annual conference, books, subscriptions, work supplies, robes, etc. There may be a cap or dollar amount on the total reimbursable business expenses that will be paid. The organization may also want to require pre-approval by the treasurer or responsible person of business expenses in excess of $500 (or any other amount deemed appropriate). Any additional requirements should be included in the policy.

C. Employee Business Expenses To Include

Employees and volunteers need to understand what expenses are considered valid business or professional expenses.

Reimbursement Policy Resolution

The following resolution is hereby adopted by the organization board/board of ____________________. It will be effective for the calendar year _____ and all future years unless specifically revoked or superseded.

The organization executive director and/or staff will be reimbursed for ordinary and necessary business expenses incurred in the performance of his or her responsibilities when he/she substantiates the amount, business purpose, date, and place of the expense.

This substantiation must be provided to the organization treasurer within sixty (60) days of incurring the expense. The individual must return to the charity any amounts received in excess of the substantiated expenses within one hundred twenty (120) days of receipt.

The organization will not report any properly substantiated reimbursement payments as income on any Form W-2.

____
(Organization Title)

____
(Organization Title)

Generally, this would include mileage (based on the standard federal rate), tolls and parking, travel expenses, postage, office supplies, as well as professional dues, subscriptions, and certain books. Personal expenses such as dry cleaning and salon services are not valid business expenses.

D. Examples of Proper Reimbursement Items

By no means is the following list all-inclusive, but here are more nonprofit-specific expenses that are correctly reimbursable:

- Reasonable travel and related expenses for attending annual conferences, district meetings, continuing education conferences, etc.

- Trips to visit members at hospitals, nursing homes, or their homes
- Lunch meetings with officers of the charity to discuss nonprofit business
- Supplies for the nonprofit office (e.g., paper, pens, notebooks, etc.)
- A computer required for organization work
- Organization-related books and periodicals
- Uniforms
- Office furnishings and equipment (e.g., desk, chairs, telephone, etc.)

Review Schedule C of the Form 1040 tax return for other business-related (non-personal) expenses allowed.

Note: If the nonprofit organization has reimbursed someone for equipment or other non-consumables, the purchased items belong to the charity

E. **Examples of Improper Reimbursement Items**

For further clarification, it is essential to recognize what is not considered a proper reimbursable item.

- Mileage to the organization from home for daily work (it is considered personal commuting by the IRS)
- A computer used primarily by family
- Everyday clothing, including business suits
- Childcare/dependent expenses
- Housing-related expenses, e.g., utilities, furniture, upkeep

Additionally, your organization may designate additional items as non-reimbursable if they do not feel it to be an appropriate use of their members' donations. Be certain all of the employees of the organization, including the executives, understand appropriate business expenses. One of the most common ways to steal from a charity is to use the organization's credit card or reimbursements for personal items. With a written policy, there will be no dispute on what is allowed and what is not.

Using donated funds to pay for personal items is STEALING!

If you are thinking, "But we've always allowed the executive director to pay for personal expenses through the charity—it's just part of his compensation," you are incorrect. If your organization pays the executive director's personal expenses instead of a larger salary, he is not paying the full amount of his required taxes, and you could lose your tax-exempt status.

A written compensation plan that adheres to IRS regulations will also protect the executive director. What if the governing board member who permitted him to pay for personal items through the charity leaves the organization? The executive could be exposed to accusations of fraud or theft. Protect your organization and your executive director by following regulations and having written policies.

F. Standard Mileage Rates

The IRS determines the standard mileage rates every year based on a study of fixed and variable costs of operating an automobile, including gas. For 2020, the following rates were in effect:

- Business travel=57.5 cents per mile is the rate to reimburse employees for their nonprofit-related travel. Mileage from your home to the office is considered commuting miles and is not reimbursable.
- Charitable organization travel=14 cents per mile is the rate given to your volunteers for any mileage they incur while assisting the charity. It is only deductible for them if they itemize deductions on their tax return.

*As these allowances change annually, you will need to check **www.irs.gov** and search standard mileage each December for the following year's rates.*

G. Reimbursing the Expense

Your staff may submit a bill and ask the organization to pay it through the typical bill paying process, or they can substantiate the expense and ask your organization to reimburse them.

1. Required Documentation For Substantiation

The IRS requires the organization to maintain proper records and have actual receipts for any expense over $75 and proper documentation to back up expenses. Your organization may wish to set a lower limit.

The documentation provided by the requestor must include:

- a description of what was purchased,
- the amount,
- the date,
- the location from where it was purchased, and
- the business nature of the expense.

The documentation for some requests is obvious. A detailed cash register receipt from the office supply store will have the list of items purchased, the amounts, the date, and the name of the store. The requestor will need to notate on the receipt or an expense report what the business purpose was (e.g., folders purchased for the adult education class project). This information will also help the bookkeeper code the expenses to the correct program.

Paper register receipts often fade over time. Digital is better. Take a picture of the receipt, get a digital copy, or scan a copy.

Organize the files and BACK UP your data!

I strongly recommend designing an expense reimbursement request form (like the one below) that is signed by the person requesting the money. It should be reviewed and approved by the appropriate nonprofit representative to ensure you have all the documentation required for the IRS as well as a concise summary for bookkeeping purposes.

2. Example of a Simple Expense Form

Here is an example of a simple expense form. You may want to add columns for any additional information your organization may need.

YOU CAN'T STOP THE BEETS CHARITY

EXPENSE REIMBURSEMENT REQUEST

REQUEST DATE: November 28, 2019

Date	Vendor	Purpose	Program	Amount
11/1/2019	Kinkos	Posters for Root Vegetable Concert	Youth	$38.00
11/21/2019	Music Supply	Metronome	Education	$65.30
11/23/2019	Harris Teeter	Snacks for R.V.C.	Youth	$135.00
			Total*	$238.30

PRINT NAME: Red Riding Hood

SIGNATURE: RRHood

APPROVED BY:

3. Sample Mileage Reimbursement

We discussed earlier the standard rate for mileage reimbursement. I find it useful to have a spreadsheet form for the employees to fill out to calculate this amount.

In the next example, the organization reimbursed an employee $156.80 for a 280 mile or 2-day trip. If a car could be rented for $40 a day and cost $30 more in gas, it would make more sense to rent a car rather than have the employee use his.

If your organization has a lot of long-distance travel, I recommend going to a local car rental and negotiating a rate. Then calculate the breakeven point between reimbursement costs vs. the rental car plus gas. Adopt a policy requiring employees to rent a car if they will be going over 150 miles (or whatever your breakeven point is).

TRUCKS FOR TUITION

EMPLOYEE MILEAGE REIMBURSEMENT FORM

Your Name Tony Talksalot

Month January

Federal Standard Rate 57.5 Cents Per Mile

Verify this Amount Annualy

Date	Reason for trip	Destination	Miles Driven	Reimbursable Amount (= Fed Rate x Mileage)	Program
1/10/2020	Pick up More wheels	High Point, NC	83.5	$48.01	Service
1/14/2020	Training Semenar	Daytona, FL	543.5	$312.51	Administration
		Total	627	$360.52	

Approved By ______________

NOTE: MILEAGE FROM YOUR HOME TO TRUCKS FOR TOTS OFFICE IS NOT REIMBURSABLE

H. Volunteer Mileage

The IRS allows people to deduct the miles spent helping a nonprofit but at a reduced rate. The 2020 rate for charities is 14 cents per mile. If your nonprofit would like to know how many miles are being driven by your volunteers, you may ask them to document it for you. A representative from the charity would then sign, and the volunteer would have documentation for their tax purposes.

The volunteer may not be able to afford to donate both their time and their gas. You could use a similar form as an employee reimbursement request that asks if it is for reimbursement or documentation purposes. It should also explain to the volunteer that if they are reimbursed, they can't request the deduction from their taxes.

If your executives and employees have smartphones, you may want to research the apps available for tracking expenses (and time if that would help). Your accounting system (like QuickBooks) may have a mobile app with these capabilities. Then design your expense reimbursement forms and requirements around the app's capabilities for a more efficient data flow.

> *Save Time, Avoid Headaches!*
>
> *Similar spreadsheets and the example forms are available for purchase in reusable spreadsheet and word processing documents at www.accountantbesideyou.com. I understand the monetary restraints of nonprofits, so we give you all of the data for you to design them yourself, but if you'd like to save time, please check out accountantbesideyou.com.*

I. Timing

The IRS requires that all substantiation of expenses occur within a "reasonable" time of the expense being paid or incurred. A reasonable time frame would be 30 or 60 days. The amount of time your company sets should be included in the resolution and detailed policy plan.

J. Advance Payments

If your staff or volunteers travel, your organization may need to issue advance payments for expenses. The process can be handled in a couple of different ways.

The first is to estimate the employee's expenses and issue him a check for that amount. The employee will then keep track of eligible expenses and reimburse the organization for any amount exceeding the total of the business expenses. If the advance were not sufficient, the organization would reimburse the employee for the remaining amount.

In this case, the receipts must be given to the charity with the request for additional reimbursement. If there are leftover funds, they are returned with the receipts. Expense reports must be submitted within a "reasonable" amount of time (as defined in your policy).

The second approach is to use the federal per diem rates. These can be found at www.gsa.gov. You can type in a city or zip code, and the government will give you the standard rate for meals and lodging. The meals are then broken down to breakfast, lunch, dinner, and incidentals. If an employee will be gone for two days to a town with a meal per diem of $46, you would issue an advance of $92. As you are using the government rates, you don't need to have them bring back receipts, but they should keep them for their records.

Many businesses and charities use a combination of per diem advances and reimbursements. For example, they may pay for meals on a per diem basis but require hotel rooms to be reimbursed.

If your policy is to use the per diem rates, the employee must use it all year; he can't choose to use it in some cities and not others within a single tax year.

> *Per the IRS, the first and last days of travel should be calculated at 75% of the per diem rate.*

If your director's compensation package includes a flat amount paid to him for accountable expenses like gas or books, define how frequently the expense documentation must be provided to the organization. Failure to maintain and provide the documentation may cause the advance to be treated as taxable income.

K. Ticketless Airline Expenses

It is unusual to see an airline ticket anymore—boarding passes are sometimes even sent as a text message to the traveler's smartphone! That doesn't mean documentation isn't necessary. An email from the airline or travel agency showing the date, place, and cost of the ticket can be used to keep track of the expense. Attach it to the credit card receipt form or the reimbursement request form with the business reason for the trip.

L. Ramifications of Not Following the Policy

If an executive director or organization is audited, and no supporting documents are backing up the reimbursement claims are available, the reimbursements could be considered income for the director or staff member. They would then owe penalties for not claiming the income, and it could snowball from there.

Do NOT give any leftover funds in your accountable reimbursement plan to any staff person, including the director, at the end of the year. It would null and void your whole policy, and you would have to include all reimbursements for the year on a W-2 as income. If the charity has more cash at the end of the year than expected and wants to reward the employees, treat it as a bonus, not part of the accountable reimbursement plan.

M. Inability To Reimburse a Valid Expense

There may be times when an employee incurs a valid expense, but the organization simply cannot afford to reimburse the employee. In a 2012 court case, Stidham, T.C. Summ. Op. 2012-61, the court ruled that a taxpayer is not entitled to take a tax deduction for unreimbursed businesses. Unreimbursed business expenses were phased out in the TCJA for tax years beginning 2018-2026, so the employee will not be allowed to take the deduction anyway.

N. Summary

A written reimbursement plan is a necessary tool for employees and volunteers to understand what is reimbursable and at what rate. It keeps misunderstandings and hard feelings from occurring, and, just as important, it keeps employees from accidentally incurring taxable income.

Some of the key rules to remember with your Accountable Reimbursement Plan are:

- Define appropriate business expenses,
- Inform employees of time limits for requesting reimbursement,
- Get supporting documents such as receipts and mileage logs,
- Include who, what, when, where, and why in all documentation,
- Have forms approved,
- Properly file them, and
- Appoint someone to oversee administrating the accountable reimbursement plan.

It is time to move on to the most significant expense for most organizations—payroll.

11. Payroll, Part I: Basic Steps

For many organizations, payroll is the largest expense item. It is also one you want to get perfect every time as it affects your employees and legal situation. In this chapter, I'll start out with the basics, including:

- terminology,
- required forms,
- necessary steps to set up the payroll, and
- how to calculate, pay, and file the necessary taxes and forms.

A. Terminology

When dealing with employees and payroll, there are many terms you may hear thrown around. I'll define a few.

Gross Pay—Total amount earned in a pay period by an employee *before* withholding taxes.

Net Pay—The paycheck amount the employee takes home *after* withholding taxes.

Employers Identification Number (EIN)—Before you start hiring employees or open a bank account, you will need an EIN from the IRS. It is the number that will identify your organization to the IRS, like the Social Security Number (SSN) does for an individual.

Employees—Persons you pay for their work. They may be paid based on an hourly rate or a set salaried amount.

Independent Contractors—These are people you pay to do a specific job. Taxes are not withheld. Be careful who you classify as independent contractors versus employees as the IRS frowns upon (and punishes) organizations who try to treat employees as independent contractors. We'll go over this in more detail later.

Pay Period—The frequency with which you pay your employees. It may be weekly, semi-monthly, bi-monthly, or monthly.

Exemptions—These determine the amount of taxes withheld and are determined by factors such as marital status, children, and other employee-specific needs.

Taxable Wages— The total dollar amount of wages paid before taxes are withheld (this is not the total amount paid to an employee).

Withholding—The federal, state, and local income taxes withheld from an employee's check.

Social Security and Medicare Tax Withholding—The amount withheld from the employee's check specifically for Social Security and Medicare. The Social Security portion is also referred to as FICA (Federal Insurance Contribution Act).

Employer Taxes or **"Match"**—The employer's share of Social Security and Medicare taxes.

Unemployment Tax—A payment to a state or federal government to cover unemployed workers.

Workers' Compensation—Money paid to a state to fund support for workers hurt on the job. Most states require workers' compensation, so you will need to check with your state agency.

Disability Insurance Program—Money paid by the employer to an insurance company to help cover any worker's disability claims with no requirement of contribution from employees and is only required in a few states. If you live in California, Hawaii, New Jersey, New York, Rhode Island, or Puerto Rico, contact your state's appropriate agency to see if this applies.

Electronic Federal Tax Payment System (EFTPS)—This allows employers to submit taxes and withholding electronically.

Self-Employment Taxes—A director and any other self-employed person must file and pay quarterly the Social Security and Medicare taxes at the rate of both the employee and employer.

That sums up a few of the possibly unfamiliar terms. I'll try to define others as we go. Next, I'd like to describe the various forms you may be using.

B. Forms & Publications

Please Note: Due dates may change. Check irs.gov for the latest information.

Form Number	Description	Due Date
SS-4	Application for EIN	Before hiring employees
IRS Pub. 15 Circular E	The Employers Tax Guide	N/A
W-4	Employee's Social Security Number and allowances being claimed	When an employee is hired or has a change in the number of exemptions requested
I-9	Employment Eligibility Verification—an employee must present documents proving citizenship or work permit.	Before hiring
941	Employer's Quarterly Federal Tax Return—summarizes the income, Social Security, and Medicare taxes withheld and paid to the government during the previous quarter.	Due the last day of the month following the quarter-end. 1st qtr—April 30; 3rd qtr—October 31 2nd qtr—July 31; 4th qtr—January 31
W-2	Wage and Tax Statement—showing total earnings and taxes withheld. It is used by employees to fill out their tax returns.	By January 31 of the following year
W-3	Transmittal of the W-2s, the summary form sent to the IRS with copies of all the W-2s.	By the end of February
1099 Misc.	Shows total amount paid to independent contractors over $600 that year.	End of January the following year
W-9	Form completed by an independent contractor with their SSN or EIN. Used to fill out the 1099 Misc.	When hiring the independent contractor
1096	Transmittal form for the 1099 Misc.	By the end of January in the following year
1040 ES	Estimated taxes for self-employed. This is filed by the person, not by the organization.	Due the 15th of the month following the quarter-end. 1st qtr—April 15; 3rd qtr—October 15 2nd qtr—July 15; 4th qtr—January 15

For your convenience, I've included a page of links to the IRS forms on my website, accountantbesideyou.com.

C. Setting Up the Payroll

In this section, I'll take you step-by-step through the process of setting up your payroll.

1. Employer Identification Number (EIN)

Whether you have started hiring employees or opening a bank account, your nonprofit will need an EIN. The EIN is easy to obtain. Go to the IRS website and search for SS-4. There is a simple step by step application that can be filled out online, tailored explicitly for nonprofits.

If you are not comfortable or cannot fill out an online application, the government will allow you to apply by mail, fax, or over the phone.

If you do apply over the phone, I suggest filling out the form to ensure you have all the information ahead of time.

If you mail or fax the form, it should then be signed, dated, before sending it to the IRS. Find the current contact information on their website.

We will go over the PDF version of this application. This should ease any questions you have, even if you are applying online.

Line 1: The legal name must tie to any filings you have with your state government. This is not the place to abbreviate your nonprofit's name.

Line 2: The trade name is only filled in if the nonprofit uses a name different from their legal name in the normal course of doing business. If not, leave it blank.

Lines 4-6: The address of the organization.

Form **SS-4** (Rev. December 2019) Department of the Treasury Internal Revenue Service

Application for Employer Identification Number
(For use by employers, corporations, partnerships, trusts, estates, churches, government agencies, Indian tribal entities, certain individuals, and others.)
▶ Go to www.irs.gov/FormSS4 for instructions and the latest information.
▶ See separate instructions for each line. ▶ Keep a copy for your records.

OMB No. 1545-0003

EIN

Type or print clearly.

1 Legal name of entity (or individual) for whom the EIN is being requested

2 Trade name of business (if different from name on line 1) | 3 Executor, administrator, trustee, "care of" name

4a Mailing address (room, apt., suite no. and street, or P.O. box) | 5a Street address (if different) (Don't enter a P.O. box.)

4b City, state, and ZIP code (if foreign, see instructions) | 5b City, state, and ZIP code (if foreign, see instructions)

6 County and state where principal business is located

7a Name of responsible party | 7b SSN, ITIN, or EIN

Line 3: Will probably be blank for a nonprofit.

Line 7a: The name of the responsible party should be the director, the governing board's president, or other legal representative of the organization. His SSN will be required.

Line 11: Date your charity started.

Line 12: The closing month of the accounting year. This is usually December, but many nonprofits have a June year-end.

Line 13: Your expected number of employees will be listed under Other.

11 Date business started or acquired (month, day, year). See instructions.

12 Closing month of accounting year

13 Highest number of employees expected in the next 12 months (enter -0- if none). If no employees expected, skip line 14.

Agricultural	Household	Other

14 If you expect your employment tax liability to be $1,000 or less in a full calendar year **and** want to file Form 944 annually instead of Forms 941 quarterly, check here. (Your employment tax liability generally will be $1,000 or less if you expect to pay $5,000 or less in total wages.) If you don't check this box, you must file Form 941 for every quarter. ☐

15 First date wages or annuities were paid (month, day, year). **Note:** If applicant is a withholding agent, enter date income will first be paid to nonresident alien (month, day, year) . . . ▶

Line 14: Allows you to request only filing payroll reports annually instead of quarterly if a tax liability is expected to be under $1000 for the year. If you have few employees, this may be an option, especially as a nonprofit does not pay self-employment tax on the director.

Line 15: List the date of your first expected payroll.

Line 8: Most likely, the answer will be No

Line 9a: Asks for the type of entity. Select Nonprofit.

8a Is this application for a limited liability company (LLC) (or a foreign equivalent)? . . . ☐ Yes ☒ No

8b If 8a is "Yes," enter the number of LLC members . . . ▶

8c If 8a is "Yes," was the LLC organized in the United States? . . . ☐ Yes ☐ No

9a **Type of entity** (check only one box). **Caution:** If 8a is "Yes," see the instructions for the correct box to check.

☐ Sole proprietor (SSN) ________
☐ Partnership
☐ Corporation (enter form number to be filed) ▶ ________
☐ Personal service corporation
☐ Church or church-controlled organization
☒ Other nonprofit organization (specify) ▶ ________
☐ Other (specify) ▶
☐ Estate (SSN of decedent) ________
☐ Plan administrator (TIN) ________
☐ Trust (TIN of grantor) ________
☐ Military/National Guard ☐ State/local government
☐ Farmers' cooperative ☐ Federal government
☐ REMIC ☐ Indian tribal governments/enterprises
Group Exemption Number (GEN) if any ▶

9b If a corporation, name the state or foreign country (if applicable) where incorporated | State | Foreign country

10 **Reason for applying** (check only one box)

☐ Started new business (specify type) ▶ ________
☐ Hired employees (Check the box and see line 13.)
☐ Compliance with IRS withholding regulations
☐ Other (specify) ▶
☐ Banking purpose (specify purpose) ▶ ________
☐ Changed type of organization (specify new type) ▶ ________
☐ Purchased going business
☐ Created a trust (specify type) ▶ ________
☐ Created a pension plan (specify type) ▶ ________

Line 10: Your reason for applying will probably be either: started a new business, hired employees, or banking purpose.

Line 16: Asks for your activities. Select Other and specify Nonprofit activities.

Line 17: Services offered would be Nonprofit Services.

16 Check **one** box that best describes the principal activity of your business. ☐ Health care & social assistance ☐ Wholesale-agent/broker ☐ Construction ☐ Rental & leasing ☐ Transportation & warehousing ☐ Accommodation & food service ☐ Wholesale-other ☐ Retail ☐ Real estate ☐ Manufacturing ☐ Finance & insurance ☒ Other (specify) ▶ Nonprofit Activities

17 Indicate principal line of merchandise sold, specific construction work done, products produced, or services provided.
Nonprofit Services

18 Has the applicant entity shown on line 1 ever applied for and received an EIN? ☐ Yes ☐ No
If "Yes," write previous EIN here ▶

Third Party Designee
Complete this section **only** if you want to authorize the named individual to receive the entity's EIN and answer questions about the completion of this form.
Designee's name | Designee's telephone number (include area code)
Address and ZIP code | Designee's fax number (include area code)

Under penalties of perjury, I declare that I have examined this application, and to the best of my knowledge and belief, it is true, correct, and complete. | Applicant's telephone number (include area code)
Name and title (type or print clearly) ▶ | Applicant's fax number (include area code)
Signature ▶ Date ▶

For Privacy Act and Paperwork Reduction Act Notice, see separate instructions. Cat. No. 16055N Form **SS-4** (Rev. 12-2019)

Line 18: If the organization had previously applied for an EIN, note it here.

2. State and Local Identification Numbers

Once you have your federal number, you will need to apply for any state, and possibly local, numbers. Check your state's Secretary of State or Department of Revenue websites for any additional requirements. It is rare, but your city or county may have additional requirements.

3. Independent Contractor Vs. Employee

You probably already understand what an employee is. An independent contractor is a little less clear. The IRS website states:

> *People such as doctors, dentists, veterinarians, lawyers, accountants, contractors, subcontractors, public stenographers, or auctioneers who are in an independent trade, business, or profession in which they offer their services to the general public are generally independent contractors. However, whether these people are independent contractors or employees depends on the facts in each case.*
>
> *The general rule is that an individual is an independent contractor if the payer has the right to control or direct only the result of the work and not what will be done and how it will be done[‡]. The earnings of a person who is working as an independent contractor are subject to Self-Employment Tax. (ref: Independent Contractor Defined, IRS.gov)*

The key passage above is if the payer has the right to control or direct only the result of the work and not what will be done and how it will be done. In the simplest terms, this means you hire someone to do something and pay them when it is finished. The IRS assumes individuals working for the charity are employees unless it is proven otherwise. When auditing an organization, they have a list of 20 questions to determine if the worker is an independent contractor or not.

---

*Note to organizations based in California: California Assembly Bill 5 severely limits the types of workers that can be considered independent contractors. Please contact a local CPA for additional guidance.

In case you are wondering why it matters, income tax and payroll taxes are withheld on employees but not independent contractors. Independent contractors must pay the full (employee and employer) Social Security and Medicare taxes on their earnings. Businesses sometimes like to classify workers as independent contractors to save on the additional employer payroll taxes.

Contractor vs. Employee

A bookkeeper comes to the charity once a week to do the bookkeeping. If he has other clients, controls when the work will be done, and gives the nonprofit the results (i.e. monthly financial statements), it is pretty clear he is an independent contractor.

If the bookkeeper is required to come in for a specified number of hours each week determined by the director and is given detailed instructions on how to do the bookkeeping, he may be considered an employee.

The gardener who uses his own equipment and is paid to keep the cemetery mowed and clear of branches may be treated as an independent contractor, as can the plumber who just comes in for a particular problem.

Scheduled employees such as nursery workers and administrative assistants, however, must be treated as employees as they do not have the right to control or direct the work. The nursery attendant must work when the children will be there.

4. W-9 (Request for Taxpayer Identification Number)

If you have determined the person should be paid as an independent contractor, you will need to have him complete a W-9 Request for Taxpayer Identification Number. The form may be downloaded from the IRS website, http://www.irs.gov/pub/irs-pdf/fw9.pdf.

Form **W-9**
(Rev. August 2013)
Department of the Treasury
Internal Revenue Service

Request for Taxpayer Identification Number and Certification

Give Form to the requester. Do not send to the IRS.

Name (as shown on your income tax return)

Business name/disregarded entity name, if different from above

Contractor's name or business name.

Check appropriate box for federal tax classification:
☐ Individual/sole proprietor ☐ C Corporation ☐ S Corporation ☐ Partnership ☐ Trust/estate

Exempt payee co

Exemption from
code (if an

☐ Limited liability company. Enter the tax classification (C=C corporation, S=S corporation, P=partnership) ▶

☐ Other (see instructions) ▶

Address (number, street, and apt. or suite no.)

Requeste (optional)

City, state, and ZIP code

List account number(s) here (optional)

Print or type See Specific Instructions on page 2.

Part I Taxpayer Identification Number (TIN)

Enter your TIN in the appropriate box. The TIN provided must match the name give the "Name" line to avoid backup withholding. For individuals, this is your social security number (S However, for a resident alien, sole proprietor, or disregarded entities, it is your employer identification number (EIN). If TIN on page 3.

Note. If the account is in number to enter.

Social security number

Employer identification number

One of these should be filled out, not both.

Part II Certification

Under penalties of perjury, I certify that:

1. The number shown on th ayer identification number (or I am waiting for a number to be issued to me), and
2. I am not subject to backup withholding because: (a) I am exempt from backup withholding, or (b) I have not been notified by the Internal Revenue Service (IRS) that I am subject to backup withholding as a result of a failure to report all interest or dividends, or (c) the IRS has notified me that I am no longer subject to backup withholding, and
3. I am a U.S. citizen or other U.S. person (defined below), and
4. The FATCA code(s) entered on this form (if any) indicating that I am exempt from FATCA reporting

Certification instructions. You must cross out item 2 above if you have been notified by the currently subject to backup withholding because you have failed to report all interest and dividends on your tax return. For real e item 2 does not apply. For mortgage interest paid, acquisition or abandonment of secured property, cancellation of debt, c an individual retirement arrangement (IRA), and generally, payments other than interest and dividends, you are not required to sign t ut you must provide your correct TIN. See the instructions on page 3.

Must be signed.

Sign Here | **Signature of U.S. person ▶** | **Date ▶**

The contractor fills out the form with his own name or his business name, if applicable. He checks his type of business organization and his address. If he used his personal name, the SSN area should be completed. If he filled the form out as a business, he should use an EIN, if he has one.

The form must be signed and dated and given to the organization. I require contractors to fill out the form before I will give them a check for their services.

> *You only need this form if you expect to pay the contractor at least $600 throughout the year or pay at least $10 in royalties (as of 2020). If you aren't sure, go ahead and have him complete it, so you won't have to track it down at the end of the year.*

D. Wages Vs. Salaries

How long do you need your staff? How many hours a week do they put in? Do they work overtime?

These fundamental questions will help you in determining an hourly worker vs. a salaried worker. Hourly workers will be paid for the amount of time they are at work and are eligible for overtime pay. Salaried workers are generally allotted wages for the year, so their payment amount will not vary per pay period.

You may also want to consider how your company operates and what funds are available for workers. It may be easier to pay your employees a salary, so you know exactly how much money you will need to fund payroll each month.

All of these considerations need to fall within the purview of your state and federal guidelines. Failing to do so could result in lawsuits, or at the minimum, having to compensate employees that have not been compensated fairly.

E. Determining the Pay Period

Now that you know who you will be paying as an employee, you should determine how often you will pay them. The frequency is referred to as the pay period.

From an efficiency standpoint, the less frequently, the better. But it is often hard to go an entire month between paychecks, so most organizations pay either bi-monthly (15th and the end of the month) or bi-weekly (every two weeks). Weekly payroll is also an option but requires more bookkeeping time and costs.

F. Employee Forms

There are a couple of forms you must have new employees complete. Check with your state for additional requirements.

1. Form I-9 (Employment Eligibility Verification)

Before an employee can be hired, the organization must determine if he is legally able to work in this country. An I-9 Employment Eligibility Verification form is required and must be completed by every employee.

Employment Eligibility Verification
Department of Homeland Security
U.S. Citizenship and Immigration Services

USCIS
Form I-9
OMB No. 1615-0047
Expires 03/31/2016

►**START HERE. Read instructions carefully before completing this form. The instructions must be available during completion of this form.**
ANTI-DISCRIMINATION NOTICE: It is illegal to discriminate against work-authorized individuals. Employers **CANNOT** specify which document(s) they will accept from an employee. The refusal to hire an individual because the documentation presented has a future expiration date may also constitute illegal discrimination.

Section 1. Employee Information and Attestation *(Employees must complete and sign Section 1 of Form I-9 no later than the first day of employment, but not before accepting a job offer.)*

Last Name *(Family Name)*	First Name *(Given Name)*	Middle Initial	Other Names Used *(if any)*

Address *(Street Number and Name)*	Apt. Number	City or Town	State	Zip Code

Date of Birth *(mm/dd/yyyy)*	U.S. Social Security Number	E-mail Address	Telephone Number
	- -		

I am aware that federal law provides for imprisonment and/or fines for false statements or use of false documents in connection with the completion of this form.

I attest, under penalty of perjury, that I am (check one of the following):

☐ A citizen of the United States

☐ A noncitizen national of the United States *(See instructions)*

☐ A lawful permanent resident (Alien Registration Number/USCIS Number): ____________

☐ An alien authorized to work until (expiration date, if applicable, mm/dd/yyyy) ____________. Some aliens may write "N/A" in this field. *(See instructions)*

Some aliens may write "N/A" on the Foreign Passport Number and Country of Issuance fields. *(See instructions)*

Signature of Employee:	Date *(mm/dd/yyyy)*:

The employee fills out the first section (shown), then the employer reviews his documents and completes the second section. A list of approved documents is available in the instructions included with the form.

Once the documents are reviewed, and the paper is signed by both the employer and the employee, a W-4, Employee's Withholding Allowance Certificate, is given to the employee to be completed.

2. Form W-4 (Employee's Withholding Certificate)

The W-4 was dramatically changed in 2020, so if an employee has not updated for a while, he should consider redoing his W-4.

The employee calculates the recommended number of allowances based on marital status and children to compute a guideline for the number of exemptions he would like. The number of allowances determines how much federal tax is withheld from his check.

The employee is not required to use the number on the worksheet. If he has significant deductible expenses outside this job, he may wish to have less money withheld.

Form **W-4**
Department of the Treasury
Internal Revenue Service

Employee's Withholding Certificate

▶ Complete Form W-4 so that your employer can withhold the correct federal income tax from your pay.
▶ Give Form W-4 to your employer.
▶ Your withholding is subject to review by the IRS.

OMB No. 1545-0074
2020

Step 1: Enter Personal Information

(a) First name and middle initial | Last name | (b) Social security number

Address

City or town, state, and ZIP code

▶ **Does your name match the name on your social security card?** If not, to ensure you get credit for your earnings, contact SSA at 800-772-1213 or go to www.ssa.gov.

(c) ☐ **Single or Married filing separately**
☐ **Married filing jointly** (or Qualifying widow(er))
☐ **Head of household** (Check only if you're unmarried and pay more than half the costs of keeping up a home for yourself and a qualifying individual.)

Complete Steps 2–4 ONLY if they apply to you; otherwise, skip to Step 5. See page 2 for more information on each step, who can claim exemption from withholding, when to use the online estimator, and privacy.

Step 2: Multiple Jobs or Spouse Works

Complete this step if you (1) hold more than one job at a time, or (2) are married filing jointly and your spouse also works. The correct amount of withholding depends on income earned from all of these jobs.

Do **only one** of the following.

(a) Use the estimator at *www.irs.gov/W4App* for most accurate withholding for this step (and Steps 3–4); **or**

(b) Use the Multiple Jobs Worksheet on page 3 and enter the result in Step 4(c) below for roughly accurate withholding; **or**

(c) If there are only two jobs total, you may check this box. Do the same on Form W-4 for the other job. This option is accurate for jobs with similar pay; otherwise, more tax than necessary may be withheld . . . . . ▶ ☐

TIP: To be accurate, submit a 2020 Form W-4 for all other jobs. If you (or your spouse) have self-employment income, including as an independent contractor, use the estimator.

Complete Steps 3–4(b) on Form W-4 for only ONE of these jobs. Leave those steps blank for the other jobs. (Your withholding will be most accurate if you complete Steps 3–4(b) on the Form W-4 for the highest paying job.)

Step 3: Claim Dependents

If your income will be $200,000 or less ($400,000 or less if married filing jointly):

Multiply the number of qualifying children under age 17 by $2,000 ▶ $

Multiply the number of other dependents by $500 . . . . ▶ $

Add the amounts above and enter the total here . . . . **3** $

Step 4 (optional): Other Adjustments

(a) Other income (not from jobs). If you want tax withheld for other income you expect this year that won't have withholding, enter the amount of other income here. This may include interest, dividends, and retirement income . . . . **4(a)** $

(b) Deductions. If you expect to claim deductions other than the standard deduction and want to reduce your withholding, use the Deductions Worksheet on page 3 and enter the result here . . . . **4(b)** $

(c) Extra withholding. Enter any additional tax you want withheld each **pay period** . **4(c)** $

Step 5: Sign Here

Under penalties of perjury, I declare that this certificate, to the best of my knowledge and belief, is true, correct, and complete.

▶ **Employee's signature** (This form is not valid unless you sign it.) ▶ **Date**

Employers Only

Employer's name and address | First date of employment | Employer identification number (EIN)

For Privacy Act and Paperwork Reduction Act Notice, see page 3. Cat. No. 10220Q Form **W-4** (2020)

Likewise, if he had a large tax bill the previous year and expects to have another, he may wish to have additional money taken from his check. If not enough money is withheld, the employee may have to pay a penalty. On the other hand, if too much is withheld, the employee has lost the use of those funds and any potential interest for the year.

A new W-4 needs to be completed anytime an employee's marital status or number of dependents change or there is a significant change in tax policy.

A tax witholding estimater is available at the IRS website https://www.irs.gov/individuals/tax-withholding-estimator.

Once completed, the employee must sign and date the W-4. As this is the federal form only, you will need to see if your state also requires one. If your state has a state income tax, there is probably a state exemption certificate to be filled out also.

Always do a criminal background check before hiring a new employee! This is especially important if the person will be working with children or the finances. It is not expensive and can save the organization embarrassment and extra work later.

G. Establish Your Payroll Records

For federal tax purposes, you must keep the following information on file:

- the name, address, and SSN of each employee
- the total amount and date of each payment
- the portion of each payment that constituted taxable wages
- each employee's I-9
- each employee's W-4
- copies of returns you filed
- copies of any undeliverable W-2 forms

As this information has confidential data such as SSNs and salary information, it must be kept in a locked, secure file. If you are keeping the information electronically, it needs to be securely password protected.

H. Summary

Not only is payroll a significant expense, but there are also so many rules and regulations, it is difficult to keep track of everything you need to do. In this chapter, you learned how to:

- Understand the terminology,
- Determine which forms are required,
- Apply for an EIN,
- Determine if a person is an employee or an independent contractor,
- Set pay periods, and
- Establish your payroll records.

You now understand the basic terminology and what is required. Let's learn how to calculate and pay the payroll.

12. Payroll, Part II: Calculating & Filing

Now comes the fun part—actually calculating the payroll. You can use a payroll service, but it isn't too hard to do yourself. The first thing you need is to get a copy of the IRS Publication 14 (Circular E) and supplement Publication 15-T. They are available online at IRS.gov or at the local IRS office.

Ministers are treated differently than other employess.

If you are paying a salary to an ordained minister, please read my book:

Church Accounting: The How-To Guide for Small & Growing Churches

where I explain pastor salaries and withholding in great detail.

Payroll federal tax withholding can be calculated manually by one of two methods, the **wage bracket method** or **percentage method**. The wage bracket method uses the tax tables listed in the Publication 15-T. They are listed by pay period and marital status and show the amount of withholding required after calculating the Adjusted Wage Amount. The Percentage Method uses the schedules in the Publication 15-T to compute the withholding.

In this chapter, I'll show you how to:

- Calculate taxes based on both methods,
- Calculate Social Security and Medicare taxes,
- Compute the employee's paycheck,
- Post the payroll expense in the general ledger,
- Handle tax deposits and filings, and
- Handle the year-end requirements.

A. Wage Bracket Method

The **wage bracket method** is only used for employees who make less than $100,000 annually. For those making over $100,00, you will need to use the percentage method. To use the wage bracket method, you will need to have all your employees update their W-4 to the 2020 or later form.

The IRS has a worksheet for you to fill out to help:

2. Wage Bracket Method Tables for Manual Payroll Systems With Forms W-4 From 2020 or Later

If you compute payroll manually, your employee has submitted a Form W-4 for 2020 or later, and you prefer to use the Wage Bracket method, use the worksheet below and the Wage Bracket Method tables that follow to figure federal income tax withholding.

The Wage Bracket Method tables cover only up to approximately $100,000 in annual wages. If you can't use the Wage Bracket Method tables because taxable wages exceed the amount from the last bracket of the table (based on filing status and pay period), use the Percentage Method tables in section 4.

Worksheet 2. Employer's Withholding Worksheet for Wage Bracket Method Tables for Manual Payroll Systems With Forms W-4 From 2020 or Later

Keep for Your Records 

Table 4	Monthly	Semimonthly	Biweekly	Weekly	Daily
	12	24	26	52	260

Step 1. Adjust the employee's wage amount

1a	Enter the employee's total taxable wages this payroll period	1a	$ 2307.69
1b	Enter the number of pay periods you have per year (see Table 4)	1b	26
1c	Enter the amount from Step 4(a) of the employee's Form W-4	1c	$ 2000.00
1d	Divide the amount on line 1c by the number of pay periods on line 1b	1d	$ 76.92
1e	Add lines 1a and 1d	1e	$ 2384.61
1f	Enter the amount from Step 4(b) of the employee's Form W-4	1f	$
1g	Divide the amount on line 1f by the number of pay periods on line 1b	1g	$
1h	Subtract line 1g from line 1e. If zero or less, enter -0-. This is the **Adjusted Wage Amount**	1h	$ 2384.61

Step 2. Figure the Tentative Withholding Amount

2a	Use the amount on line 1h to look up the tentative amount to withhold in the appropriate Wage Bracket Table in this section for your pay frequency, given the employee's filing status and whether the employee has checked the box in Step 2 of Form W-4. This is the **Tentative Withholding Amount**	2a	$ 157.00

Step 3. Account for tax credits

3a	Enter the amount from Step 3 of the employee's Form W-4	3a	$ 4000.00
3b	Divide the amount on line 3a by the number of pay periods on line 1b	3b	$ 153.85
3c	Subtract line 3b from line 2a. If zero or less, enter -0-	3c	$ 3.15

Step 4. Figure the final amount to withhold

4a	Enter the additional amount to withhold from Step 4(c) of the employee's Form W-4	4a	$
4b	Add lines 3c and 4a. **This is the amount to withhold from the employee's wages this pay period**	4b	$ 3.15

I think an example to step you through this method will help. Assume you have a nonprofit administrator who is married with two children, is paid $60,000 annually, and has $2000 of outside income she would like taxes taken out. Your organization runs payroll on a bi-weekly system.

For line 1a, you would enter $2307.69 (salary over 26 pay periods).

Line 1b is 26 for biweekly payroll.

Line 1c is $2000 for outside income per line 4(a) of her W-4.

Line 1d equals $76.92 ($2000 over 26 pay periods).

Line 1e adds the wages and the additional amount for the period and would equal $2384.61 ($2307.69 + $76.92).

Line 1f and 1g would be used if extra deductions had been requested.

Line 1h is the **adjusted wage amount**. In this example, it is $2384.61, the same value as line 1e.

Now we will go to the **Wage Bracket Table** in the Publication 15-T and look for "BIWEEKLY Payroll Period."

2020 Wage Bracket Method Tables for Manual Payroll Systems With Forms W-4 From 2020 or Later

BIWEEKLY Payroll Period

If the **Adjuste[illegible]** **Amount** (line 1h) [illegible]		Married Filing Jointly		[illegible]d of Household		Single or Married Filing Separately	
At least	But less than	Standard withholding	Form W-4, Step 2, Checkbox withholding	Standard withholding	Form W-4, Step 2, Checkbox withholding	Standard withholding	Form W-4, Step 2, Checkbox withholding
		The Tentative Withholding Amount is:					
$1,135	$1,155	$19	$73	$43	$89	$73	$118
$1,155	$1,175	$21	$75	$45	$91	$75	$123
$1,175	$1,195	$23	$77	$47	$94	$77	$127
$1,195	$1,215	[illegible]	$80	$49	$96	$80	$132
$1,215	$1,235	$51	$82	$51	$99	$82	$136
	$1,255		$85		$101		$140
$2,255		$143		$175		$233	
$2,285	$2,315	$146	$239	$179	$324	$239	$381
$2,315	$2,34[illegible]	$150	$246	$183	$332	$246	$388
$2,345	$2,3[illegible]	$154	$252	$186	$339	$252	$395
$2,375	$2,405	$157	$259	$190	$346	$259	$403
$2,405	$2,435	$161	$266	$193	$353	$266	$410
$2,435	$2,465	$164	$272	$197	$360	$272	$417
$2,465	$2,495	$168	$279	$201	$368	$279	$424

Find the Adjusted Wage Amount in the columns to the left. In this situation, $2384.61 is between $2375 and $2405, so you will use the withholding on this line.

Next, look for Married Filing Jointly. There are two options, **standard withholding** or **Form W-4 Step 2 Checkbox withholding**. If the employee had checked the box in Step 2 (relating to other jobs held by her or her spouse), you would use the right column. But in this example, the step 2 box was not checked, so her tentative withholding amount is $157 for the pay period.

If the administrator was single or head of household, you would use one of the columns to the right.

Step 3 of the worksheet is to account for children and other dependents. For our example, the administrator has two children and therefore should enter $4000 in line 3a. ($2000x2)

Line 3b divides 3a by 26 periods and will equal $153.85.

Line 3c subtracts 3b from the tentative withholding amount on line 2a. It is greater than $0, so enter $3.15 ($157 - $153.85).

If there is no additional withholding from Step 4 of the W-4, then we will withhold the $3.15 for federal taxes.

All of that seems tedious, but it only takes a couple of minutes after you've done it the first time.

B. Percentage Method

The second approach is to use the **percentage method**. If you have an employee making over $100,00, you will need to use this method. You will calculate the tentative withholding amount with a worksheet similar to the Wage Bracket Method. Before you start, request 2020 or later versions of all employees W-4s.

Find the worksheet in Publication 15-T, Percentage Method Tables for Manual Payroll Systems with Forms W-4 From 2020 or later. We'll fill this out using information from the previous example.

Step 1, Line 1a asks for the total taxable wages for the payroll period. Using our previous example, we would enter $2307.69.

Line 1b is the number of pay periods, so we are using 26 for bi-weekly.

Line 1c reflects any additional income the employee recorded on Step 4a of the W-4, so we have $2000.

Line 1d divides the $2000 by 26 weeks for $76.92.

Line 1e adds the $76.92 to the bi-weekly gross payroll of $2307.69. The sum is $2384.61.

Line 1f records any additional deductions from the W-4.

4. Percentage Method Tables for Manual Payroll Systems With Forms W-4 From 2020 or Later

If you compute payroll manually, your employee has submitted a Form W-4 for 2020 or later, and you prefer to use the Percentage Method or you can't use the Wage Bracket Method tables because the employee's annual wages exceed $100,000, use the worksheet below and the Percentage Method tables that follow to figure federal income tax withholding. This method works for any amount of wages.

Worksheet 4. Employer's Withholding Worksheet for Percentage Method Tables for Manual Payroll Systems With Forms W-4 From 2020 or Later

Keep for Your Records 

Table 5	Monthly	Semimonthly	Biweekly	Weekly	Daily
	12	24	26	52	260

Step 1. Adjust the employee's wage amount

1a	Enter the employee's total taxable wages this payroll period	1a	$ 2307.69
1b	Enter the number of pay periods you have per year (see Table 5)	1b	26
1c	Enter the amount from Step 4(a) of the employee's Form W-4	1c	$ 2000.00
1d	Divide line 1c by the number on line 1b	1d	$ 76.92
1e	Add lines 1a and 1d	1e	$ 2384.61
1f	Enter the amount from Step 4(b) of the employee's Form W-4	1f	$
1g	Divide line 1f by the number on line 1b	1g	$
1h	Subtract line 1g from line 1e. If zero or less, enter -0-. This is the **Adjusted Wage Amount**	1h	$ 2384.61

Step 2. Figure the Tentative Withholding Amount

based on your pay frequency, the employee's Adjusted Wage Amount, filing status (Step 1(c) of Form W-4), and whether the box in Step 2 of Form W-4 is checked.

2a	Find the row in the *STANDARD Withholding Rate Schedules* (if the box in Step 2 of Form W-4 is NOT checked) or the *Form W-4, Step 2, Checkbox, Withholding Rate Schedules* (if it HAS been checked) of the Percentage Method tables in this section in which the amount on line 1h is at least the amount in column A but less than the amount in column B, then enter here the amount from column A of that row	2a	$ 1713.00
2b	Enter the amount from column C of that row	2b	$ 75.90
2c	Enter the percentage from column D of that row	2c	12 %
2d	Subtract line 2a from line 1h	2d	$ 671.61
2e	Multiply the amount on line 2d by the percentage on line 2c	2e	$ 80.59
2f	Add lines 2b and 2e. This is the **Tentative Withholding Amount**	2f	$ 157.00

Step 3. Account for tax credits

3a	Enter the amount from Step 3 of the employee's Form W-4	3a	$ 4000.00
3b	Divide the amount on line 3a by the number of pay periods on line 1b	3b	$ 152.85
3c	Subtract line 3b from line 2f. If zero or less, enter -0-	3c	$ 3.15

Step 4. Figure the final amount to withhold

4a	Enter the additional amount to withhold from Step 4(c) of the employee's Form W-4	4a	$
4b	Add lines 3c and 4a. **This is the amount to withhold from the employee's wages this pay period**	4b	$ 3.15

Line 1g divides 1f by 26 weeks.

Line 1h is the **Adjusted Wage Amount,** which is the $2384.61 without any additional deductions.

Step 2 calculates the Tentative Withholding Amount using the Withholding Rate Schedules.

The worksheet will walk you through the calculation. First, make sure you have the correct payroll period. We are using BIWEEKLY. If the employee checked the box in Step 2 of the W-4, use the tables on the right. In this example, she did not, so we are using the **STANDARD Withholding Rate Schedule**. Look for the filing status (in this case, Married Filing Jointly). Then find the row in which the **Adjusted Wage Amount** of $2384.61 falls within.

2020 Percentage Method Tables for Manual Payroll Systems With Forms W-4 From 2020 or Later

BIWEEKLY Payroll Period

STANDARD Withholding Rate Schedules (Use these if the box in Step 2 of Form W-4 is **NOT** checked)					Form W-[illegible] Checkbox, Withholding Rate Schedules (Use the[illegible] in Step 2 of Form W-4 **IS** checked)				
If the Adjusted Wage Amount (line 1h) is: At least—	But less than—	The tentative amount to withhold is:	Plus this percentage—	of the amount that the Adjusted Wage exceeds—	If the Adjusted Wage Amount (line 1h) is: At least—	But less than—	The tentative amount to withhold is:	Plus this percentage—	of the amount that the Adjusted Wage exceeds—
A	B	C	D	E	A	B	C	D	E
Married Filing Jointly					**Married Filing Jointly**				
$0	$954	$0.00	0%	$0	$0	$477	$0.00	0%	$0
$954	$1,713	$0.00	10%	$954	$477	$857	$0.00	10%	$477
$1,713	$4,040	$75.90	12%	$1,713	$857	$2,020	$38.00	12%	$857
$4,040	$7,533	$355.14	22%	$4,040	$2,020	$3,766	$177.56	22%	$2,020
$7,533	$13,515	$1,123.60	24%	$7,533	$3,766	$6,758	$561.68	24%	$3,766
$13,515	$16,904	$2,559.28	32%	$13,515	$6,758	$8,452	$1,279.76	32%	$6,758
$16,904	$24,879	$3,643.76	35%	$16,904	$8,452	$12,439	$1,821.84	35%	$8,452
$24,879		$6,435.01	37%	$24,879	$12,439		$3,217.29	37%	$12,439
Single or Married Filing Separately					**Single or Married Filing Separately**				
$0	$477	$0.00	0%	$0	$0	$238	$0.00	0%	$0
$8,452	$20,415	$1,821.84	35%	$8,452	$4,226	$10,208	$910.98	35%	$4,226
$20,415		$6,008.89	37%	$20,415	$10,208		$3,004.68	37%	$10,208

For Line 2a, enter $1713 from column A.

On Line 2b, enter $75.90 from column C.

Line 2c reflects the related percentage of 12%.

For line 2d, subtract line 2a from 1h. This gives us $671.61.

On line 2e, you will multiply line 2c (12%) by the amount on line 2d ($671.61) for a total of $80.59.

The **Tentative Withholding Amount** is Line 2f, calculated by adding lines 2b and 2e or $156.50, which rounds to the same $157 we saw using the Wage Bracket Method.

Step 3 is the same as the previous method to reflect any tax credits.

Line 3a is the dependents valued at $4000.

Line 3b divides the above line by the number of pay periods (26) for a total of $153.85.

Line 3c subtracts 3b from 2f the Tentative Withholding Amount for a net of $3.15.

Step 4 reflects any additional amounts to be withheld from Step 4c of the W-4.

Line 4a brings in any additional amount to withhold.

Line 4b adds lines 3c and 4a for a total amount to withhold from the employee's wages of $3.15.

As up can see, both methods calculate substantially the same federal withholding tax due.

C. State Tax Withholding

No matter which method you choose, the formulas above are for the federal withholding only. If your state has a state income tax, you will need to do a similar calculation with your state withholding rates. Check your state's Department of Revenue website or office for more information.

D. FICA—Social Security & Medicare Taxes

The Federal Insurance Contributions Act (FICA) is a federal system of old-age, survivors, disability, and hospital insurance. The old-age, survivors, and disability insurance part is financed by the Social Security tax while the hospital insurance part is financed by the Medicare tax.

The taxes are required to be withheld on all part-time and full-time employees. Once an employee is paid $137,700 (in 2020), you no longer need to withhold Social Security tax on the excess, but you will continue withholding for the Medicare portion of the tax. Any earnings over $137,700 are not taxed with Social Security because the benefits are capped to that earning rate.

The Social Security tax rate is 6.2% to be withheld from the employee and 6.2% matched by the employer. Thus, the total Social Security tax is 12.4% (in 2020) of the employee's wages without withholding allowances, equally split between the employer and employee.

The Medicare rate is 1.45% of the employee's wages without withholding allowances each for the employee and employer. If you pay an employee over $200,000 per year, you will need to withhold an additional .9% for **Additional Medicare Tax**. There is no employer match for the .9%.

Let me walk you through the SS and Medicare tax withholding calculation using the earlier example. The administrator had $2308 of gross earnings. To calculate her taxes:

Multiply $2308 times 6.2% to equal $143.10 for SS.

Multiply $2308 times 1.45% to equal $33.47 for Medicare.

Reduce her paycheck by $176.57 ($143.10 +$33.47).

Additionally, the organization will need to calculate its employer tax liability by multiplying the gross wages by the employer tax percentages.

Add the 6.2% for SS tax to 1.45% for Medicare to equal 7.65% employer tax percentage.

Multiply gross wages of $2308 times 7.65% to equal $176.57 of employer tax liability.

Now you have enough information to prepare the employee's paycheck.

E. The Employee's Payroll Check

After all of the deductions have been calculated, it is time to compute the net amount due to the employee. I like to do this in a spreadsheet to make it easier to double-check my calculations and to see the total amount of money I need to have available in the checking account. Use the example on the following page to follow the process.

The formulas in the spreadsheet check to see if there are hours included, in which case, the gross pay is calculated based on the number of hours times the rate. If no hours are included, it assumes the rate is a salary.

Federal and state withholding can be manually input. If you are experienced with spreadsheet calculations, you can link it to another spreadsheet with the percentage tax rate calculation.

G6 fx Employee FICA

	A	B	C	D	E	F	G	H	I	J
1		**Your Charity**								
2		**Net Payroll**								
3	**Biweekly ending**	**5/31/2020**								
4										
5							6.20%	1.45%		
6	**Employee**	**Hourly Rate or Salary**	**# of Hours**	**Gross Pay**	**Federal W/H**	**State W/H**	**Employee FICA**	**Employee Medicare**	**Additional Medicare**	**Net Pay**
7	Susan Administrator	$2,308.00		$2,308.00	$ 3.15		$ 143.10	$ 33.47		$2,128.79
8	Albert Assistant	15	20	300	0		18.6	4.35		277.05
9										
10	**Total**	**$2,323.00**	**$ 20.00**	**$2,608.00**	**$ 3.15**	**$ -**	**$ 161.70**	**$ 37.82**	**$ -**	**$2,405.84**
11										
12	Employer Portion Tax Due						161.70	37.82		
13										
14	**Total Taxes Due to Federal**				**$ 3.15**	**$ -**	**$ 323.39**	**$ 75.63**	**$ -**	**$ 402.17**
15	**Total Taxes Due to State**					**$ -**				**$ -**
16										
17	**Total Cash Required for Payroll**									**$2,808.01**
18										

The spreadsheet is set up with formulas for the SS and Medicare tax rates, so if they change next year, I only have to adjust those percentages, and the spreadsheet will calculate the new rates.

The net pay column subtracts the withholding (which you need to calculate as discuss previously), SS, and Medicare taxes from the gross pay to compute the net pay. Net pay is the amount of the paycheck due to the employee.

Additionally, I want the spreadsheet to tell me how much I need to send to the government. It calculates the employer match and then adds it to the employee withholding. These are added together with the federal withholding to calculate a total due to the Federal and State governments.

The "Total Cash Required" line is the total amount needed in the checking account for payroll.

F. Posting the Payroll Expense

Once the checks are cut, you need to post this to your accounting system. For a spreadsheet system, input the gross wages as the wages expense item and the employer taxes as a payroll tax expense item. Cash will be reduced by the amount of the net pay and the payments to the government, whether EFTPS (electronic payment to IRS) or by check.

If you are using a computerized accounting program, you can post it as a journal entry. In this example, the gross payroll was $2608, and the employer tax expense was $199.52. Check 1010 was issued for one employee's net pay of $277.05, and the second employee's net pay of $2128.79 went via direct deposit. The federal income, Social Security, and Medicare taxes withheld plus the employer's tax totaled $401.67 and is recorded as a payable.

	A	B	C	D
1		**Your Charity**		
2		**Payroll Journal Entry**		
3	**Biweekly ending**	**(Payroll Date)**		
4				
5	**Account**	**Debit**	**Credit**	
6	Payroll Expense	2,608.00		
7	Payroll Tax Expense	199.52		
8	Cash-Check # 1010		277.05	
9	Cash-Direct Deposit		2,128.79	
10	Federal Taxes Payable		401.67	
11	State Taxes Payable		-	
12				
13	**Total**	**2,807.52**	**2,807.51**	
14				

When the taxes are paid to the government, the payable accounts will be debited and cash credited.

> *The reductions in cash are broken out by checks and the electronic payments to make reconciling the bank account easier.*

G. Other Taxes

1. Unemployment Taxes

Charities are exempt from federal unemployment taxes but not necessarily from state unemployment taxes. Consult your state agency to see if your state grants exemptions to nonprofits and if there are any filing requirements associated with it.

2. Workers' Compensation

Most states require nonprofit organizations to provide workers' compensation insurance. It is usually purchased through a company, not through the payroll system, but it is based on your level of payroll. Again, you will need to check with your specific state for requirements.

3. Temporary Disability Insurance Program

If you live in California, Hawaii, New Jersey, New York, Rhode Island, or Puerto Rico, contact your state's appropriate agency to see if this applies.

H. Payroll Tax Deposits

Once your employees have been paid, you need to remit the money withheld and the employer match to the federal government. For most organizations, this needs to be done monthly. Late payments may incur penalties. We'll now look at when and how to pay these deposits.

1. Tax Deposit Schedule

The frequency of your payroll deposits is determined by the tax liability due.

If your tax liability is expected to be less than $1000 annually, you can call the IRS at 1-800-829-4933 before April 1st of the year and request permission to file a Form 944. Once you have written notification from the IRS, you will only need to file and pay annually. The filing and the payment are due by January 31st of the following year.

If you have less than $50,000 of tax deposits due per quarter in the past, you will need to file monthly. The payments must be made by the 15th day of the following month for the last month's payroll.

If your payroll tax deposits are greater than $50,000, you will follow the semiweekly deposit schedule. If the payday falls on a Wednesday, Thursday, or Friday, deposit the taxes by the following

Wednesday. If the payday is any other day of the week, deposit the taxes by the following Friday.

2. Electronic Federal Tax Payment System (EFTPS)

The federal government is requiring all federal tax deposits to be made using electronic funds. The Electronic Federal Tax Payment System (EFTPS) is a free service provided by the Department of Treasury. The website for EFTPS is www.eftps.gov, and the telephone number is 1-800-555-4477.

If you are just receiving your EIN, you will be pre-enrolled in EFTPS and should receive information on activating the assigned PIN (personal identification number). Once you have enrolled and have an activated PIN, you can submit your federal deposits directly from your bank to the government.

Login

In order to make, view or cancel a Payment, you must first login.

Please enter your Employer Identification Number (EIN) or your Social Security Number (SSN), PIN, and Internet password in the fields below. If you do not have a PIN, please enroll first.

EIN (for Business) -

or

SSN (for Individual) - -

PIN

Internet Password

Need a Password

CANCEL LOGIN ▶

Once you are logged in, it will take you step-by-step through how to input your bank account and routing number. Payments can be scheduled in advance, so even if you are not working on the due date, the payment can be made on time.

I. Payroll Tax Filings With Form 941

Just because you have deposited the withholding and taxes, don't think you are finished yet. Unless you are a very small filer and been told by the IRS to file an annual Form 944, you will need to prepare a Form 941-Employer's Quarterly Tax Return.

Form 941 reconciles the monthly payments you made to the total liability for the quarter. It is due the last day of the month following the end of the quarter (i.e., April 30, July 31, October 31, and

January 31). It reports to the IRS the number of employees, total wages paid during the quarter, and withholdings and total payroll taxes paid.

On the IRS website is a fileable version of the form: http://www.irs.gov/pub/irs-pdf/f941.pdf. I have included screens shots of the form, so you can see what is required. To get started, you will need the last quarter's payroll information.

1. 941 Line-By-Line Instructions

The top section is for your EIN, legal name of the organization, and address. To the right, you will notice a box listing the months. Mark the months on which you will be reporting.

Form **941 for 2019: Employer's QUARTERLY Federal Tax Return** 950117
(Rev. January 2019) Department of the Treasury — Internal Revenue Service OMB No. 1545-0029

Employer identification number (EIN)
Name (not your trade name)
Trade name (if any)
Address
Number Street Suite or room number
City State ZIP code
Foreign country name Foreign province/county Foreign postal code

Report for this Quarter of 2019 (Check one.)
☐ 1: January, February, March
☐ 2: April, May, June
☐ 3: July, August, September
☐ 4: October, November, December
Go to www.irs.gov/Form941 for instructions and the latest information.

Read the separate instructions before you complete Form 941. Type or print within the boxes.

Part 1, Line 1: Enter the number of employees you had receiving wages during the quarter.

Line #2: Enter the wages paid to employees.

Line #3: Enter the amount of federal income tax withheld from employees' checks for the quarter.

Line #4: Check this box only if NO wages or compensations were subject to Social Security and Medicare.

Line #5a, Column 1: Enter the amount of taxable wages paid to employees subject to the Social Security limits.

Line #5a, Column 2: Multiply line 5a by the percentage shown.

Line #5b: Does not apply to nonprofits.

Line #5c, Column 1: Enter the amount of taxable wages paid to employees.

Line #5c, Column 2: Multiply line 5a by the percentage shown.

Line #5d: Only needed for employees paid over $200,000.

Part 1: Answer these questions for this quarter.

Line	Description	Column 1		Column 2 / Amount
1	Number of employees who received wages, tips, or other compensation for the pay period including: *Mar. 12* (Quarter 1), *June 12* (Quarter 2), *Sept. 12* (Quarter 3), or *Dec. 12* (Quarter 4)			1
2	Wages, tips, and other compensation			2 .
3	Federal income tax withheld from wages, tips, and other compensation			3 .
4	If no wages, tips, and other compensation are subject to social security or Medicare tax			☐ Check and go to line 6.
		Column 1		Column 2
5a	Taxable social security wages	.	× 0.124 =	.
5b	Taxable social security tips	.	× 0.124 =	.
5c	Taxable Medicare wages & tips	.	× 0.029 =	.
5d	Taxable wages & tips subject to Additional Medicare Tax withholding	.	× 0.009 =	.
5e	Add Column 2 from lines 5a, 5b, 5c, and 5d			5e .
5f	Section 3121(q) Notice and Demand—Tax due on unreported tips (see instructions)			5f .
6	**Total taxes before adjustments.** Add lines 3, 5e, and 5f			6 .
7	Current quarter's adjustment for fractions of cents			7 .
8	Current quarter's adjustment for sick pay			8 .
9	Current quarter's adjustments for tips and group-term life insurance			9 .
10	**Total taxes after adjustments.** Combine lines 6 through 9			10 .
11	**Qualified small business payroll tax credit for increasing research activities.** Attach Form 8974			11 .
12	**Total taxes after adjustments and credits.** Subtract line 11 from line 10			12 .
13	**Total deposits for this quarter, including overpayment applied from a prior quarter and overpayments applied from Form 941-X, 941-X (PR), 944-X, or 944-X (SP) filed in the current quarter**			13 .
14	**Balance due.** If line 12 is more than line 13, enter the difference and see instructions			14 .
15	**Overpayment.** If line 13 is more than line 12, enter the difference	.	Check one: ☐ Apply to next return. ☐ Send a refund.	

► **You MUST complete both pages of Form 941 and SIGN it.** Next ►

Line #5e: Enter the total Social Security and Medicare taxes due.

Line #5f: Skip assuming your employees probably do not receive tips.

Line #6: Add lines 3 and 5e.

Line #7: Adjustment for calculations to make the pennies match. Use a minus sign if it is a decrease.

Line #8: Use if you have a third-party sick pay payer.

Line #9: Nonprofits will not usually need to use these lines.

Line #10: Add lines 6 thru 9.

Line #11: Not applicable to nonprofits.

Line #12: Use amount from Line 10.

Line #13: Total deposits for the quarter. (This is for medium category organizations with a payroll tax liability over $2500 per quarter that have been making monthly deposits.)

Line #14: If line 12 is more than line 13, enter the difference. Hopefully, this is 0.

Line #15: If line 13 is more than line 12, enter the overpayment and select if you will be applying it to the next return or if you would like a refund sent.

The second page requires you to type in the charity name and EIN at the top.

Part 2

Part 2: Tell us about your deposit schedule and tax liability for this quarter.

If you are unsure about whether you are a monthly schedule depositor or a semiweekly schedule depositor, see section 11 of Pub. 15.

16 Check one: ☐ **Line 12 on this return is less than $2,500 or line 12 on the return for the prior quarter was less than $2,500, and you didn't incur a $100,000 next-day deposit obligation during the current quarter.** If line 12 for the prior quarter was less than $2,500 but line 12 on this return is $100,000 or more, you must provide a record of your federal tax liability. If you are a monthly schedule depositor, complete the deposit schedule below; if you are a semiweekly schedule depositor, attach Schedule B (Form 941). Go to Part 3.

☐ **You were a monthly schedule depositor for the entire quarter.** Enter your tax liability for each month and total liability for the quarter, then go to Part 3.

Tax liability: Month 1 ______ .

Month 2 ______ .

Month 3 ______ .

Total liability for quarter ______ . **Total must equal line 12.**

☐ **You were a semiweekly schedule depositor for any part of this quarter.** Complete Schedule B (Form 941), Report of Tax Liability for Semiweekly Schedule Depositors, and attach it to Form 941.

Part 3: Tell us about your business. If a question does NOT apply to your business, leave it blank.

17 If your business has closed or you stopped paying wages . . . . ☐ Check here, and

enter the final date you paid wages / / .

18 If you are a seasonal employer and you don't have to file a return for every quarter of the year . . ☐ Check here.

Line 16: This explains to the IRS the frequency of your deposits. Select the first option only if you consistently have deposits due of less than $2500 per quarter. If you have been depositing monthly, even if less than $2500 per quarter, you need to select the second box and enter your monthly deposit amounts. The totals MUST equal Line 12 on the first page. If your charity was large enough to be depositing semiweekly, select the third box instead and complete a Schedule B (available on the IRS website).

Part 3: It is usually unnecessary.

Part 3:	Tell us about your business. If a question does NOT apply to your business, leave it blank.
17	If your business has closed or you stopped paying wages . . . . ☐ Check here, and enter the final date you paid wages [/ /].
18	If you are a seasonal employer and you don't have to file a return for every quarter of the year . . ☐ Check here.
Part 4:	May we speak with your third-party designee?
	Do you want to allow an employee, a paid tax preparer, or another person to discuss this return with the IRS? See the instructions for details.
	☐ Yes. Designee's name and phone number [ ] [ ]
	Select a 5-digit Personal Identification Number (PIN) to use when talking to the IRS. ☐☐☐☐☐
	☐ No.
Part 5:	Sign here. You MUST complete both pages of Form 941 and SIGN it.
	Under penalties of perjury, I declare that I have examined this return, including accompanying schedules and statements, and to the best of my knowledge and belief, it is true, correct, and complete. Declaration of preparer (other than taxpayer) is based on all information of which preparer has any knowledge.
X	Sign your name here [ ] — Print your name here [ ] — Print your title here [ ]
	Date [/ /] — Best daytime phone [ ]

Part 4: This allows you to have someone else discuss the tax return with the IRS. This could be your outside accountant or an organization member who is helping. It is not required.

Part 5: This part must be signed by an official of the organization. The bookkeeper is NOT an allowed signer per the IRS. The executive director, treasurer, and president of the board are all options.

The form also includes a voucher to use only if your total taxes for the preceding quarter were less than $2500.

If not submitted electronically, the form must be mailed by the due date to the address listed in the instructions. The address is dependent on which state your nonprofit is located in.

> *Form 941 may be filed electronically or mailed, though the IRS prefers electronic filing. If you are using an accounting software package, see if there is an e-file option.*

2. State Filings

Don't forget most states have their unique payroll tax forms and filing deadlines. Most are due the same month as the 941, but you will need to verify it with your state department of revenue.

J. Year-End Filings

At year-end, you may have several forms you will need to complete and submit to the IRS.

1. W-2 (Wage and Tax Statement)

After the calendar year-end, your employees need to know the total amount of wages received and how much was taken out for taxes in the previous year. The W-2 gives them this information and is also sent to the federal government.

A W-2 has at least three copies. The first (Copy A) is in red and is sent to the Social Security Administration with a transmittal form (W-3). Copy B in black is to be filed with the employee's federal return. Copy C is included for the employee's records. There is a Copy 1 (and 2, if needed) for the state, city, or local department of revenue.

The W-2 is a relatively simple form to complete. At the very top, enter your employee's SSN in Box a. Box b is the charity's EIN, followed by the charity's legal name and address in Box c. The Control number in box d is for your use if you are numbering the W-2 for tracking purposes. It can be left blank. Box e and f are for the employee's name and address.

Let's step through the numbered boxes next.

Box 1: Total wages and compensation paid to the employee. This amount is before any deductions. It should include any other taxable compensation, such as travel advances—not per diems—for which receipts were not received, as discussed previously.

Keep in mind this box is asking for wages paid, not earned.

If you paid your employees on January 2 for the previous two weeks of work, you would not include those wages.

22222 | VOID ☐ | a Employee's social security number | For Official Use Only ▶ OMB No. 1545-0008

b Employer identification number (EIN)
1 Wages, tips, other compensation
2 Federal income tax withheld
c Employer's name, address, and ZIP code
3 Social security wages
4 Social security tax withheld
5 Medicare wages and tips
6 Medicare tax withheld
7 Social security tips
8 Allocated tips
d Control number
9
10 Dependent care benefits
e Employee's first name and initial | Last name | Suff.
11 Nonqualified plans
12a See instructions for box 12
13 Statutory employee | Retirement plan | Third-party sick pay
12b
14 Other
12c
12d
f Employee's address and ZIP code
15 State | Employer's state ID number | 16 State wages, tips, etc. | 17 State income tax | 18 Local wages, tips, etc. | 19 Local income tax | 20 Locality name

Form **W-2** Wage and Tax Statement **2020**

Department of the Treasury—Internal Revenue Service
For Privacy Act and Paperwork Reduction Act Notice, see the separate instructions.
Cat. No. 10134D

Copy A—For Social Security Administration. Send this entire page with Form W-3 to the Social Security Administration; photocopies are not acceptable.

Do Not Cut, Fold, or Staple Forms on This Page

Box 2: Federal income tax withheld. This is the total amount of federal taxes withheld from the employee for the year.

Box 3: Social Security wages are usually the same as total wages. Differences may occur if the employee was paid more than the $117,000 base or other compensation was included.

Box 4: Tax withheld on Social Security wages and should equal 6.2% of box 3.

Box 5: Medicare wages and tips will usually be the same as Box 1 unless there is other compensation included.

Box 6: Tax withheld on the amount in box 5. This amount should equal 1.45% of box 5.

Boxes 7-9: These are not commonly used by nonprofit organizations.

Boxes 10-14: These relate to dependent care benefits, retirement plans, and other miscellaneous items too detailed for the scope of this book. Your accountant or retirement benefits administrator will need to give you specific directions for your organization.

Boxes 15-20: This is where you input the nonprofit's state and local identification number and the state and local income and taxes withheld for the employee.

Once all the employee's information is entered, double-check the SSN and address. Then total each of the boxes of all the W-2s. This information will be entered into the **W-3 Transmittal of Wage and Tax Statement**.

2. W-3 (Transmittal of Wage and Tax Statements)

DO NOT STAPLE

33333 | a Control number | For Official Use Only ▶ OMB No. 1545-0008

b Kind of Payer (Check one): 941, 943, 944, CT-1, Hshld. emp., Medicare govt. emp.

Kind of Employer (Check one): None apply, 501c non-govt., State/local non-501c, State/local 501c, Federal govt.

Third-party sick pay (Check if applicable)

c Total number of Forms W-2 / d Establishment number	1 Wages, tips, other compensation / 2 Federal income tax withheld
e Employer identification number (EIN)	3 Social security wages / 4 Social security tax withheld
f Employer's name	5 Medicare wages and tips / 6 Medicare tax withheld
	7 Social security tips / 8 Allocated tips
	9 / 10 Dependent care benefits
g Employer's address and ZIP code	11 Nonqualified plans / 12a Deferred compensation
h Other EIN used this year	13 For third-party sick pay use only / 12b
15 State / Employer's state ID number	14 Income tax withheld by payer of third-party sick pay
16 State wages, tips, etc. / 17 State income tax	18 Local wages, tips, etc. / 19 Local income tax
Employer's contact person	Employer's telephone number / For Official Use Only
Employer's fax number	Employer's email address

Under penalties of perjury, I declare that I have examined this return and accompanying documents, and, to the best of my knowledge and belief, they are true, correct, and complete.

Signature ▶ Title ▶ Date ▶

Form **W-3** Transmittal of Wage and Tax Statements 2020 Department of the Treasury Internal Revenue Service

Send this entire page with the entire Copy A page of Form(s) W-2 to the Social Security Administration (SSA). Photocopies are not acceptable. Do not send Form W-3 if you filed electronically with the SSA.
Do not send any payment (cash, checks, money orders, etc.) with Forms W-2 and W-3.

Before you start entering data in the W-3, pull out the four quarterly reports (941s) for the year. Compare the total wages for the four quarters to the totals of all your W-2s. If there is a discrepancy, you will need to see if a W-2 is incorrect, if your 941 filing is wrong, or if you just added them up incorrectly.

Notice the W-3 looks similar to the W-2.

Starting at the top, **Box a** is for your use as a control number if desired.

Box b reflects the **Kind of Payer** you are. Unless you are small enough to be a 944 filer (discussed earlier in the chapter), you will select 941. The **Kind of Employer** option for a nonprofit is 501c non-govt.

Box c asks for the total number of forms you are submitting with the transmittal statement.

Box d allows for an establishment number in case you have several locations using the same EIN. The other lettered boxes request your legal name, address, federal and state EINs, etc.

The numbered boxes are the totals of that box from all the attached W-2s. For example, **Box 1** will reflect the total of all the W-2 Box 1 wage amounts. The amount will also equal the four quarters of Total Taxable Wages on your 941s.

Box 2 will equal the total of all the W-2 Box 2 federal tax withheld amounts (and ties to the federal taxes withheld on the four quarters of the 941).

The remaining numbered boxes are the totals from their respective W-2 boxes. Once you are sure your totals reconcile with the four 941s, complete the form, sign, title, and date. Include (but do NOT staple) the red Copy A for each W-2 and mail to the address listed in the instructions on the form. These are typically due by the last day of February.

> *You cannot download a usable W-2 and W-3 from the web! The original that's filed with the IRS is printed in red ink and is read by a scanner.*

K. Ordering IRS Forms

You can order forms from the IRS at no charge or purchase them from an office supply store. You can reach the IRS at 1-800-TAX-FORM to request the ones you need or order them online at irs.gov. Order your W-2 and W-3 forms from the IRS as early as possible. If you wait until January, you may not get them in time, and office supply stores may run short as well.

L. Summary

I know this chapter was rather complicated, but you now have the tools and ability to calculate and pay the regular payroll, which can save your organization a lot of money.

The amount of an employee's payroll check is determined by calculating the federal tax withholding using either the wage rate method or the percentage method. If your state has an income tax, you will calculate that withholding based on the state charts. Next, calculate Social Security and Medicare withholding. From the gross wages, subtract the total of the withholdings. The net of the two will give you the net payroll check amount.

The taxes withheld and the employer taxes must be deposited with the US Treasury and quarterly reports filed (unless you have been approved for an annual filing). The taxes are filed electronically, so the charity needs to set up an account through the IRS. After year-end, the employees need to receive a W-2 showing annual earnings and taxes withheld. A copy of these is filed with a W-3 transmittal form to the government.

You have learned how to:

- Calculate payroll withholding,
- Prepare the payroll checks,
- Recording the journal entry,
- Make the tax deposit, and
- File the required forms for a standard payroll.

In the next chapter, we will go over how to prepare budgets and forecasts for an organization.

13. Budgeting For Nonprofit Organizations

So many people dread the concept of budgeting. I don't know if it's because I'm an accountant (and maybe a bit of a geek) or just odd, but I find budgeting the most interesting part of the accounting process. Think of preparing an annual budget as a way to prioritize its efforts to achieve the group's mission.

> *Approach the budgeting process as a way to garner consensus around the priorities of your charity.*

There is a limit to the donations expected to be received, and therefore a limit to the services that can be offered. The budgeting process can assist with the prioritization of your nonprofit's goals.

In this chapter, you will learn:

- The process necessary to prepare a budget,
- How to do monthly budgeting,
- The difference between budgets and forecasts, and
- How to use your forecast for analyzing cash flow.

A. The Budget Process

Budgets are typically done on operating income and expenses. Income and expenses outside of normal nonprofit operations (like the receipt of a bequest or repaving the parking lot) only need to be budgeted if they are substantial. Budgets may be helpful for specific grants or funds (such as a new building project) in which there will be numerous transactions and cash implications.

The budget process will have several steps. First, you must consider if you need budgets at a top-level (total nonprofit only) or program by program. Budgeting at the program level will take more time but will also give you more information.

You may also wish to budget by program and grant. If you prepare program budgets for all areas (including administration), this will then be summarized into a total organization budget.

For example, if donations have consistently been close to $50,000 for the last five years, you are probably safe budgeting $50,000 for next year. But if a large donor has died, consider reducing the expected pledges by their usual donation.

Next, you will need to determine what donations and other revenues you are expecting. Unless your membership and contributions are stable, this is often difficult to budget. Economic factors, like the unemployment rate in your area or changes in the stock market, may impact your members' giving. If your nonprofit membership and donations have been fairly consistent over the years, use historical trends, and tweak them for any likely changes and economic conditions.

Some organizations prefer to ask for the annual donations or pledge commitments before they begin the budgeting process. This gives the treasurer a more accurate idea of the minimum amount of donations that will be received. The difficulty with this approach is the timing. If you start asking members for their commitments in October, it may be late December before you have them nailed down.

A hybrid approach is to use historical data and update it with known donations before you finalize the budgets. This incorporates the best of both worlds and also allows the treasurer to do what accountants call a "smell test." A smell test really means "does it make sense?" If donations committed are 50% less than last year's, but membership is stable, you either have an entry error or need to follow up with your members to see what has changed.

Non-pledged donations are usually budgeted at historical rates. This would include money received for a fundraiser, rental of space, etc. Investment income can be budgeted based on expected returns of the investments. If you had $100,000 in a money market account that is currently paying 2% interest, you would budget $2000 of investment income.

For the expense budgets, I like to get buy-in from the heads of the programs. Start by giving a report to the directors of each program showing how much money they have spent this year. Then, ask your program heads to submit their budget proposal of expected needs for the next year, and if it is substantially different than this year, an explanation should be included. I refer to this as "the wish list." Be sure to remind the program heads that it is not part of the budget until approved by the finance committee or governing board.

Preparing their proposal and explanation encourages the program directors to think about what they would like to do differently. The written documentation is a good resource for the governing board as they deliberate on how to divide the budget dollars. This also gives you the information to put in your budget.

Besides program expenses, your charity has facilities and other overhead expenditures. These can usually be calculated based on historical information or contracts. If you are allocating this expense across the programs, save yourself time by waiting until all the direct program costs have been budgeted. Then you can do a one-time calculation based on the percentage of space used, the number of employees, or the percentage of total costs to allocate the overhead.

For example, use a spreadsheet to estimate all your building expenses. If you have three programs, Administration, Program 1, and Program 2, you would add one-third of the expected building expenses to each of these three budgets. You can do the same thing for salaries if you allocate people over more than one program. Some charities use different allocation percentages for facilities costs versus supplies and administrative costs.

One of the most common questions asked by directors as they work on the budget is,

"What is the average percentage of salaries in a nonprofit budget?"

The consensus seems to be there is no consensus, but you must sure that the compensation is reasonable for the services provided.

Excess compensation may jeopardize the tax exempt status of the organization.

B. Example Budget Spreadsheet

On the next page is an example of a simple top-level budget spreadsheet. Input your prior year amounts for each account in the Actual (D) column. The Budget (E) column is for your current budget. The next column (F) becomes the year-to-date budget. It assumes the budget should be spread evenly throughout the year, so there is a formula to divide Column F by 12 and multiply it by the number of months (in the box in the heading) you are reporting on. This allows you to compare your actual year-to-date income and expenses (G) with the expected budget. The final column (h) shows the percentage change.

In this example, the January (Month #1) donations are close to expectations, and the capital campaign appears to be doing better than expected. Under "Expenses," the salaries and related tax should be right on the budget unless an unbudgeted hire was brought on or hourly people worked more hours than expected. Program expenses are showing at only 80% of expected. This would be an area you would want to investigate to see if an outstanding invoice had not yet been paid or something had been incorrectly charged.

If you are using the cash method of accounting, you can put your beginning-of-the-year cash at the top. The system will add the "Net Income Actual" line to it so you can see ending cash all on one report.

NAME

BUDGET TO ACTUAL YTD

DATE: [illegible] Month # 1

		Actual Previous Yr	Budget 2021	Linear Budget YTD 13-Feb-20	YTD Actuals 2021	%
	Cash Beginning of Period:					$ 15,000
Revenue						
4001	Donations	$ 98,780	$ 110,000	$ 9,167	$ 9,000	98%
4002	Capital Campaign	$ 20,000	$ 30,000	$ 2,500	$ 4,000	160%
4003	Venue Rentals	$ 3,000	$ 3,000	$ 250	$ -	0%
4004	Investment Income	$ 500	$ 550	$ 46	$ 45	98%
	Total Revenue:	$ 122,280	$ 143,550	$ 11,963	$ 13,045	
Expenses:						
5001	Salaries	$ 50,000	$ 52,500	$ 4,375	$ 4,375	100%
5002	Payroll Tax Expense	$ 3,825	$ 4,016	$ 335	$ 335	100%
5003	Rent	$ 4,000	$ 4,120	$ 343	$ 343	100%
5004	Utilities	$ 600	$ 618	$ 52	$ 50	97%
5005	Program Expenses	$ 62,000	$ 82,000	$ 6,833	$ 5,500	80%
	Total Expenses:	$ 120,425	$ 143,254	$ 11,938	$ 10,603	
Net : Income Gain / (Loss)		$ 1,855	$ 296	$ 25	$ 2,442	
Cash End of Period						$ 17,442

C. Monthly Budgeting

A strong monthly budget can help nonprofit administrators plan for resources and cash flow. It also gives them a better understanding of how the organization is doing compared to its budget at any point in the year.

Your charity's income may not be received equally throughout the year. Contributions are probably higher near the end of the year, and whichever months you may have fundraising events or mailings. If you have historical data, use it to track your contributions.

For your members who pledge, budget their gifts based on how they would like to pay—weekly, monthly, quarterly, or annually. Membership dues can be budgeted based on the number of members and the dues amount. You will want to estimate a little less due to people moving away or more if your organization is growing. Donation income and other non-pledged support are harder to nail down, but historical trends should help.

For example, an organization was concerned that by the end of June, they had only recieved 40% of their budgeted contributions. At that run rate, they risked running out of cash and having to lay off staff.

However, by going back three years and tracking contributions by month, they noticed that 32% of the contributions were received in December.

Using this information, they realized they were likely on track to reach their budget goals and did not need to reduce their staff.

For expenses, consider during which month they are most likely to occur. As you are probably using the cash basis method of accounting, you will need to budget the expense when you think the bill will be paid. If supplies are typically ordered and paid two months before a big summer event, budget the expense in April, not June. If each September, the organization requires the professional landscaper to prepare the lawn for winter, but the bill doesn't usually come until October, budget the expense for October.

There also may be significant expenses in certain months that are planned but do not occur every year. If your organization sends several people to a large conference in the summer or you have a fall gala, you may have additional expenses those months.

Most computerized software packages, like QuickBooks, allow you to design budgets down to the program level by month. This allows you to run reports monthly, quarterly, or annually at the top-level or by individual program.

A well-thought-out monthly budget is more work, but it can also be a strong internal control and give the executives and governing board a feel for changes in the congregation. Revenue coming in below expectations may be due to several things, including unhappy members or fraud. If you didn’t recognize the trend, how could you investigate it? Large unbudgeted expenses could be related to growth at the charity, a program director who is not following protocol, or even theft. The administrators of the charity need to understand which one it could be.

Comparing the actual income and expenses to the budget monthly allows the organization to spot errors and catch fraud on a timely basis.

> *If reviewed regularly with the executive and governing board, monthly budgets are instrumental in understanding the financial situation of the nonprofit organization.*

D. **Forecasts**

No matter how carefully and thoughtfully you work through your budget, situations may change. To help you anticipate what these changes will mean for your organization, you may want to prepare a forecast.

Budgets are typically created annually and stay stable throughout the year. **Forecasts** are used as a "what if" tool and are useful when change is anticipated. A forecast is not meant to replace the budget, but to give the administration tools to understand and plan for changes before they occur.

> *Perhaps you are considering hiring some new personnel to run an expanded children's program. You could create a forecast making assumptions on the additional costs of payroll and program expenses offset by any anticipated growth in your organization.*

To create a forecast, I like to start with a schedule of current actual income and expenses year to date. Input these in a summary fashion in a spreadsheet. Add columns for the remaining months of the year and populate those columns with the budgeted data.

C	D	E	F	L	M	N	O
January Actual	February Actual	March *Forecast	Apr *Forec	ober ecast	November *Forecast	December *Forecast	Total YTD

Next, adjust the monthly budgeted amounts for the items you know will be changing. For example, if you expect a grant which will fund staff, increase the budget for grants by the amount of the gift in the month you expect the money. Then increase salaries, benefits, and payroll taxes for the cost of the new position or project.

Anytime you are forecasting for new staff, do not forget to add any additional expenses (e.g., a cell phone, computer, desk, additional supplies the person may need). It is a common error to only think of the monthly salary, not the associated day-to-day costs of doing a job.

Now let's look at the forecast in more detail. After you have input the actual revenue received and expenses paid for any months that have already passed and keyed in your budget, you can start to analyze how the forecast may differ from the budget. To help my analysis, I added three columns: total budget, expected variance, and actual run rate.

First, adjust for financial events you are aware of and include the total budget. Let's say you are receiving a grant in November that will require additional program and labor expenses. Those need to be added to the November and December forecast. Include a column with the **total budget** so you can compare what money the organization

Next, look at your **run rate**. The run rate is the average actual cost of each month. For example, if actual telephone costs were $600 in total for January and February, the run rate for telephone expense is $300 per month. If you have only budgeted $200 per month for the rest of the year, consider whether you need to increase the budgeted amount for your forecast. Run rate analysis can be very useful but requires careful evaluation.

The **actual run rate** column sums up all the months with revenue and expenses that have already occurred and divides the sum by the number of months passed to give an average revenue or expense for the periods. In the above example, it would add columns C and D and then divide by 2. The next month, the formula would need to add C, D, and E and divide by 3.

Use this calculation to compare your current run rate to your monthly budget. For example, if the run rate for program expenses is $1450 per month and the budget is $1200 per month, you may need to investigate if there were unusual expenses in the first months or if the budget was simply too low. In the next screenshot, I assume the higher run rate will continue and have adjusted my forecast to the run rate.

When I did that, the amount in the "Total YTD" column for program expenses has increased to $17,400 and is now showing an **expected variance** of $3000.

	A	B	C	D	E	F	M	N	O	P	Q	R
1			January Actual	February Actual	March *Forecast	Ap *Fore	lovember Forecast	December *Forecast	Total YTD	Total Budget	Expected Variance	Actual Run Rate
2												
4												
5	Revenue											
6	#	Donations	$2,250	$1,800	$1,800	$1,	$1,800	$1,800	$22,050	$20,000	$2,050	$2,025
7	#	Misc. Income	55	200	100		100	100	1,255	1,200	55	128
8	#	Fundraisers		20,000					48,000	50,000	(2,000)	10,000
9	#	Grant					26,000		26,000	26,000	-	0
10		Total Revenue	$2,305	$22,000	$1,900	$1	$27,900	$1,900	$97,305	$97,200	$105	$ 12,153
11	Expenses											
12	#	Salary/Benefits	$4,000	$4,000	$4,000	$4	$4,000	$5,000	$49,000	$48,000	($1,000)	$4,000
13	#	Travel					$2,000		[illegible]	[illegible]	[illegible]	$0
14	#	Program Expenses	1,500	1,400	1,450	1	1,450	1,450	17,400	14,400	(3,000)	$1,450
15	#	Office Supplies	120	80	110		110	110	[illegible]	1,320	20	$100
16	#	Phone/ Internet	300	300	200		200	200	2,600	2,400	(200)	$300
17	#	Rent	800	800	800		800	800	9,600	9,600	0	$800
18	#	Fundraising Expense			5,000				11,000	12,000	1,000	$0
19	#	Insurance	500	500	500		500	500	6,000	6,000	0	$500
20	Total Expenses		$7,220	$7,080	$12,060	$7	$9,060	$8,060	$98,900	$96,720	($2,180)	$7,150
21	Net Income		$ (4,915)	$ 14,920	$ (10,160)	$ (5	18,840	$ (6,160)	$ (1,595)	$ 480	$ (2,075)	$ 5,003

Actual Run Rate does not match budget.
Were there any unusual expenses?

Review the significant amounts in the "Expected Variance" column to decide how to make up any shortfall. Consider options for additional revenues or reductions of other expenses and adjust your forecast based on the decisions made.

To develop a forecast:

- Adjust the budget column numbers to the most likely amounts you will be spending based on your current run rate and experience.
- Adjust any numbers you expect to change based on changing conditions or expected donations or expenses.
- Look at the column titled "Expected Variance." Are you substantially over or under in any category?

- If you are substantially worse than budget, use the forecast as a tool to determine the best way to get closer to your budgeted goals.

> *The earlier you can make the nonprofit administration aware of potential financial shortfalls, the earlier they can address the issues.*

E. Cash Flow Analysis

The forecast can also be used to help track cash flow. If you are a small nonprofit, you probably use the cash basis method of accounting (i.e., only record revenue and expenses when the cash is received or paid out). With a well-thought-out forecast, the cash requirements can be tracked. With an advance warning that the cash flow will not be sufficient, the nonprofit can apply for a line of credit, have additional fundraisers, or put off non-critical purchases.

The worksheet from the previous example also takes the beginning cash balance and adjusts it with the monthly net income to reach a **Cash End of Period** amount. This amount is then copied into the next month's **Cash Beginning of Period** line.

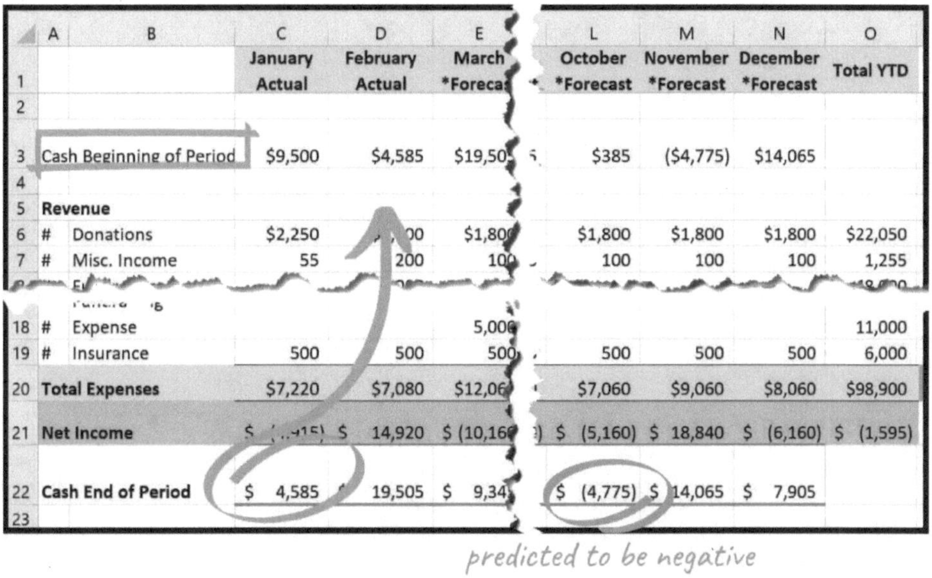

	A	B	C	D	E	L	M	N	O
1			January Actual	February Actual	March *Foreca	*Forecast October	November *Forecast	December *Forecast	Total YTD
2									
3	Cash Beginning of Period		$9,500	$4,585	$19,50	$385	($4,775)	$14,065	
4									
5	Revenue								
6	#	Donations	$2,250	[illegible]00	$1,80	$1,800	$1,800	$1,800	$22,050
7	#	Misc. Income	55	200	10	100	100	100	1,255
18	#	Expense			5,00				11,000
19	#	Insurance	500	500	500	500	500	500	6,000
20	Total Expenses		$7,220	$7,080	$12,06	$7,060	$9,060	$8,060	$98,900
21	Net Income		$ [illegible]	$ 14,920	$ (10,16	$ (5,160)	$ 18,840	$ (6,160)	$ (1,595)
22	Cash End of Period		$ 4,585	19,505	$ 9,34	$ (4,775)	$ 14,065	$ 7,905	
23									

predicted to be negative

It appears the organization will run short of money in October but should have a cash balance of $7905 at the end of the year.

Using this information can help you determine the best approach to guard against cash shortfalls and plan for contingencies.

F. Summary

In this chapter, we discussed how to:

- Approach your budget as a way to prioritize for the coming year,
- Design a spreadsheet for the budget,
- Go through the budget process and break it out into monthly increments,
- Use the budget as a strong internal control feature to catch mistakes and theft early,
- Use a combination of actual data and the budget to design a forecast, and
- Use the budget as a cash-flow analysis that will guide your nonprofit activities.

The transactions have been entered, and budgets and forecasts prepared. Let's look at month-end financial requirements.

14. Month-End Financial Requirements

It's the end of the month, and your monthly board meeting is coming up. There are things you will want to do to ensure the financial information you give them is accurate and complete. In this chapter, we will:

- Review the steps needed to assure complete financials,
- Learn how to reconcile the bank accounts, and
- Learn what reports to generate for comprehensive information.

A. Monthly Processes for Complete Financials

Before we can put together any financial reports for the executive director, treasurer, or governing board, we need to confirm the information is complete and accurate. At a minimum, you will need to:

- Check unopened mail for any checks or donations received and for any unpaid bills,
- Make sure all contributions have been deposited in the bank and recorded in the financial records,
- Record and verify payment of all paid bills in the appropriate expense account and against the checking account,
- Record payroll and pay payroll liabilities to the appropriate agencies,
- Record credit card charges to the correct expense accounts,
- Look at your bank statement or online banking transactions and record interest earned, bank charges, and any automatic withdrawals into the correct accounts, and
- Record any online donations received minus the processing charge.

B. Bank Reconciliation

Once all transactions have been recorded, you will need to reconcile your bank account. This is the process of determining what you have in your records that the bank has not yet recorded or what has cleared the bank but has not yet been recorded by you. It is a simple process but can be very tedious.

Start with the bank statement.

First, scan the "Other Withdrawals," "Debits," and "Service Charges" sections of the statement and make sure each of the charges has been properly recorded in your general ledger account. If you don't know what a charge is for, call the bank immediately. Banks rarely make mistakes, but they do make them. If you do not bring it to the bank's attention on a timely basis, you may lose any recourse.

Next, look at the *deposits* that have cleared the bank and compare them to the deposits recorded in the general ledger cash account. Sometimes the last deposits of the month are not yet recorded in the bank. These are called **outstanding deposits**. If it appears to be a timing issue, it should not be a problem.

If your accounting records show an outstanding deposit was made early in the month, you need to research why the bank is not showing it. It could be a bank error, it could be recorded in the accounting system incorrectly, or the deposit may never have been made. It may even be sitting in someone's car where someone forgot about it, or it could have been stolen.

Less frequently, there will be deposits recorded by the bank but not in the accounting records. The most common of these are credit card donations. If your website allows donors to make donations online, the credit card processor may automatically move the money into your checking account. In this case, go to the website donation site and print out a report by donor and amount for the month. Record these donations and restart your bank reconciliation.

Thirdly, review your *withdrawals*. Compare each of the checks you wrote to the checks that cleared the bank. List any checks not on the bank statement as an **outstanding check**. If there are checks on the bank statement that are not in the accounting records, you will need to investigate these. Were they properly approved and signed by an authorized signer? If so, why weren't they recorded?

Once you know the outstanding deposits and checks, you are ready to complete the reconciliation.

- Set up a spreadsheet and input the ending balance from the bank statement.
- Add to this balance the outstanding deposits.
- Subtract any outstanding checks. The net effect should be the balance of the cash account in your accounting records.

	A	B	C	D	E
1		**Your Charity**			
2		**Bank Reconciliation**			
3		**as of 06/30/xx**			
4					
5	**Date**	**Description**	**Check #**	**Amount**	**Totals**
6					
7	xx/xx/xx	**Bank Balance per Statement**			**$5,789.14**
8					
9		**Outstanding Deposits**			
10	06/29/xx			150.00	
11	06/30/xx			1,250.00	
12	**Total Outstanding Deposits**				1,400.00
13					
14					
15		**Outstanding Checks**			
16	06/15/xx	Jane Smith	1052	25.00	
17	06/20/xx	USPS	1061	37.00	
18	06/28/xx	Utilitie Inc	1075	125.00	
19	06/29/xx	Janet Director (payroll)	1076	1,250.00	
20	**Total Outstanding Checks**				(1,437.00)
21		**Ending Book Balance***			**$5,752.14**
22					
23	*This should be the general ledger checking account balance. If it doesn't tie,				
24	make sure all of the bank charges and withdrawals have been recorded.				

If the reconciled balance does NOT equal the accounting records, you will need to go back through everything that was recorded in the general ledger and everything that was recorded in the bank.

A common error is from transposition (a check written for $93.00 but is recorded on accounting as $39.00). If the amount you are off is divisible by 9, this is likely the case.

If outstanding checks from the previous month still have not cleared, your reconciliation will not balance. Look at the previous reconciliation and verify that all checks on the outstanding list have cleared this month. If not, add the un-cleared check to the outstanding checks list.

Great! Now you have the bank and accounting records reconciled, but you aren't quite done.

- Look at the reconciling items for outdated or unusual items. Outstanding deposits that were recorded on the last couple of days of the month are usually just a timing error.

In the example spreadsheet above, we aren't surprised to see Janet Director's payroll check outstanding because it is dated near the last day of the month. She may have not been able to get to the bank in time.

You can also see Jane Smith was reimbursed for some expenses earlier in the month. This check appears to be outstanding as well. You may want to call her to see if the check was lost or if it is still in her purse.

- Reconcile the petty cash fund and any gift cards. Petty cash is reconciled by totaling the receipts and counting the remaining cash as discussed in Chapter 1. Gift cardholders should have receipts for any reduction in the value of the gift card. Record the receipts in the appropriate expense categories.
- Give the completed bank reconciliation with the bank statement and cleared checks (or bank images) to the director or treasurer (if he is not the bookkeeper) each month for review. They should scrutinize the checks for unusual payees, duplicate payments, and long-outstanding checks or deposits.

C. Investment Account Reconciliations

If your organization holds funds in an investment account with a broker, you should receive statements monthly or quarterly. These need to be reconciled in a similar manner to the checking account. The most significant difference is the income earned on the account.

Most investment accounts will list several types of income: interest, dividend, realized gain or loss from the sale of stock, and unrealized gain or loss based on market value. The *interest* and *dividends* are recorded in the general ledger in operating income accounts called "Interest and Dividends."

Realized gain or loss from the sale of stock is the money change in the value of the investment based on the sale of some of the stock. The gain or loss is treated as "other income/loss" and is usually shown at the bottom of the Income Statement. It is differentiated from the regular income as it is not from donations or services offered to donors.

Unrealized gain or loss reflects the change in the market value of the stock since the last brokerage statements. It should be recorded in a separate Other Income or Loss account (usually called "Unrealized Gain/Loss"). This income is considered "unrealized" as the stock has not been sold, so its value will change with the stock market.

D. Generate Reports

Once all of your accounts are reconciled, it is time to start looking at the financial reports. I like to start with a **Balance Sheet** or **Statement of Financial Position** (which is the correct title for nonprofits). The Statement of Financial Position is a snapshot of the charity's current financial situation. It lists the assets (the things owned), the liabilities (those owed), and the net assets (the cumulative amount of what's left). The balance sheet can be as simple as the example on the next page, or, if the charity is using the accrual basis of accounting, it may include pledges or grants receivable and accounts payable.

2	**Basic Balance Sheet**		
3	**06/30/xx**		
4			
5	**Assets**		
6			
7	Cash	$5,752.14	
8	Petty Cash	100.00	
9	Gift Cards	100.00	
10	Computer	1,200.00	
11			
12	**Total Assets**	**$7,152.14**	
13			
14	**Liabilities**		
15	Credit card	850.45	
16	Payroll Taxes Due	356.00	
17			
18	**Total Liabilities**	**$1,206.45**	
19			
20	**Net Assets**		
21	Without Donor Restriction	4,945.69	
22	With Donor Restriction	1,000.00	
23			
24	**Total Net Assets**	**$5,945.69**	
25			
26	**Total Liabilities & Net Assets**	**$7,152.14**	
27			

Either way, review each line item on the balance sheet. Any cash and investment accounts should have reconciliations. An aging of the amounts owed to the organization as receivable should be compared to the amount on the balance sheet. The fixed assets (e.g., equipment, land, and buildings) should have a list of items to support the amount. The treasurer and/or executive director should have a detailed understanding of the items in any "Other Assets" category.

The liabilities should be identifiable and paid in a timely fashion. The Net Assets are divided between Without Donor Restrictions (normal operating balances) and With Donor Restrictions (grants or designated programs).

Once you feel the balance sheet is correct, it is time to review the Profit and Loss statement, known as a **Statement of Activity** for nonprofits. The Profit & Loss statement reflects all the operating revenues and related expenses to give you the change in net assets. This can be looked at from a top-level basis as well as a program-by-program basis. Here is an example by program from a QuickBooks file.

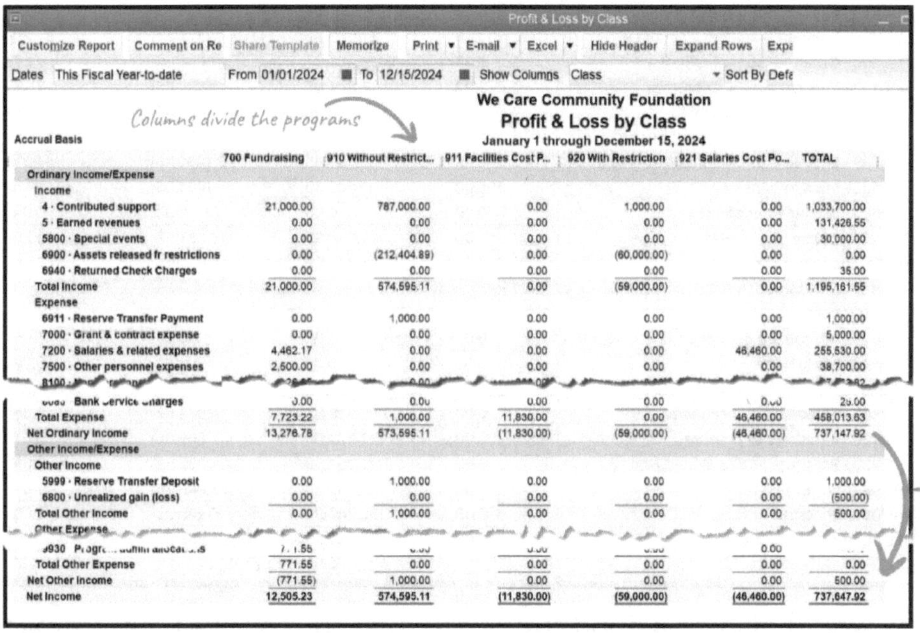

Profit & Loss by Class

Customize Report | Comment on Re | Share Template | Memorize | Print ▾ | E-mail ▾ | Excel ▾ | Hide Header | Expand Rows | Exp

Dates This Fiscal Year-to-date | From 01/01/2024 | To 12/15/2024 | Show Columns Class | Sort By Defa

Columns divide the programs

We Care Community Foundation
Profit & Loss by Class
January 1 through December 15, 2024

Accrual Basis

	700 Fundraising	910 Without Restrict...	911 Facilities Cost P...	920 With Restriction	921 Salaries Cost Po...	TOTAL
Ordinary Income/Expense						
Income						
4 · Contributed support	21,000.00	787,000.00	0.00	1,000.00	0.00	1,033,700.00
5 · Earned revenues	0.00	0.00	0.00	0.00	0.00	131,426.55
5800 · Special events	0.00	0.00	0.00	0.00	0.00	30,000.00
6900 · Assets released fr restrictions	0.00	(212,404.89)	0.00	(60,000.00)	0.00	0.00
6940 · Returned Check Charges	0.00	0.00	0.00	0.00	0.00	35.00
Total Income	21,000.00	574,595.11	0.00	(59,000.00)	0.00	1,195,161.55
Expense						
6911 · Reserve Transfer Payment	0.00	1,000.00	0.00	0.00	0.00	1,000.00
7000 · Grant & contract expense	0.00	0.00	0.00	0.00	0.00	5,000.00
7200 · Salaries & related expenses	4,462.17	0.00	0.00	0.00	46,460.00	255,530.00
7500 · Other personnel expenses	2,500.00	0.00	0.00	0.00	0.00	38,700.00
8100 · [illegible]	[illegible]	0.00	[illegible]	[illegible]	[illegible]	[illegible]
[illegible] · Bank Service Charges	0.00	0.00	0.00	0.00	0.00	25.00
Total Expense	7,723.22	1,000.00	11,830.00	0.00	46,460.00	458,013.63
Net Ordinary Income	13,276.78	573,595.11	(11,830.00)	(59,000.00)	(46,460.00)	737,147.92
Other Income/Expense						
Other Income						
5999 · Reserve Transfer Deposit	0.00	1,000.00	0.00	0.00	0.00	1,000.00
6800 · Unrealized gain (loss)	0.00	0.00	0.00	0.00	0.00	(500.00)
Total Other Income	0.00	1,000.00	0.00	0.00	0.00	500.00
Other Expense						
9930 · Program admin allocations	771.55	0.00	0.00	0.00	0.00	[illegible]
Total Other Expense	771.55	0.00	0.00	0.00	0.00	0.00
Net Other Income	(771.55)	1,000.00	0.00	0.00	0.00	500.00
Net Income	12,505.23	574,595.11	(11,830.00)	(59,000.00)	(46,460.00)	737,647.92

The total **Net Income** will add to (or net loss will subtract from) the "Net Assets" area of the balance sheet/statement of financial position.

The most useful report to review is the Profit & Loss Comparison to Budget. Depending on your accounting system, this can be as easy as the one fund spreadsheet we discussed earlier or a program-by-program comparison to the budget, which can be generated by computerized software systems.

Either way, it is important to understand any variances to the budget. If contributions are below expectations, you can research the issues and make appropriate adjustments. As we discussed in the previous chapter, the use of the comparison-to-budget report can be a powerful control.

We Care Community Foundation
Profit & Loss Budget vs. Actual
October 2024

	Oct 24	Budget	$ Over Budget	% of Budget
Ordinary Income/Expense				
Income				
4 · Contributed support	27,000.00	25,250.00	1,750.00	106.9%
5 · Earned revenues	338.02	9,666.66	(9,328.64)	3.5%
5800 · Special events	30,000.00	29,000.00	1,000.00	103.4%
6900 · Assets released fr restrictions	0.00	0.00	0.00	0.0%
Total Income	57,338.02	63,916.66	(6,578.64)	89.7%
Expense				
7000 · Grant & contract expense	0.00	416.67	(416.67)	0.0%
7200 · Salaries & related expenses	23,230.00	27,602.34	(4,372.34)	84.2%
7500 · Other personnel expenses	0.00	4,066.67	(4,066.67)	0.0%
8100 · Non-personnel expenses	1,076.00	8,696.65	(7,620.65)	12.4%
8200 · Occupancy expenses	3,650.00	5,299.99	(1,649.99)	68.9%
8300 · Travel & meetings expenses	3,000.00	2,616.67	383.33	114.6%
8400 · Depreciation & amortization e...	350.00	791.65	(441.65)	44.2%
8500 · Misc expenses	305.00	508.33	(203.33)	60%
8600 · Business expenses	0.00	0.00	0.00	0.0%
Total Expense	31,611.00	49,998.97	(18,387.97)	63.2%
Net Ordinary Income	25,727.02	13,917.69	11,809.33	184.9%
Other Income/Expense				
Other Income				
6800 · Unrealized gain (loss)	0.00	0.00	0.00	0.0%
Total Other Income	0.00	0.00	0.00	0.0%
Other Expense				
9800 · Fixed asset purchases	0.00	6,666.67	(6,666.67)	0.0%
9920 · Additions to reserves	0.00	27,500.00	(27,500.00)	0.0%
9930 · Program admin allocations	0.00	1,082.58	(1,082.58)	0.0%
Total Other Expense	0.00	35,249.25	(35,249.25)	0.0%
Net Other Income	0.00	(35,249.25)	35,249.25	0.0%
Net Income	25,727.02	(21,331.56)	47,058.58	(120.6%)

This would also be a good time to look at the forecast you prepared in Chapter 13 to give the governing board an understanding of the remainder of the rest of the year. If you track pledges and donations as receivables, an **accounts receivable report** will show the treasurer which members still have outstanding balances.

We Care Community Foundation
A/R Aging Summary
As of December 15, 2018

	Current	1 - 30	31 - 60	61 - 90	> 90	TOTAL
Bayshore City Schools	855.00	0.00	0.00	0.00	0.00	855.00
Easley, Paula						
Mexico Trip	250.00	0.00	0.00	0.00	0.00	250.00
Total Easley, Paula	250.00	0.00	0.00	0.00	0.00	250.00
HHS						
Research Next Year	250,000.00	0.00	0.00	0.00	0.00	250,000.00
StudentEd Next Year	200,000.00	0.00	0.00	0.00	0.00	200,000.00
Total HHS	450,000.00	0.00	0.00	0.00	0.00	450,000.00

This assortment of reports should give your director and treasurer a complete understanding of the financial situation of the organization.

Talk to your executive director, treasurer, and governing board to determine the information they would like to see. Some prefer details into the programs, others want to keep it top-level and have the bookkeeper available to answer questions.

The reports can then be designed around the organization's requirements and any other reporting requirements (i.e. the IRS).

E. **Summary**

Closing out the month can be nerve-racking, but you now have the tools to know what to look for and how to make sure everything has been recorded. You have learned:

- What is required each month when closing the books,
- How to prepare a bank reconciliation,
- How to reconcile your investment accounts, and
- How to determine what reports are needed.

Next, we'll be reviewing how to handle year-end requirements.

In the appendix, I've included the Month-End Checklist I designed for QuickBooks users.

Feel free to use it as a guide and adjust for your nonprofit.

15. Year-End

At the end of the calendar year, there are a few more things to do. In this chapter, we will cover how to:

- Complete and file year-end payroll forms to employees and the government,
- Complete and file forms for independent contractors,
- Send year-end donor acknowledgments,
- Review possible state-required filings,
- Determine if UBIT (unrelated business income tax) is applicable,
- File Forms 990-N, 990-EZ, or 990 if required, and
- Assess potential audit needs.

A. Forms W-2 (Wages) and W-3 (Taxes)

In Chapter 12 on payroll, we discussed the W-2s that must be sent to employees as well as the W-3 used to send a copy of the W-2s to the Social Security Administration. For non-employees, you will need to send 1099s. Details on completing the forms are in Chapter 12.

B. Form 944 (Employer's Annual Federal Tax Return)

This is an annual return for employers with very little payroll and is used in lieu of the quarterly 941s. It can ONLY be used if the IRS has notified you in writing. See Chapter 12 on payroll for the requirements.

It is a two-page form and is similar to Form 941. Input the wages paid for the year and the related taxes. If the total taxes are greater than $2500, you will need to show the monthly amounts.

Be sure to sign, title, and date before mailing. If you have not deposited the taxes, use the voucher at the end of the form.

Form **944 for 2019: Employer's ANNUAL Federal Tax Return**

Department of the Treasury — Internal Revenue Service

OMB No. 1545-2007

Employer identification number (EIN)

Name (not your trade name)

Trade name (if any)

Address: Number / Street / Suite or room number; City / State / ZIP code; Foreign country name / Foreign province/county / Foreign postal code

Who Must File Form 944

You must file annual Form 944 instead of filing quarterly Forms 941 only if the IRS notified you in writing.

Go to www.irs.gov/Form944 for instructions and the latest information.

Read the separate instructions before you complete Form 944. Type or print within the boxes.

Part 1: Answer these questions for this year. Employers in American Samoa, Guam, the Commonwealth of the Northern Mariana Islands, the U.S. Virgin Islands, and Puerto Rico can skip lines 1 and 2, unless you have employees who are subject to U.S. income tax withholding.

1 Wages, tips, and other compensation . . . 1

2 Federal income tax withheld from wages, tips, and other compensation . . . 2

3 If no wages, tips, and other compensation are subject to social security or Medicare tax 3 ☐ Check and go to line 5.

4 Taxable social security and Medicare wages and tips:

	Column 1		Column 2
4a Taxable social security wages	.	× 0.124 =	.
4b Taxable social security tips	.	× 0.124 =	.
4c Taxable Medicare wages & tips	.	× 0.029 =	.
4d Taxable wages & tips subject to Additional Medicare Tax withholding	.	× 0.009 =	.

4e Add Column 2 from lines 4a, 4b, 4c, and 4d . . . 4e

5 Total taxes before adjustments. Add lines 2 and 4e . . . 5

6 Current year's adjustments (see instructions) . . . 6

7 Total taxes after adjustments. Combine lines 5 and 6 . . . 7

8 Qualified small business payroll tax credit for increasing research activities. Attach Form 8974 8

9 Total taxes after adjustments and credits. Subtract line 8 from line 7 . . . 9

10 Total deposits for this year, including overpayment applied from a prior year and overpayments applied from Form 944-X, 944-X (SP), 941-X, or 941-X (PR) . . . 10

11 Balance due. If line 9 is more than line 10, enter the difference and see instructions . . . 11

12 Overpayment. If line 10 is more than line 9, enter the difference . Check one: ☐ Apply to next return. ☐ Send a refund.

▶ You MUST complete both pages of Form 944 and SIGN it. Next ➡

For Privacy Act and Paperwork Reduction Act Notice, see the back of the Payment Voucher. Cat. No. 39316N Form 944 (2019)

Name (not your trade name) | Employer identification number (EIN)

Part 2: Tell us about your deposit schedule and tax liability for this year.

13 Check one: ☐ Line 9 is less than $2,500. Go to Part 3.

☐ Line 9 is $2,500 or more. Enter your tax liability for each month. If you're a semiweekly depositor or you became one because you accumulated $100,000 or more of liability on any day during a deposit period, you must complete Form 945-A instead of the boxes below.

	Jan.		Apr.		July		Oct.
13a	.	13d	.	13g	.	13j	.
	Feb.		May		Aug.		Nov.
13b	.	13e	.	13h	.	13k	.
	Mar.		June		Sept.		Dec.
13c	.	13f	.	13i	.	13l	.

Total liability for year. Add lines 13a through 13l. Total must equal line 9. 13m

Part 3: Tell us about your business. If question 14 does NOT apply to your business, leave it blank.

14 If your business has closed or you stopped paying wages...

☐ Check here and enter the final date you paid wages.

Part 4: May we speak with your third-party designee?

Do you want to allow an employee, a paid tax preparer, or another person to discuss this return with the IRS? See the instructions for details.

☐ Yes. Designee's name and phone number

Select a 5-digit Personal Identification Number (PIN) to use when talking to the IRS.

☐ No.

Part 5: Sign here. You MUST complete both pages of Form 944 and SIGN it.

Under penalties of perjury, I declare that I have examined this return, including accompanying schedules and statements, and to the best of my knowledge and belief, it is true, correct, and complete. Declaration of preparer (other than taxpayer) is based on all information of which preparer has any knowledge.

✗ Sign your name here | Print your name here | Print your title here

Date | Best daytime phone

Paid Preparer Use Only Check if you're self-employed ☐

Preparer's name | PTIN

Preparer's signature | Date

Firm's name (or yours if self-employed) | EIN

Address | Phone

City | State | ZIP code

Page 2 Form 944 (2019)

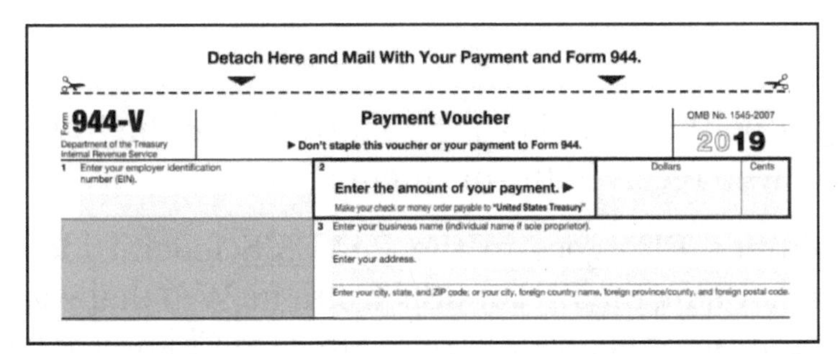

Detach Here and Mail With Your Payment and Form 944.

Form **944-V** Department of the Treasury Internal Revenue Service

Payment Voucher

▶ Don't staple this voucher or your payment to Form 944.

OMB No. 1545-2007

2019

1 Enter your employer identification number (EIN).

2 **Enter the amount of your payment.** ▶ Make your check or money order payable to "United States Treasury" | Dollars | Cents

3 Enter your business name (individual name if sole proprietor).

Enter your address.

Enter your city, state, and ZIP code; or your city, foreign country name, foreign province/county, and foreign postal code.

Find Form 944 at www.irs.gov/pub/irs-pdf/f944.pdf.

C. Form 1099 (Miscellaneous Income)

In Chapter 11, we discussed the difference between employees and independent contractors. Non-employees may include your bookkeeper, plumber, or yard service. The IRS requires the nonprofit (and any other organization) to send independent contractors a Form 1099 after the end of the calendar year.

If the person works for a corporation (i.e., the business name ends in "Inc."), you are not required to send a Form 1099. A possible exception to this is that all attorneys paid over $600 annually must receive a Form 1099.

Any person (not a corporation) to whom the organization paid over $600 (amount changes—check the IRS website), cumulatively, will need a 1099. Keep in mind this is cumulative, so be sure to total ALL payments through the year to them.

9595 ☐ VOID ☐ CORRECTED

PAYER'S name, street address, city or town, state or province, country, ZIP or foreign postal code, and telephone no.		1 Rents	OMB No. 1545-0115	Miscellaneous Income
Slippers for Kids Foundation 23 Anywhere St., Any City, State, Country 12345 Phone # 123-456-789		$ 2 Royalties $	2020 Form 1099-MISC	
		3 Other income $ (amount paid)	4 Federal income tax withheld $	Copy A For Internal Revenue Service Center
PAYER'S TIN (Nonprofit's EIN)	RECIPIENT'S TIN (Contractor's SSN or EIN)	5 Fishing boat proceeds $	6 Medical and health care payments $	File with Form 1096.
RECIPIENT'S name (Your Contractor)		7 Payer made direct sales of $5,000 or more of consumer products to a buyer (recipient) for resale ☐	8 Substitute payments in lieu of dividends or interest $	For Privacy Act and Paperwork Reduction Act Notice, see the 2020 General Instructions for Certain Information Returns.
Street address (including apt. no.)		9 Crop insurance proceeds $	10 Gross proceeds paid to an attorney $	
City or town, state or province, country, and ZIP or foreign postal code		11	12 Section 409A deferrals $	
Account number (see instructions)	FATCA filing requirement ☐ · 2nd TIN not. ☐	13 Excess golden parachute payments $	14 Nonqualified deferred compensation $	
		15 State tax withheld $ $	16 State/Payer's state no.	17 State income $ $

Form 1099-MISC Cat. No. 14425J www.irs.gov/Form1099MISC Department of the Treasury - Internal Revenue Service

Do Not Cut or Separate Forms on This Page — Do Not Cut or Separate Forms on This Page

The PAYER on this form is your nonprofit, and the RECIPIENT is the person who received the payments.

The nonprofit's EIN goes in the PAYER'S federal identification number box. Using the EIN or SSN from the W-9 that was received from the contractor before you paid him (see Chapter 11), fill in the RECIPIENT'S identification number, name, and address.

Use “Box 3 Other Income” to record the amount paid unless another box is more appropriate (e.g., royalties or attorney’s fees).

Like the W-2, there is a red Copy A to send to the government and several black copies. Copy B is for the recipient to use to fill out his tax return, and Copy C is for the organization to retain and file. If required, Copies 1 and 2 are for the state and local tax department and to be filed with the recipient's state and local tax returns, respectively. The 1099s must be mailed to the recipients by January 31st of the following year.

D. Form 1096 (Transmittal of U.S. Information Returns)

After mailing the black copies of the 1099s to the recipients, the red Copy As are sent to the Internal Revenue Service along with a transmittal Form 1096. The transmittal form summarizes the total number of 1099s and the total dollars reported.

Do Not Staple 6969

Form **1096**

Department of the Treasury
Internal Revenue Service

Annual Summary and Transmittal of U.S. Information Returns

OMB No. 1545-0108

2020

FILER'S name

Street address (including room or suite number)

City or town, state or province, country, and ZIP or foreign postal code

For Official Use Only

Name of person to contact	Telephone number
Email address	Fax number

1 Employer identification number	2 Social security number	3 Total number of forms	4 Federal income tax withheld	5 Total amount reported with this Form 1096
			$	$

6 Enter an "X" in only o[illegible] box below to indicate the type of form being filed.

W-2G 32	1097-BTC 50	[illegible]	1098-C 78	1098-E 84	1098-F 03	1098-Q 74	1098-T 83	1099-A 80	1099-B 79	1099-C 85	1099-CAP 73	1099-DIV 91	1099-G 86	1099-INT 92	1099-K 10	1099-LS 16
☐	☐	☐	☐	☐	☐	☐	☐	☐	☐	☐	☐	☐	☐	☐	☐	☐
1099-LTC 93	1099-MISC 95	1099-NEC 71	1099-OID 96	1099-PATR 97	1099-Q 31	1099-QA 1A	1099-R 98	1099-S 75	1099-SA 94	1099-SB 43	3921 25	3922 26	5498 28	5498-ESA 72	5498-QA 2A	5498-SA 27
☐	☐	☐	☐	☐	☐	☐	☐	☐	☐	☐	☐	☐	☐	☐	☐	☐

Return this entire page to the Internal Revenue Service. Photocopies are not acceptable.

Under penalties of perjury, I declare that I have examined this return and accompanying documents and, to the best of my knowledge and belief, they are true, correct, and complete.

Signature ▶ **Title ▶** **Date ▶**

This form is used to transmit other types of forms, so select the box labeled 1099-Misc 95 near the bottom. Fill in the organization's name and address, the contact person (this may be the bookkeeper), the telephone number, and the email. If the group does not have an Employer Identification Number, the director or primary person's SSN is used. Box 3 asks for the total number of forms. Box 4 is usually 0, as the charity probably did not withhold taxes on any payments. To compute the amount for box 5, add all the amounts listed in Box 3 on the individual 1099s.

The form must be signed by an appropriate representative of the nonprofit with that person's title and the date. The title bookkeeper is not considered an appropriate representative. The executive director, the treasurer, and the chairman of the board are all considered representatives of the organization.

The form will also tell you where the transmittal and all of the Copy As of the 1099s are to be sent. Make a complete copy for your records and file in a locked, secure location as these documents have sensitive information like SSNs.

> *All payroll and employee information, as well as W-9s, should be kept in a locked, secure location. It is not uncommon for employees, cleaning crews, or other workers to access the information for use in identity theft.*

E. **Year-End Donor Acknowledgements**

In Chapter 6, we discussed the value and requirements of the donor acknowledgment. A nonprofit organization is not penalized by the government for not acknowledging received gifts, except in the case of vehicles. Still, as the donor needs the acknowledgment for tax purposes, it should be considered a required mailing. Most charitable organizations send the acknowledgments out by January 31st.

Remember, the basic donor acknowledgment must include:

- Name of the organization,
- Amount of cash contribution,
- Description (but not value) of non-cash contribution,
- A statement that no goods or services were provided in return for the contribution (unless there was), and
- The description and good faith estimate of the value of goods or services, if any, that the organization provided in return for the contribution.

As these acknowledgements are going to your donors, it would behoove you to include thanks and an explanation of the good their gifts have done.

F. State Filings

Each state has its own rules and filing requirements. You will need to research the payroll, income tax, sales tax, and license requirements in your state. If you are a registered 501(c)3, your state may require an annual filing. Check with the office of your Secretary of State. On my website, www.accountantbesideyou.com, I have a page with links to each state's website for your convenience.

G. Other IRS Requirements

If you have received your 501(c)3 status, you will need to file a Form 990-N, 990-EZ, or the full 990 with the IRS annually. Which one is filed is determined by the size of your organization. In the next chapter, I'll explain these and show how to fill out the 990-EZ. If you are large enough to file the full 990, I highly recommend hiring a CPA with nonprofit experience to help.

Another year-end filing requirement is the 990-T for **unrelated business expense tax (UBIT)**. You may have to file this if you have income from non-exempt sources like sales of products or rental of parking spaces. I'll explain this in detail in Chapter 16.

H. Audit Needs

EVERY organization should have an audit each year. Having a CPA firm perform the audit is preferred but may be cost-prohibitive. Many nonprofits use an audit committee instead. The audit committee should consist of people who have some accounting knowledge but are not involved in the day-to-day accounting of the charity. If your group is associated with a larger organization, there are probably audit committee guidelines.

In preparation for the audit, the bookkeeper, treasurer, or executive director should do the following:

- For each **cash account**, look at the bank reconciliation and tie it to the balance on the balance sheet. While you have them out, take the time to look for checks that haven't cleared in months. Do you need to make some calls and reissue the checks? Don't forget to reconcile your petty cash and gift cards!
- **Investment account statements** should be compared to the balance sheet. If the ending balance does not match, you probably need to record interest earned and any investment income or loss.
- Print an **aging schedule** for each of your receivable accounts. An aging schedule is a list of money *due* to the organization by a certain date. Any old receivables should be reviewed to see if follow up is needed or if they should be written off. Also, think about any recent grants awarded for which you have not received the money. Are they reflected as a receivable as required by accounting principles? (Only required if using the accrual basis of accounting).
- Do you carry any **inventory**? Books or T-shirts? Now is the time to do a physical inventory and verify that the number of items you have ties to the value on your balance sheet.
- **Prepaid expenses** often need to be investigated. Tie the balance of prepaid postage to the postage meter. Did part of the insurance bill get coded to prepaid last year? Is it time to record the expense? Look at anything in the prepaid accounts and determine if they should stay on the balance sheet or be moved to the statement of activities (income statement).

- Do you have a list of **assets,** such as furniture and equipment? Does it match the value on your balance sheet? Even if your accountant records depreciation for you, it is a good idea to walk around and see if the assets are still there. Notate any that have been lost or sold. Add any new assets that are not on the list if they are substantial. If the total dollars on your list do not equal your balance sheet account, some items may have been recorded to the expenses.

- Print out the **accounts payable aging report**. The accounts payable aging report shows which bills are *owed* and how old they are. Are bills incurred in the last fiscal year missing? If so, you may need to record those charges. Are your credit cards current? If you have charges since the last statement, you may need to accrue these in an accrued liability account. An **accrued liability** is an expense you have incurred but not yet received the bill for.

- **Payroll tax liabilities** should tie to your payroll reports. Any other accrued liabilities should be documented.

After making any adjustments, reprint your balance sheet and place all the documentation you have compiled behind it. To keep it organized, order the papers to follow the listing on the balance sheet.

In planning for your audit, I'd recommend you gather, print, or have in an electronic file the following information as of the last day of the period being audited:

- Board Minutes
- Contracts, including employment, rent, insurance, etc.
- Payroll reports from the outside service or detail files
- Copies of the year-end donor acknowledgments
- Copies of Form 1099s and Form 1096
- Copies of W-2s and the W-3
- Copies of any 990s and related schedules

Additionally, you will need to review your internal accounting controls and policies with the auditors. Reread the first chapter of this book and document your procedures. Once you have all this data gathered, the audit should go very smoothly.

I. Summary

In this chapter, you learned what to do at the end of the year, including:

- Send employees W-2s,
- Send vendors 1099s,
- Prepare a transmittal W-3 and send it with Copy A of the W-2s to the government,
- Prepare a transmittal 1096 and send it with a copy of the 1099s to the government,
- Prepare and file quarterly or annual tax deposits,
- Send donor acknowledgments, and
- And what to pull together for your audit committee.

Wow! You now know how to record your transactions, produce financial reports, and survive an audit. In the next chapter, you will learn how to recognize unrelated business income and how to file the appropriate return.

16. Unrelated Business Income Taxes (UBIT)

In my opinion, the most confusing IRS regulation for nonprofits is the concept of unrelated business income. You have applied for your 501(c)3 status, so you should be exempt from taxes, right? Not necessarily!

When you applied for your exemption, you told the IRS what charitable or educational purpose your organization had. The IRS then granted you tax relief for activities related to that mission. Your 501(c)3 status does not allow you to add in for-profit businesses without paying taxes on the business income.

I'll try not to get too technical here. There are many specific rules, so if your situation isn't as clear cut as the ones I'll be sharing, it is worth the time and money to consult with a nonprofit accountant to be sure you comply with the UBIT regulations.

A. What is Unrelated Business Income?

A nonprofit isn't taxed on the income coming from actions *substantially* related to its designated purpose. Donations, membership dues, etc. are usually exempt from tax as they allow you to fulfill your charitable or educational mission.

Exceptions to this, such as selling advertising space in your monthly newsletter, can be taxed. Why? Although this revenue is useful to your mission, it does not fulfill your education mission or the charitable requirement of your organization. It is therefore required to be taxed at the current corporate rate.

If you do not bring in more than $1000 (as of 2020; check IRS.gov for current levels) on unrelated business income, you do not have to file. The $1000 threshold is <u>GROSS</u> income, <u>not</u> net income (i.e., what is left after expenses).

To determine if something is unrelated business income (UBI) for the IRS, you must see if all three of the following requirements are met:

1. "It is a trade or business,
2. It is regularly carried on, **and**
3. It is not substantially related" to the stated purpose of the organization. *(IRS Publication 598)*

I'll step you through these one at a time, but remember, you must meet all three requirements before your income is taxable.

B. "Trade or Business"

The IRS defines a trade or business as "any activity conducted for the production of income from selling goods or performing services. An activity must be *conducted with the intent to make a profit* ..." (ref: Tax on Unrelated Business Income, IRS Publication 598, italicized for emphasis).

There are two essential pieces to this. First is the **production of income**, and the second is the **intent to make a profit**. When considering if some of your income would be considered a trade or business, ask yourself the following:

- Are we competing with other businesses?
- Do we sell books or greeting cards or candy?
- Do we rent out our facility for a fee?
- Do we sell advertising?
- Do we rent the parking lot out to other businesses?
- Do we consult with individuals or businesses?

If you answered yes to any of these, you have a trade or business. Now, let's look at the second part of the equation:

Is our intent to make a profit to help fund the mission?

Do you use the money to buy more supplies for your organization? Or perhaps to send more kids to camp? Just because it is going into your nonprofit, it does not mean you do not intend to make a profit.

Perhaps you run a dog rescue organization. At the front entrance, you sell dog food and toys for the new "parents" to purchase on their way home. The money you make from selling these products goes to purchasing dog food for the pets in the kennels.

In the above situation, you would be considered a business because you compete with other businesses (namely dog food and toy sellers), and you intend to make a profit.

An organization whose mission is to raise awareness and develop tools to combat childhood obesity sells coloring books encouraging healthy eating habits. The books are sold at a steep discount to get them in as many children's hands as possible.

In the above example, the organization selling goods acts like a business, but there is no intention of making a profit. Donors or other sources of income must cover the remaining costs of buying and selling coloring books. Therefore you should not be required to pay taxes on this income.

C. "Regularly Conducted"

If you have determined your organization has a trade or business, the next step is to see if these activities are regularly conducted. Per the IRS, a business or trade is considered "regularly conducted" if it "shows a *frequency and continuity*, and are pursued in a manner similar to comparable commercial activities of nonexempt organizations" (from the IRS website; italics added for emphasis).

The frequency may be daily, weekly, or even annually, and not a one-time event.

Your organization in downtown Nashville owns its building and has a large parking lot. You rent the parking lot out to a company that charges people to park there on the weekends.

In the example above, it meets the first consideration of business as you are renting the lot out for profit, and it meets the second because it has a frequency and continuity of every weekend. The money is also raised the same way a for-profit business may raise money.

Your organization is downtown in a mid-sized city and has a large parking lot. A big name entertainer is coming to the convention center down the street, and you have been offered money by the promoter to allow them to use your lot as a staging area.

Though the income has nothing to do with your charitable mission, the money raised is not considered "regularly conducted" because it is a one-time event. Therefore, you should not be required to pay taxes on this income.

D. "Not Substantially Related" To The Mission

The third requirement for the money to be UBI is for the business activity not to be substantially related to the organization's overall mission or purpose. Per the IRS, *"if it doesn't contribute importantly to accomplishing that purpose (other than through the production of funds)."*(ref: Substantially Related https://www.irs.gov/charities-non-profits/substantially-related)

As you can tell, this is the most subjective of the three requirements. Income that is not substantially related to one organization may be very related to another, so this has to be determined on a case-by-case basis.

You need to examine the size and extent of the activity relative to the charitable or educational nature. There are situations where some of the income activity will be taxed as UBI, and some will stay exempt.

The IRS recommends considering the following principles to determine if a trade/business is substantially related:

1. **Selling Products Of Exempt Functions**

For nonprofits that make and sell products, whether or not the product is considered exempt from UBI is determined by the *state of the product*. To be considered exempt from taxes, the product must be in the same state as it was when the function related to the organization's mission was complete.

A farm designed to teach prospective dairy farmers how to manage a herd of dairy cattle trains students how to milk cows. The farm then sells the milk and cream procured from these trainings.

The money from milk and cream sales from the example is exempt from UBI because the product is sold in substantially the same state as it was when the related function (training the students) was completed.

The same farm, in addition to selling the milk and cream, makes and sells ice cream, changing the state of the end product.

In this instance, the money from ice cream sales is not exempt from UBI since the end product of the exempt function was changed from raw milk to ice cream. This business activity is not substantially related to the mission of the organization since the mission of the farm was to train students to become dairy farmers, not ice cream manufactures. If the mission of the organization had been to encourage farmers to extend their operations for additional revenue sources, the ice cream might have been a substantially related function. You can see that what may be exempt for some nonprofits may not be for others.

2. Dual-Use of Facilities

The IRS asserts that if an asset or facility used by the charity is also used in a commercial activity, you must determine whether the activities contribute to the accomplishment of the exempt purpose.

If your organization's mission is to support family farms and a charitable foundation contracts you to work with farmers who are failing, this is not considered a trade or business as it is substantially related to your original mission.

E. Excluded Trade/Business Activities

The IRS explicitly excludes several business activities from being considered UBI. Some are so specific that I recommend you talk to a local CPA if you think it may affect your organization. I'll briefly go through each of them:

1. Bingo Games

Bingo games are excluded IF they meet the legal definition of bingo, as defined in IRS Code section 513(f)(2).

2. Gambling Other Than Bingo In North Dakota

The specific exclusion for gambling is only for organizations in North Dakota.

3. Convenience Of Members

If your organization runs a business for the convenience of the members, the income is excluded. For example, if a nonprofit camp has a laundry facility for the campers and staff to use, this is an excluded business.

4. Convention Or Trade Show Activity

If you have an annual meeting, convention, or trade show that your organization regularly conducts as part of its mission, the income is not UBI. An example of this would be a trade association that holds an annual meeting. They may offer booth space for vendors to rent to display or sell products that the members may find useful. Even though it is a regularly occurring event, this is an excluded business.

5. Distribution Of Low-Cost Articles

Many charities distribute low-cost items in attempts to increase contributions (e.g., calendars, return address labels, etc.). As long as these articles cost less than $11.10 (in 2019, indexed for inflation), they are considered low cost. $11.10 is the aggregate amount to a single recipient, so you can't send several $10 items out to the same person.

Additionally, the distribution has to be incidental, which means:

1. The person receiving it did not request it.
2. It was sent without the express consent of the recipient.
3. It was accompanied by a request for a contribution with a statement that the receiver can keep the item whether they donate or not.

6. Employee Association Sales

The employee association sales exclusion is specific to local associations organized before 1969.

7. Exchange Or Rental Of Member Lists

If your organization rents out its member list to other charities, this is an excluded business.

8. Hospital Services

There are specific services that may be provided at or below cost to other exempt hospitals with 100 or fewer inpatients without being considered a trade or business.

9. Pole Rentals

The pole rentals exclusion is another narrow ruling for cooperative telephone and electric companies.

10. Public Entertainment Activity

This exclusion is related to agricultural fairs or to promoting the breeding of animals or the development of related equipment.

11. Qualified Sponsorship Activities

A qualified sponsorship payment is made by a person engaged in the trade or business for which the person will receive no substantial benefit other than the use or acknowledgment of the business name, logo, or product lines in connection with the organization. You see this frequently, where a corporation will have its logo on a charity's website.

Be careful here. Advertising is <u>not</u> exempted from UBI. Advertising includes information regarding price, value, savings, or comparative language, endorsements, and any inducements to purchase or use the products.

In the example above, Lowes is a sponsor, and any money paid to Habitat for Humanity would be exempted. If there were a box or pop-up ad that said, "Get 20% off at Lowes using this link", it would be considered advertising income for Habitat.

Sponsorship of a magazine or other periodicals follows the same rules. A company can sponsor your monthly magazine with a logo without a tax effect on your organization. Still, if there is any encouragement to buy, it is considered a trade or business.

12. Selling Donated Merchandise

Think thrift stores here. If substantially all of the merchandise sold has been received as gifts, this is an excluded business.

13. Volunteer Workforce

Organizations may run a trade or business where substantially all of the labor is volunteered. If so, the income is exempted. Examples of this include a retail store associated with a nonprofit or church. If it is staffed by volunteers, this may be an excluded business.

If any of these exemptions pertain to you and aren't crystal clear, please contact a local CPA for guidance. Next, I'll go through some examples.

F. Examples

I asked my readers for examples of money raised from their organizations. We'll go through several them to determine if they may be subject to UBIT. Keep in mind all three of the following requirements must be met:

1. Trade or business,
2. Regularly conducted, and
3. Not substantially related to the organization's mission

Additionally, if the total of all UBI is less than $1000, or if the money is from excluded trade or business activities as detailed in the previous section, you do not need to file.

1. Selling Coffee

Julie H. asked if churches selling coffee after services would be taxable.

It is UBI if:

They are selling every week. It meets requirements 2 and 3 (regularly conducted and not substantially related to the mission). Additionally, it is not run by volunteers, but as a coffee shop with the intent to use the profits (even if said profits went to fund the church's mission).

If gross proceeds were over $1000 a year, a tax return would need to be filed.

It is not UBI if:

There is a donation jar at the end of the refreshment table. The income is not taxable as it does not meet requirement 1 (trade or business). The intent is to simply cover the cost of the coffee and not make a profit.

It is run primarily with volunteers as a coffee shop with the intent to use the profits to fund the church's mission and is not considered taxable income.

2. Other Organizations Using Your Facility

Doris W. asked, "If other organizations are using your facility and they help with upkeep and utilities by making donations, is that other income?"

This is probably not UBI, but this one gets a bit complicated. Rents from real property are generally excluded, but rent income is NOT excluded *if* the rent:

- Includes personal services such as administrative support, catering, etc.,
- Is based on the net profit of the renter, or
- The value of personal property rented out with the real property is more than 10%.
    - If the personal property rental is between 10-50%. An allocation will have to be used.
    - If more than 50%, all of the rent is considered UBI.

As long as the other organizations' rents do not include any of the above three items, it should not be considered UBI.

Please note that there are additional rules regarding whether or not there is debt (mortgage) related to the property. If your nonprofit has substantial rental income, please contact a local CPA to ensure you comply with local and national regulations.

3. Pass-Through Expenses

Lisa C. and Becky D. asked about "pass-through" expenses. Examples include purchasing a book from a retailer for a book study or purchasing flowers that were donated for an event. Other examples are having a "memorial fund" where people can make donations in memory of someone who's passed and have pass-through honorariums for people helping at a wedding or a funeral (pastor, AV tech, musician, or singer).

These are not UBI but would be treated as you would normal pass-through donations to your organization.

4. Logo Merchandise and Candy

Heather F. says her organization offers logo merchandise and has a student store where they purchase snacks and candy.

These would most likely be considered UBI as they meet all three of the conditions: it is a trade or business, it is regularly offered, and it is not substantially related to the organization's exempt purpose.

If the store also offers educational materials for purchase that assist in her mission, those materials would not be considered UBI and should be tracked separately.

If the students do the majority of the work at the store on a volunteer basis, the sales of the candy and merchandise would not be considered UBI.

5. Parking Lot Rent

Dawn C. was wondering about renting out the organization's parking lot.

If it is done regularly, say every weekend, this would be considered UBI as it meets all three conditions: it is a business, it is regularly offered, and it is not substantially related to the organization's purpose.

If a special event came into town and the organization rented out their lot for that one event, it would not be UBI as it wasn't regularly offered.

Another way organizations keep the income from becoming taxable is by having their members handle the parking lot. If substantially all of the work is being done by volunteers, it is exempt from UBI.

6. Gifts-In-Kind

Carolyn A. asked about gifts-in-kind. The sales of donated merchandise are not considered UBI. This rule is why thrift shops dedicated to charities can thrive. Sales of art, autos, or any other non-cash contributions should be treated as donations and acknowledged as we discussed in Chapter 6.

7. Daycare Income

Jennifer W. asked about daycare income. This one is tricky; the revenue may be UBI, or it may be exempt based on the individual situation.

Usually, a daycare will meet the requirements to be considered UBI as it is run regularly.

Next, we need to ask, "Is the daycare being run with an intent to make a profit?" If the intent is to help people with low-cost child care, and they just want to cover the necessary costs, it may not be considered UBI.

If the daycare does make money, the organization must focus on the third requirement: is it substantially related to the exempt purpose? If the nonprofit assists families trying to get off welfare, offering a childcare option would be substantially related to its purpose. If the organization's mission is to educate people on how to be daycare workers, the income would not be considered UBI.

Even if the daycare is not substantially related, the income may be excluded if it is for the convenience of its members (e.g., a church runs a daycare center to assist its congregation).

G. Miscellaneous Excluded Revenues

If your total gross unrelated business income is less than $1000, you don't need to file a UBIT return.

Gross income is the total revenue from the business minus the cost of goods sold, which I will explain in the next section. Dividends, interest annuities, and other investment income are excluded from being taxed as unrelated business income. Royalties are also usually excluded.

As I discussed earlier, money from rentals is usually excluded with three exceptions: the rental includes personal services, is based on profits the renter makes (like a % of sales), or if the value of personal property (not real estate-chairs, tent) rented out with the real property is more than 10%. There are other rules if you have income from debt-financed property.

Gains and losses from the disposition of property (sale of office equipment) are generally not considered UBI.

If you have any large or unusual revenues outside your usual donations, I strongly encourage you to consult with a local CPA to ensure you are filing the correct returns.

H. 990-T (Exempt Organization Business Income Tax Return)

Once you have determined that you have unrelated business income over $1000, you will have to file a **Form 990-T (Exempt Organization Business Income Tax Return)**. If your organization has a gross income of $10,000 or less, than you will only need to complete the first two pages. If over $10,000, you will need to complete all five pages.

> *This book is written for SMALL nonprofits, and I will not be covering the more complicated issues. If you have significant UBI or unusual situations, I highly recommend consulting a local CPA.*

In this section, I will briefly summarize the form so you can see what information you will need.

1. Blocks A-J

Form **990-T** — Department of the Treasury, Internal Revenue Service

Exempt Organization Business Income Tax Return
(and proxy tax under section 6033(e))

For calendar year 2019 or other tax year beginning ______, 2019, and ending ______, 20 ___.
► Go to www.irs.gov/Form990T for instructions and the latest information.
► Do not enter SSN numbers on this form as it may be made public if your organization is a 501(c)(3).

OMB No. 1545-0047 — **2019** — Open to Public Inspection for 501(c)(3) Organizations Only

A ☐ Check box if address changed
B Exempt under section ☐ 501( )( ) ☐ 408(e) ☐ 220(e) ☐ 408A ☐ 530(a) ☐ 529(a)
C Book value of all assets at end of year

Print or Type: Name of organization (☐ Check box if name changed and see instructions.)
Number, street, and room or suite no. If a P.O. box, see instructions.
City or town, state or province, country, and ZIP or foreign postal code

D Employer identification number (Employees' trust, see instructions.)
E Unrelated business activity code (See instructions.)

F Group exemption number (See instructions.) ►
G Check organization type ► ☐ 501(c) corporation ☐ 501(c) trust ☐ 401(a) trust ☐ Other trust

H Enter the number of the organization's unrelated trades or businesses. ► ______ Describe the only (or first) unrelated trade or business here ► ______. If only one, complete Parts I–V. If more than one, describe the first in the blank space at the end of the previous sentence, complete Parts I and II, complete a Schedule M for each additional trade or business, then complete Parts III–V.

I During the tax year, was the corporation a subsidiary in an affiliated group or a parent-subsidiary controlled group? . . ► ☐ Yes ☐ No
If "Yes," enter the name and identifying number of the parent corporation. ►

J The books are in care of ► ______ Telephone number ►

Part I Unrelated Trade or Business Income — (A) Income | (B) Expenses | (C) Net

These are mostly self-explanatory, but I'll highlight a few things.

Block C (book value of all assets at the end of year) is the total assets from your statement of financial position as of the end of your fiscal year.

Block E (unrelated business activity code) is to tell the government the type of business you are running. You can find your number at the Census Bureau website: www.census.gov/cgi-bin/sssd/naics/naicsrch?chart=2017. You will want to use the most specific 6-digit code that describes the business activity. For example, a coffee and snack service could be *722515 Snack and non-alcoholic beverage bars*.

Block F (group exemption number) is only used if you are covered by a group exemption.

Block G (organization type) will be "501 (c) corporation" unless you are filing for a trust.

Block H (the number of the organization's unrelated trades or businesses) is where you will share the number of different taxable businesses your organization has. The next blank is to describe the first (or only) business with just a few words, or you can attach a statement.

If you have more than one taxable businesses, you will need to fill out Parts I and II for the primary business. For the remaining businesses, there is a separate for 990-T Schedule M that mirrors Parts I and II of the 990-T. Fill one of these forms out for each of the additional businesses.

Block I (subsidiary) is checked if you are part of an affiliated group but aren't filing a consolidated return. If this is the case, you will need to have your parent organization's EIN.

2. Part I (Unrelated Trade or Business Income)

All amounts should be entered as whole numbers.

J The books are in care of ▶ Telephone number ▶

	Part I Unrelated Trade or Business Income		(A) Income	(B) Expenses	(C) Net
1a	Gross receipts or sales				
b	Less returns and allowances c Balance ▶	1c			
2	Cost of goods sold (Schedule A, line 7)	2			
3	Gross profit. Subtract line 2 from line 1c	3			
4a	Capital gain net income (attach Schedule D)	4a			
b	Net gain (loss) (Form 4797, Part II, line 17) (attach Form 4797)	4b			
c	Capital loss deduction for trusts	4c			
5	Income (loss) from a partnership or an S corporation (attach statement)	5			
6	Rent income (Schedule C)	6			
7	Unrelated debt-financed income (Schedule E)	7			
8	Interest, annuities, royalties, and rents from a controlled organization (Schedule F)	8			
9	Investment income of a section 501(c)(7), (9), or (17) organization (Schedule G)	9			
10	Exploited exempt activity income (Schedule I)	10			
11	Advertising income (Schedule J)	11			
12	Other income (See instructions; attach schedule)	12			
13	**Total.** Combine lines 3 through 12	13			

Part II Deductions Not Taken Elsewhere (See instructions for limitations on deductions.) (Deductions must be directly

Line 1a (gross receipts) is the total of all the receipts received for your first (or only) business.

Line 1b (returns and allowances) is for any product returns or write-offs.

Line 1c (balance) is line 1b (returns/write-offs) subtracted from 1a (gross receipts)

Line 2 (cost of goods sold or COGS) needs to be calculated if you sell products and have inventory. Even if you are not required to submit Schedule A (because you received less than $10,000 gross income), you should still fill it out to get the calculation correct. Enter your total from line 7 of Schedule A.

Form 990-T (2010) Page 3

Schedule A—Cost of Goods Sold. Enter method of inventory valuation ▶

1	Inventory at beginning of year	1		6	Inventory at end of year	6	
2	Purchases	2		7	**Cost of goods sold.** Subtract line 6 from line 5. Enter here and in Part I, line 2	7	
3	Cost of labor	3					
4a	Additional section 263A costs (attach schedule)	4a		8	Do the rules of section 263A (with respect to property produced or acquired for resale) apply to the organization?	Yes	No
b	Other costs (attach schedule)	4b					
5	Total. Add lines 1 through 4b	5					

Schedule A

*Let's say you have a bookstore. You would enter the dollar value of your inventory at the beginning of the year on **Line 1.***

***Line 2** is the total of all purchases of products throughout the year.*

***Line 3** is the total payroll and benefits associated with the sales of the books (cost of labor).*

***Line 4a** is related to production and inventory valuation rules, and all non-cash basis filers should review the related regulations. These rules can get very detailed and is beyond the scope of this book.*

***Line 4b** is for any additional costs of goods sold besides purchases and labor (e.g., an e-commerce website to sell logo material).*

***Line 5** adds lines 1-4b for a total.*

***Line 6** is the value of the remaining inventory at the end of the fiscal year.*

> ***Line 7*** *is your COGS. It is calculated by subtracting your ending inventory from your Line 5 Total.*
>
> ***Line 8*** *will be "No" if you are using the cash-basis method of accounting. If you are using the accrual basis and do not produce products, it will usually be "No." If you have a production facility and are on the accrual basis of accounting, please check with a local CPA.*

You may not have a cost of goods sold to compute. If you are renting a parking lot and no labor or other direct expenses are involved, you do not need to enter an amount in Line 2.

Line 3 (gross profit) is an essential line. If the total from all businesses' Line 3 does not exceed $1000, you do not need to file this form. It is calculated by taking 1c and subtracting Line 2.

Lines 4, 5, 7, 8, 9, and 10 relate to debt-related real estate and other unusual items that most small nonprofits will not have. Please note that most capital gains and investment income for a nonprofit are exempt. These lines are for particular issues. See the IRS 990-T instructions or your CPA for more details.

Line 6 reflects any non-exempt rental income less directly related expenses. You will need to complete Schedule C if your total UBI is over $10,000. Here is another area where I recommend consulting a CPA if you have debt associated with the property you are renting.

Line 11 is the money received for advertising in an exempt organization's periodical. If the gross UBI of the organization is over $10,000, you will need to fill out Schedule J.

Schedule J below looks at the periodicals for which you receive income and subtracts the direct advertising costs. If you have a gain, you then need to show circulation income and the related readership costs. If the readership costs are more than the circulation income, you may reduce the advertising gain, but it cannot go below $0.

Schedule J—Advertising Income (see instructions)

Part I Income From Periodicals Reported on a Consolidated Basis

	1. Name of periodical	2. Gross advertising income	3. Direct advertising costs	4. Advertising gain or (loss) (col. 2 minus col. 3). If a gain, compute cols. 5 through 7.	5. Circulation income	6. Readership costs	7. Excess readership costs (column 6 minus column 5, but not more than column 4).
(1)							
(2)							
(3)							
(4)							
Totals (carry to Part II, line (5)) ▶							

Form 990-T (2019)

There is an additional section to Schedule J that may need to be completed if your organization has more than one periodical. I recommend consulting with a CPA if these are significant dollars.

Line 12 (other income) covers any unrelated business income that isn't reported elsewhere in the report. It also includes recoveries of bad debts deducted in previous years.

Line 13 adds lines 3 through 12 for your total gross income.

3. Part II (Deduction Not Taken Elsewhere)

13	Total. Combine lines 3 through 12	13			
Part II	**Deductions Not Taken Elsewhere** (See instructions for limitations on deductions.) (Deductions must be directly connected with the unrelated business income.)				
14	Compensation of officers, directors, and trustees (Schedule K)			14	
15	Salaries and wages			15	
16	Repairs and maintenance			16	
17	Bad debts			17	
18	Interest (attach schedule) (see instructions)			18	
19	Taxes and licenses			19	
20	Depreciation (attach Form 4562)	20			
21	Less depreciation claimed on Schedule A and elsewhere on return	21a		21b	
22	Depletion			22	
23	Contributions to deferred compensation plans			23	
24	Employee benefit programs			24	
25	Excess exempt expenses (Schedule I)			25	
26	Excess readership costs (Schedule J)			26	
27	Other deductions (attach schedule)			27	
28	**Total deductions.** Add lines 14 through 27			28	
29	Unrelated business taxable income before net operating loss deduction. Subtract line 28 from line 13			29	
30	Deduction for net operating loss arising in tax years beginning on or after January 1, 2018 (see instructions)			30	
31	Unrelated business taxable income. Subtract line 30 from line 29			31	

If the total on Line 13 is $10,000 or less, you don't have to complete lines 14-27 and the schedules. However, you do still have to complete lines 28-31 and Part III. These deductions in Part II must be DIRECTLY related to the unrelated business income.

Line 14 (compensation of officers, etc.) must be directly related to the UBI and cannot include any compensation already included on a schedule. For example, if you have included officer compensation on Schedule J, you would not include that officer's salary component on this line.

Line 15 includes salaries and wages of the employees who work on the business or trade. If they split their time between it and donor work, timesheets should be kept documenting this expense.

If there are expenses in **Lines 16-24** that are shared with the not-for-profit side of the organization, document your assumptions. For example, if a bookstore in a museum takes 10% of the building space, you may be able to allocate 10% of the building repairs and maintenance.

Lines 25-26 relate to Schedules I and J, which were discussed previously.

Line 27 is for other deductions that must be detailed on a separate schedule. This may include travel expenses. Meals are only 50% deductible. What is and is not deductible is the same for for-profit and not-for-profit corporations.

Line 29 will be your unrelated business taxable income before net operating losses (NOL).

Line 30 is the deductible amount for the year if you have a loss carryforward. See your CPA for the allowable amount.

4. Part III (Total Unrelated Business Taxable Income)

Form 990-T (2019) Page 2

Part III Total Unrelated Business Taxable Income

32	Total of unrelated business taxable income computed from all unrelated trades or businesses (see instructions)	32	
33	Amounts paid for disallowed fringes	33	
34	Charitable contributions (see instructions for limitation rules)	34	
35	Total unrelated business taxable income before pre-2018 NOLs and specific deduction. Subtract line 34 from the sum of lines 32 and 33	35	
36	Deduction for net operating loss arising in tax years beginning before January 1, 2018 (see instructions)	36	
37	Total of unrelated business taxable income before specific deduction. Subtract line 36 from line 35	37	
38	Specific deduction (Generally $1,000, but see line 38 instructions for exceptions)	38	
39	**Unrelated business taxable income.** Subtract line 38 from line 37. If line 38 is greater than line 37, enter the smaller of zero or line 37	39	

Part IV Tax Computation

This section tweaks the UBI calculated on the previous page to come to the taxable income.

For **Line 32**, if you have only one business, you will input the amount from line 31 here. If you have more than one, this will be the sum of line 31 from each of them. If one of them shows a negative number on line 31, do not include them in the sum reported.

Line 33 has been repealed. Leave it blank.

Line 34 is used if your organization has made a charitable contribution to another organization. Do not put pass-through donations here. The total amount claimed can not be more than 10% of the UBI figured without deductions for contributions. The remaining amount (if any) may be carried forward for five years. Still, there are some other specific rules for carryovers, and there is a temporary suspension of the limit for specific disaster relief contributions. See your CPA for how this might affect your filings.

Line 38 (specific deduction) is like the standard deduction on the personal tax return. It is $1000, no matter how many different businesses are reflected in the return. There is an exception for religious organizations associations or dioceses if they have several congregations that aren't separate legal entities. The individual parishes can deduct up to $1000 each (cannot be more than their unrelated business income).

Line 39 becomes the Unrelated Business Taxable Income that is used to calculate the tax.

5. Part IV (Tax Computation)

	enter the smaller of zero or line 37	39	
Part IV	**Tax Computation**		
40	**Organizations Taxable as Corporations.** Multiply line 39 by 21% (0.21) . . . ▶	40	
41	**Trusts Taxable at Trust Rates.** See instructions for tax computation. Income tax on the amount on line 39 from: ☐ Tax rate schedule or ☐ Schedule D (Form 1041) . . . ▶	41	
42	**Proxy tax.** See instructions . . . ▶	42	
43	Alternative minimum tax (trusts only) . . .	43	
44	**Tax on Noncompliant Facility Income.** See instructions . . .	44	
45	**Total.** Add lines 42, 43, and 44 to line 40 or 41, whichever applies . . .	45	
Part V	Tax and Payments		

This section is to calculate the tax on the UBI. Most small nonprofits that are not trusts or hospitals can ignore **Lines 41-44**.

For **Line 40**, calculate the tax due by multiplying Line 39 by 21% (for the year 2019-check your form for the current amount). If you have nothing on lines 41-44, this is your tax due.

6. Part V (Tax and Payments)

This section calculates where you have tax due or if you overpaid.

44	Tax on Noncompliant Facility Income. See instructions		44
45	**Total.** Add lines 42, 43, and 44 to line 40 or 41, whichever applies		45
Part V	**Tax and Payments**		
46a	Foreign tax credit (corporations attach Form 1118; trusts attach Form 1116)	46a	
b	Other credits (see instructions)	46b	
c	General business credit. Attach Form 3800 (see instructions)	46c	
d	Credit for prior year minimum tax (attach Form 8801 or 8827)	46d	
e	**Total credits.** Add lines 46a through 46d		46e
47	Subtract line 46e from line 45		47
48	Other taxes. Check if from: ☐ Form 4255 ☐ Form 8611 ☐ Form 8697 ☐ Form 8866 ☐ Other (attach schedule)		48
49	**Total tax.** Add lines 47 and 48 (see instructions)		49
50	2019 net 965 tax liability paid from Form 965-A or Form 965-B, Part II, column (k), line 3		50
51a	Payments: A 2018 overpayment credited to 2019	51a	
b	2019 estimated tax payments	51b	
c	Tax deposited with Form 8868	51c	
d	Foreign organizations: Tax paid or withheld at source (see instructions)	51d	
e	Backup withholding (see instructions)	51e	
f	Credit for small employer health insurance premiums (attach Form 8941)	51f	
g	Other credits, adjustments, and payments: ☐ Form 2439 ☐ Form 4136 ☐ Other Total ▶	51g	
52	**Total payments.** Add lines 51a through 51g		52
53	Estimated tax penalty (see instructions). Check if Form 2220 is attached ▶ ☐		53
54	**Tax due.** If line 52 is less than the total of lines 49, 50, and 53, enter amount owed ▶		54
55	**Overpayment.** If line 52 is larger than the total of lines 49, 50, and 53, enter amount overpaid ▶		55
56	Enter the amount of line 55 you want: Credited to 2020 estimated tax ▶ Refunded ▶		56
Part VI	Statements Regarding Certain Activities and Other Information (see instructions)		

Lines 46-48 and 50 are various tax credits and other specific taxes, most of which will not be applicable. Review the lists and see if they pertain to you.

Line 49 becomes your tax liability by taking line 45 and subtracting all the credits and adding any other taxes from line 48.

Lines 51a-e are any estimated tax payments, payments when the extension Form 8868 was filed, and withholding from investment accounts on these lines.

If you offer employer health insurance, you may be able to take a credit at **Line 51f**. See IRS Form 8941 to see if you are eligible.

Line 51g covers other tax credits related to undistributed long-term capital gains and fuel taxes.

Line 52 adds all the payments (lines 51a through g) to get the total payments.

If line 49 is greater than line 52, you owe tax and should put the amount on **Line 54 (tax due).** If line 52 is greater than line 49, you have overpaid your taxes and should put the amount on **line 55 (overpayment)**. If you have an overpayment, go to Line 56.

Line 56 Enter the amount of the overpayment you would like credited to your next tax return or refunded.

7. Part VI (Statements Regarding Certain Activities)

56 Enter the amount of line 55 you want: Credited to 2020 estimated tax ▶ Refunded ▶ 56

Part VI Statements Regarding Certain Activities and Other Information (see instructions)

		Yes	No
57	At any time during the 2019 calendar year, did the organization have an interest in or a signature or other authority over a financial account (bank, securities, or other) in a foreign country? If "Yes," the organization may have to file FinCEN Form 114, Report of Foreign Bank and Financial Accounts. If "Yes," enter the name of the foreign country here ▶		
58	During the tax year, did the organization receive a distribution from, or was it the grantor of, or transferor to, a foreign trust? . If "Yes," see instructions for other forms the organization may have to file.		
59	Enter the amount of tax-exempt interest received or accrued during the tax year ▶ $		

Sign Here — Under penalties of perjury, I declare that I have examined this return, including accompanying schedules and statements, and to the best of my knowledge and belief, it is true, correct, and complete. Declaration of preparer (other than taxpayer) is based on all information of which preparer has any knowledge.

Signature of officer | Date | Title

May the IRS discuss this return with the preparer shown below (see instructions)? ☐ Yes ☐ No

Paid Preparer Use Only	Print/Type preparer's name	Preparer's signature	Date	Check ☐ if self-employed	PTIN
	Firm's name ▶			Firm's EIN ▶	
	Firm's address ▶			Phone no.	

Form 990-T (2019)

These are questions on foreign financial information and tax-exempt interest. Answer appropriately, then sign and date your form. The form should be mailed to:

Department of the Treasury
Internal Revenue Service Center
Ogden UT 84201-0027

Check the IRS website to see if this address has changed.

It must be filed by the 15th day of the 5th month after the end of their tax year. Extensions may be filed using Form 8868, but any expected tax due should be sent at the same time.

I. Summary

Unrelated business income (UBI) is a complicated topic because it is different for each organization. In this chapter, you learned:

- What UBI is,
- What is excluded,
- How to determine if your activity is considered UBI, and
- The basics behind how to fill out the UBIT tax form 990-T.

In the next chapter, we will cover the Form 990s.

17. Form 990 Annual Filings for Exempt Organizations

If you are a 501(c)3 or other exempt organization, the IRS requires you to fill out an annual return. Different size exempt organizations have different filing requirements. In this chapter, you will learn:

- The different types of forms,
- Which form your organization requires,
- How to file the 990-N, and
- How to complete the 990-EZ.

> *I am intentionally excluding how to fill out the full IRS Form 990. I strongly recommend you use a knowledgeable CPA to ensure it is completed correctly.*

Please note if you are a private foundation, there are different filing requirements that are not covered in this book.

A. Types of 990s

There are three different annual returns, Form 990-N (also known as the e-Postcard), Form 990-EZ, and the full Form 990. The gross receipts and the total assets of a nonprofit determine which form you will complete.

Gross receipts are defined by the IRS as "the total amounts the organization received from all sources during its annual accounting period, without subtracting any costs or expenses" (ref: Gross Receipts Defined IRS).

Total assets are the value of all assets from your Balance Sheet. Remember from our discussion in Chapter 1; assets are the things you own or are owed to you (cash, pledges receivable, buildings, etc.).

1. Form 990-N e-Postcard (Small Nonprofits)

Form 990-N is a straightforward form that asks for the ending date of your organization's tax year, if the nonprofit has gone out of business, and if the gross receipts are normally $50,000 or less.

The term "normally $50,000 or less" needs a bit more explanation. According to the IRS:

An organization's gross receipts are considered to be $50,000 or less if the organization:

- *Has been in existence for 1 year or less and received, or donors have pledged to give, $75,000 or less during its first taxable year;*
- *Has been in existence between 1 and 3 years and averaged $60,000 or less in gross receipts during each of its first two tax years, and*
- *is at least 3 years old and averaged $50,000 or less in gross receipts for the immediately preceding three tax years (including the year for which calculations are being made).*

Gross Receipts Normally $50,000 or Less, IRS.

There are a couple of exceptions to the requirement to file the Form 990-N. They include:

- Organizations that are included in a group return,
- Churches, their integrated auxiliaries, and conventions, and
- Organizations required to file a different return, which includes private foundations, supporting organizations (ones that exempt purpose is to support another nonprofit), and political organizations

These organizations are specifically ineligible for filing Form 990-N:

- Section 501(c)(1) – U.S. government instrumentalities
- Section 501(c)(20) – Group legal services plans
- Section 501(c)(23) – Pre-1880 Armed Forces organizations
- Section 501(c)(24) – ERISA sec. 4049 trusts

- Section 501(d) – Religious and apostolic organizations
- Section 529 – Qualified tuition programs
- Section 4947(a)(2) – Split-interest trusts
- Section 4947(a)(1) – Charitable trusts treated as private foundations

The filing date is the 15th day of the 5th month after the close of your tax year.

If your organizations have more than $50,000 of gross receipts, you will need to file either Form 990-EZ or Form 990.

2. Form 990-EZ (Medium Nonprofits)

If your nonprofit has gross receipts less than $200,000 and total assets less than $500,000, you have the option to file either Form 990-EZ or the complete Form 990.

The 990-EZ is substantially more straightforward than the full Form 990, but some charitable organizations prefer to submit Form 990 to give donors a more complete picture of their organization.

3. Form 990 (Large Nonprofits)

Organizations with $200,000 or more of gross receipts OR $500,000 or more of total assets must file Form 990 unless they are a private foundation. It is twelve pages long (versus the 4 page 990-EZ) and asks detailed questions about your organization.

If you are large enough to require Form 990, I strongly recommend hiring a knowledgeable accountant to assist you.

4. Form 990-PF (Private Foundations)

Private foundations of any size are required to file Form 990-PF. The 990-PF is outside the scope of this book, so I will not be covering it.

B. IRS Summary of Forms to File

On the next page is a copy of the IRS.gov table for which form to file for each organization's size.

Status	Form to File
Gross receipts normally ≤ $50,000 **Note**: Organizations eligible to file the *e-Postcard* may choose to file a full return	990-N
Gross receipts < $200,000, and Total assets < $500,000	990-EZ or 990
Gross receipts ≥ $200,000, or Total assets ≥ $500,000	990
Private foundation - regardless of financial status	990-PF

C. Completing Form 990-N (e-Postcard)

Form 990-N used to be called "the Postcard" because all of the required information fit on a postcard you could mail into the IRS. It is now an e-Postcard because *it is only accepted via electronic filing*.

1. Data Required

To complete the e-Postcard, you need the following information:

1. **Employer identification number (EIN),** also known as a Taxpayer Identification Number (TIN),
2. **Tax year,**
3. **Legal name** and mailing address,
4. Any other names the organization uses,
5. Name and address of a **principal officer,**
6. **Web site address** if the organization has one,
7. Confirmation that the organization's **annual gross receipts are $50,000 or less**, and
8. If applicable, a statement that the organization has terminated or is terminating (going out of business).

Please note that you are allowed to fill out Form 990-EZ or Form 990 if you would like to have the additional information about your charity as a public record.

2. **Registering**

All filers must register at IRS.gov before filing Form 990-N. Your organization will only have to register once.

The IRS offers the following advice before you get started:

1. *Close multiple browsers before beginning, especially during registration.*
2. *Do NOT use your smartphone to register.*
3. *Use only letters, numbers, or a hyphen in text fields.*
4. *For a password, special characters are allowed except the caret (^).*
5. *Check your spam or junk email folders when looking for a response.*

Let's walk through the process of filing the e-Postcard step by step.

To register, you will need to go to IRS.gov and search 990-N. Select the link titled *"Annual Electronic Filing Requirement for Small Exempt Organizations-Form 990-N (e-Postcard)"*

Scroll down on that page, and there is an area called *Ready to File?* Click on the link to start the process.

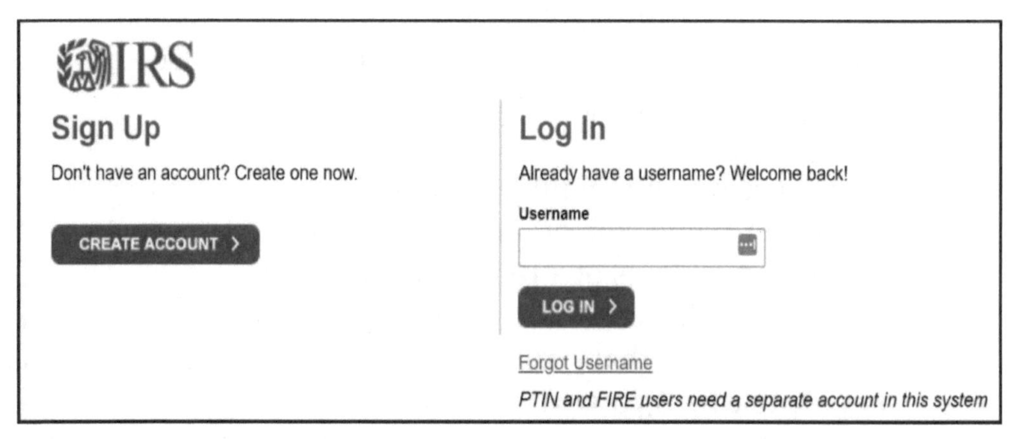

If this is your first time logging in, you will need to **Create Account**.

Please note: You will use your personal information to register. The login I.D. and related password belong to you, not the organization. With this registration, you can file a Form 990-N for multiple organizations. Each organization does not need to reregister.

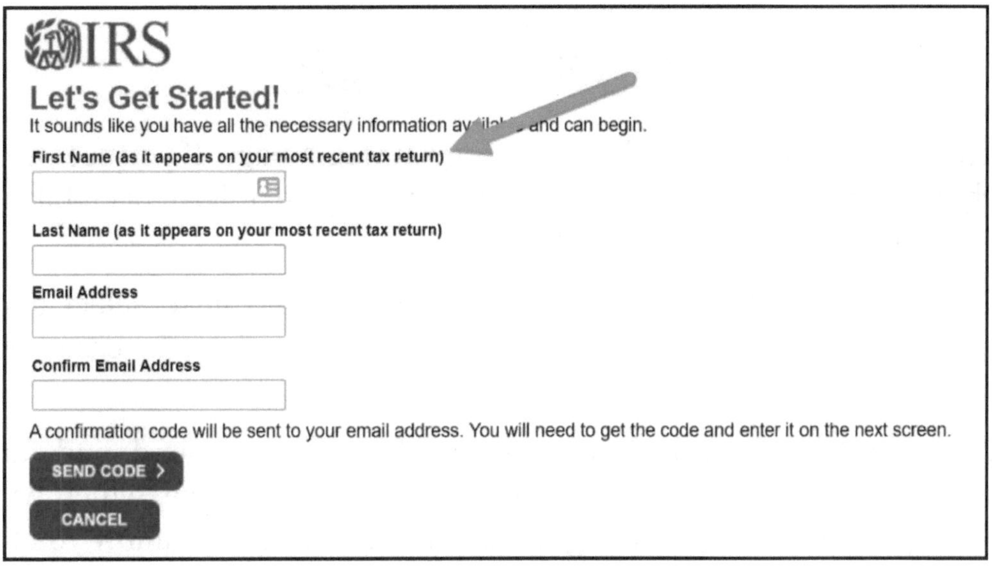

IRS

Let's Get Started!

It sounds like you have all the necessary information av[...] and can begin.

First Name (as it appears on your most recent tax return)

Last Name (as it appears on your most recent tax return)

Email Address

Confirm Email Address

A confirmation code will be sent to your email address. You will need to get the code and enter it on the next screen.

SEND CODE >

CANCEL

Enter your name as it appears on your personal tax return and your email address twice. After you select "SEND CODE," check your email and enter the code that was sent. If you can't find an email from the IRS, check your spam or junk folders.

Enter the one-time code and hit continue. You will then be asked to create a user name and password. Follow the instructions for the password rules. At the time of publication, the password needed to be between 8 and 20 characters long with at least one number and one special character and both upper and lower case letters.

As added security features, there will be a **site phrase** and a **site image**.

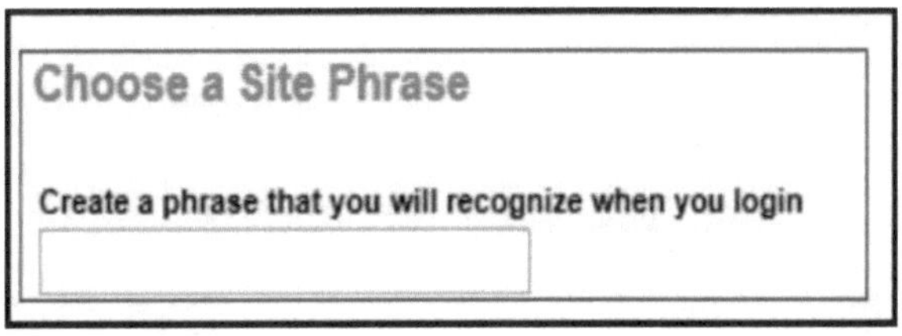

Choose a Site Phrase

Create a phrase that you will recognize when you login

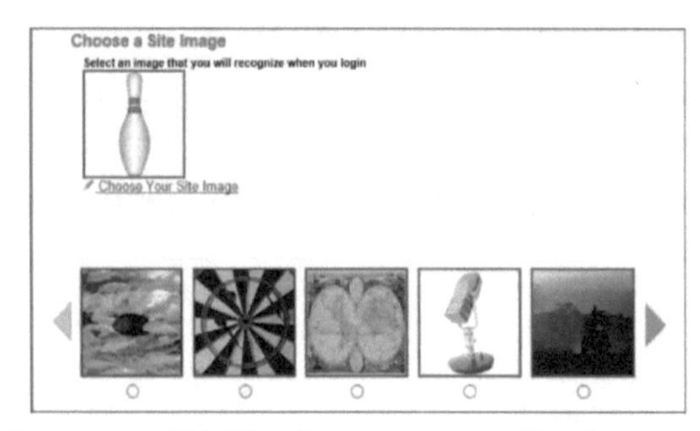

The phrase and image will display on your login page. If you see your choices, you will know you are not on a fake page or have been taken there by a scammer.

There will also be four challenge questions for you to select and answer. Don't forget to write these down somewhere in case you forget them.

Once you hit "Continue," your user profile will be created, and you will continue to the "Online Security Information" page, which will show you the most recent login history. The extra steps allow you to see if someone else is logging in with your credentials.

You are now registered and ready to submit the e-Postcard.

3. Electronic Submission

The next screen allows you to set up your organization's profile. Select "MANAGE E-POSTCARD PROFILE."

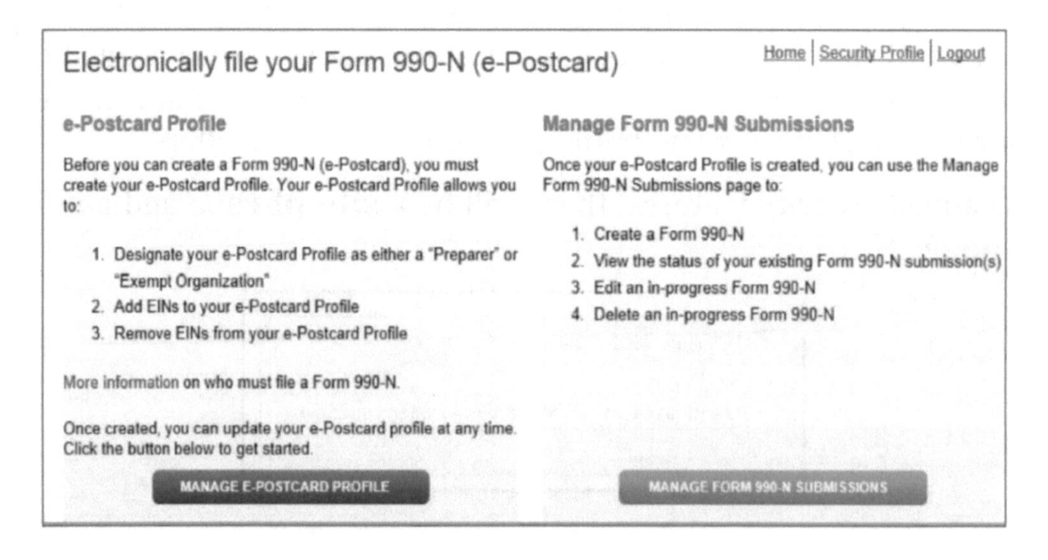

Start by selecting the user type from the drop-down arrow at the bottom.

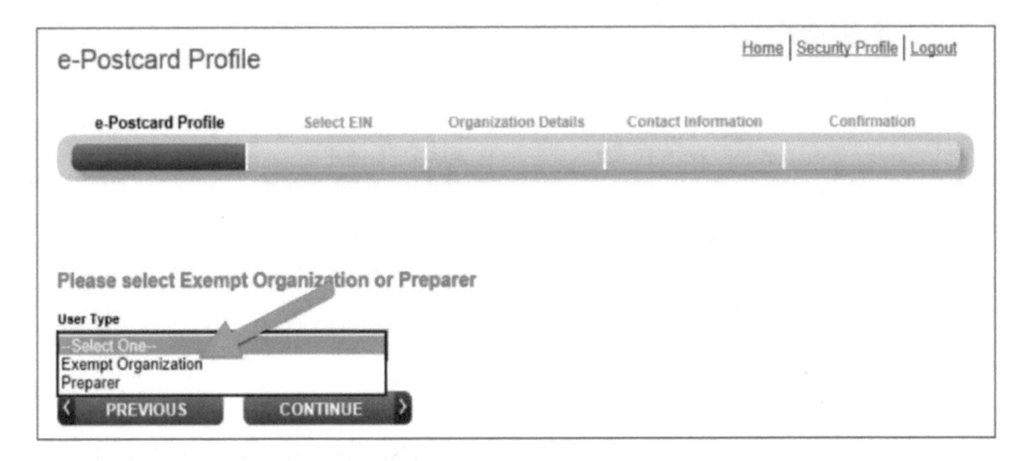

Choose "Exempt Organization" if you are only responsible for one charity. Choose "Preparer" if you work with several organizations.

Next, you will add your EIN.

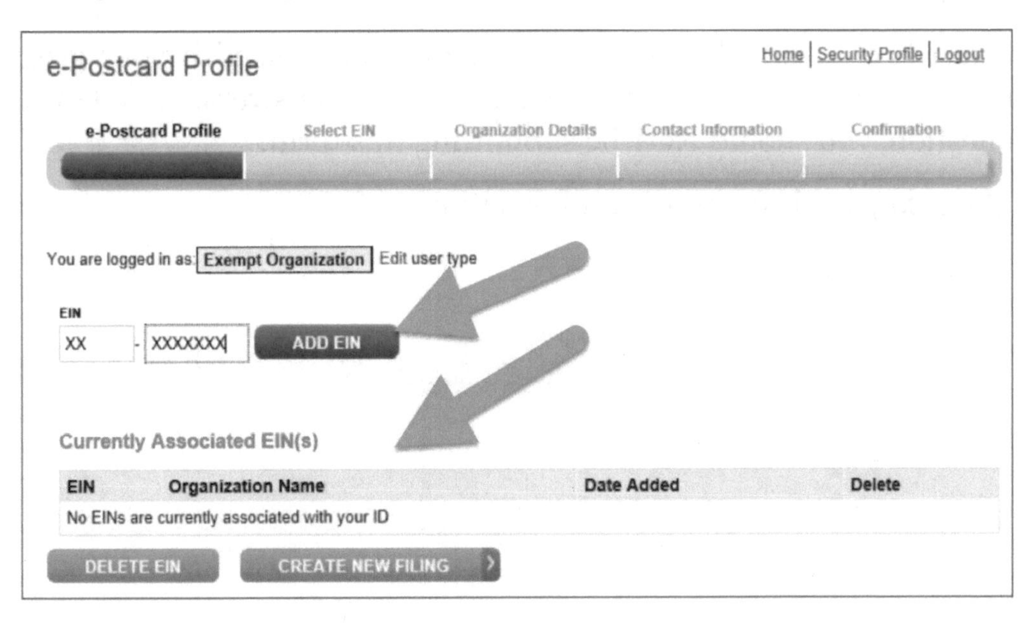

If you add more than one, you will select the appropriate one from a drop-down arrow.

Once you have selected your EIN, you will be entering the organization details.

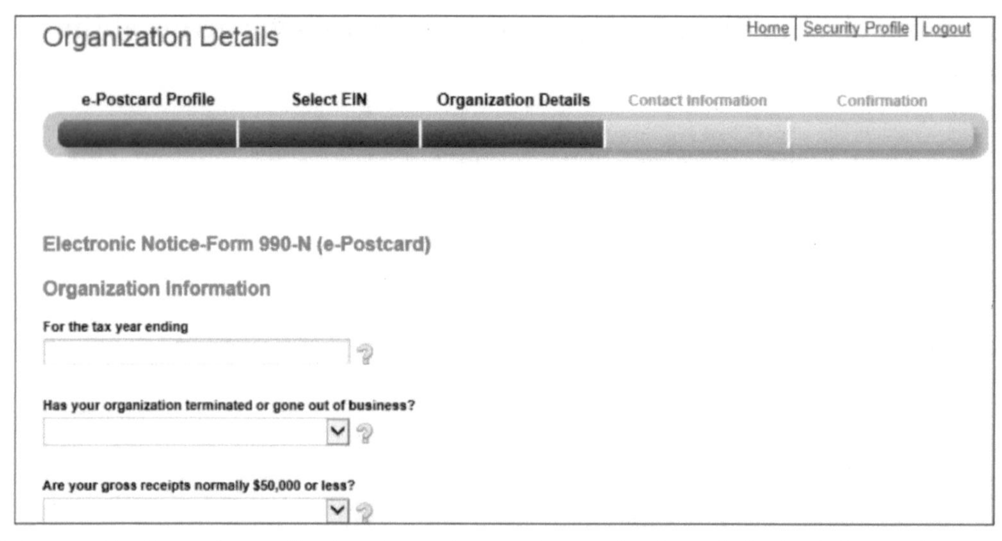

Organization Details

Home | Security Profile | Logout

e-Postcard Profile | Select EIN | Organization Details | Contact Information | Confirmation

Electronic Notice-Form 990-N (e-Postcard)

Organization Information

For the tax year ending

Has your organization terminated or gone out of business?

Are your gross receipts normally $50,000 or less?

Enter the last day of your fiscal year into the box labeled "For the tax year ending."

If your organization has not gone out of business, select "No" from the next drop-down option.

Select "Yes" from the drop-down arrow when asked if your gross receipts are normally less than $50,000. If the answer is "No" to this question, you should NOT be submitting this form.

The next page is for contact information

Contact Information

Home | Security Profile | Logout

e-Postcard Profile | Select EIN | Organization Details | Contact Information | Confirmation

Electronic Notice-Form 990-N (e-Postcard)

Organization Address and Principal Officer Information

Organization's legal name:

If your organization conducts business using another name (DBA), enter other name:

* = required field

Organization:

DBA Name

Enter the LEGAL name of the organization first and then the "Doing Business As (DBA)" name. This page will also ask for the address of the organization, website, and the principal officer's name and address.

Once you have gone through all of the questions, you can "Save Filing" to allow you to return later or "Submit Filing" if it is complete.

Once it has been submitted, you will see a screen similar to this one, recommending you PRINT or screenshot a copy for your record.

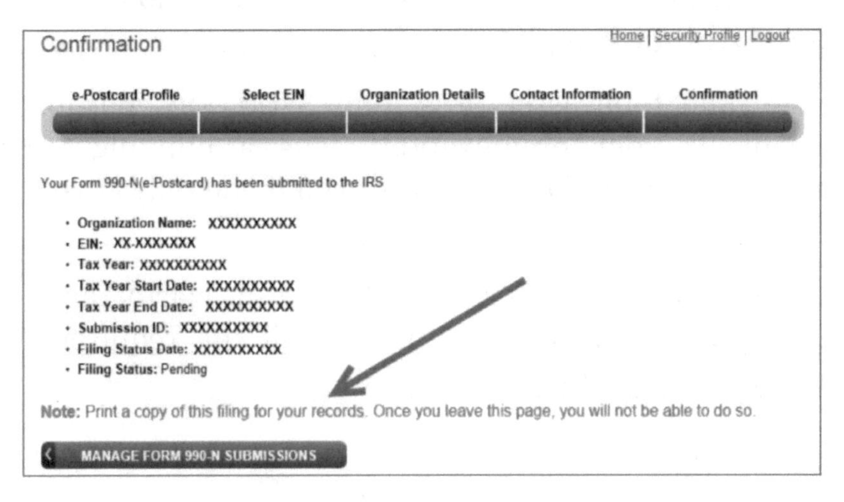

The bottom button "MANAGE FORM 990-N SUBMISSIONS" will take you to a summary screen. The report you just submitted will show the status as "Pending." If you refresh the page after five or so minutes, the status will be either "Accepted" or "Rejected."

If it is rejected, follow the **submission I.D.** hyperlink on the screen for additional details.

The 990-N is now complete. In subsequent years, you will not need to reregister. Instead, you will log into your account and update the organization's information.

4. Form 990-N Filing Dates

Form 990-N must be filed by the 15th day of the fifth month after the end of the fiscal year. If you have a December 31st year-end, your 990-N is due by May 15th. If you have a June 30th year-end, your filing is due by Nov 15th.

If you need to file an extension, use Form 8868 to receive an automatic three-month extension. You only need to fill out Part I of the form. Now, let's go onto filling out Form 990-EZ.

D. Completing Form 990-EZ Short Form Return

If your nonprofit has gross receipts greater than $50,000, you will have to complete a more comprehensive annual return. As I mentioned earlier, if you have gross receipts less than $200,000 and total assets less than $500,000, you have the option to file either Form 990-EZ or the complete Form 990.

Notice the "and total assets less than $500,000" portion of the requirement. If your organization owns a building valued at $600,000, you cannot file the 990-N even if you only have $10,000 of gross receipts.

Before I step you through Form 990-EZ, let me clarify that I cannot cover in detail all the regulations and all the requirements for different types of charities.

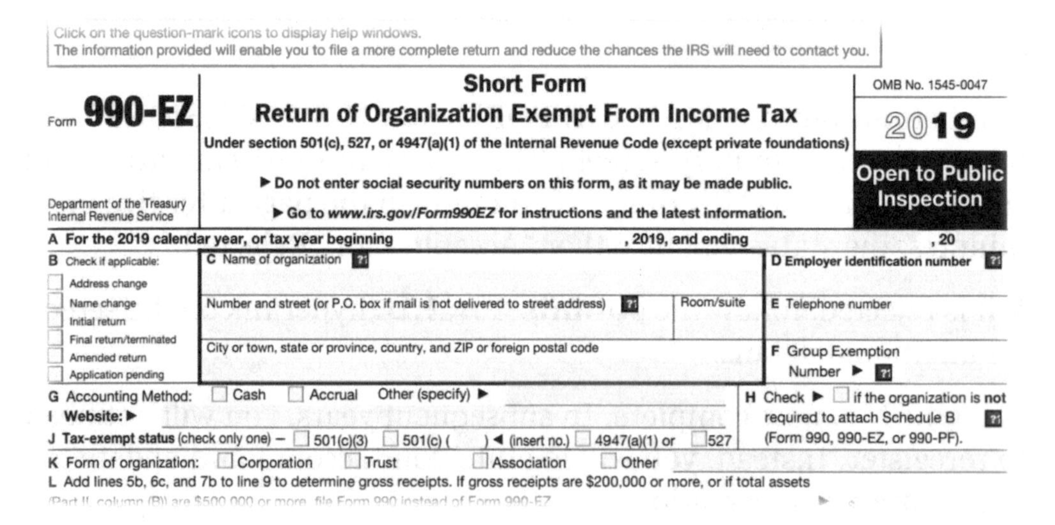

Click on the question-mark icons to display help windows.
The information provided will enable you to file a more complete return and reduce the chances the IRS will need to contact you.

Form **990-EZ**
Department of the Treasury
Internal Revenue Service

Short Form
Return of Organization Exempt From Income Tax
Under section 501(c), 527, or 4947(a)(1) of the Internal Revenue Code (except private foundations)
▶ Do not enter social security numbers on this form, as it may be made public.
▶ Go to www.irs.gov/Form990EZ for instructions and the latest information.

OMB No. 1545-0047
2019
Open to Public Inspection

A For the 2019 calendar year, or tax year beginning , 2019, and ending , 20

B Check if applicable:
- Address change
- Name change
- Initial return
- Final return/terminated
- Amended return
- Application pending

C Name of organization
Number and street (or P.O. box if mail is not delivered to street address) | Room/suite
City or town, state or province, country, and ZIP or foreign postal code

D Employer identification number
E Telephone number
F Group Exemption Number ▶

G Accounting Method: Cash Accrual Other (specify) ▶
I Website: ▶
J Tax-exempt status (check only one) – 501(c)(3) 501(c) ( ) ◀ (insert no.) 4947(a)(1) or 527
H Check ▶ if the organization is not required to attach Schedule B (Form 990, 990-EZ, or 990-PF).
K Form of organization: Corporation Trust Association Other
L Add lines 5b, 6c, and 7b to line 9 to determine gross receipts. If gross receipts are $200,000 or more, or if total assets (Part II, column (B)) are $500,000 or more, file Form 990 instead of Form 990-EZ

1. Top Sections Blocks A-L

These are mostly self-explanatory and are similar to the top section of the 990-T we discussed in the last chapter.

Block A can be left blank if your fiscal year is the same as the calendar year. If not, enter the beginning month and day and the ending month and day.

Block B checks to see if this is the first (initial) or last (final) return for the organization, if there have been an address or name change, or if you still have your exempt application as pending.

Blocks C-E is for your organization's name and address, employer identification number, and contact telephone number.

Block F (group exemption number) is only used if you are covered by a group exemption.

Block G tells the IRS what accounting method you are using. Most small nonprofits use the cash method.

Block H will be checked if you are not required to attach Schedule B Schedule of Contributors. If you did not receive a contribution of greater than $5000 from a single donor, you have met the general rule and can select this box. Otherwise, leave it blank, and you will be required to attach a Schedule B (Schedule of Contributors).

Block I is for your organization's website.

Block J (tax-exempt status) will usually be the 501(c)3. Select one of the other boxes if you have a different exempt status.

Block K is to show what type of organization. Select whether yours is a "Corporation" or an "Association."

Block L shows you how to calculate your gross receipts to ensure you are filing the correct form.

2. Part I (Revenue, Expenses, And Changes In Net Assets)

Part I of Form 990-EZ is your statement of activity. You may not have all these types of revenues and expenses, so don't worry if you leave many of these blank. Alternatively, you may have others not listed. Supporting schedules can be attached to the form to list any other items.

At the top is a checkbox to be used if **Schedule O** will be attached. Schedule O is a simple form to provide the IRS with narrative information on specific questions.

Part I **Revenue, Expenses, and Changes in Net Assets or Fund Balances** (see the instructions for Part I)

Check if the organization used Schedule O to respond to any question in this Part I . . . . ☐

Section	Line	Description	Box	Line
Revenue	1	Contributions, gifts, grants, and similar amounts received		1
	2	Program service revenue including government fees and contracts		2
	3	Membership dues and assessments		3
	4	Investment income		4
	5a	Gross amount from sale of assets other than inventory	5a	
	b	Less: cost or other basis and sales expenses	5b	
	c	Gain or (loss) from sale of assets other than inventory (subtract line 5b from line 5a)		5c
	6	Gaming and fundraising events:		
	a	Gross income from gaming (attach Schedule G if greater than $15,000)	6a	
	b	Gross income from fundraising events (not including $ ______ of contributions from fundraising events reported on line 1) (attach Schedule G if the sum of such gross income and contributions exceeds $15,000)	6b	
	c	Less: direct expenses from gaming and fundraising events	6c	
	d	Net income or (loss) from gaming and fundraising events (add lines 6a and 6b and subtract line 6c)		6d
	7a	Gross sales of inventory, less returns and allowances	7a	
	b	Less: cost of goods sold	7b	
	c	Gross profit or (loss) from sales of inventory (subtract line 7b from line 7a)		7c
	8	Other revenue (describe in Schedule O)		8
	9	**Total revenue.** Add lines 1, 2, 3, 4, 5c, 6d, 7c, and 8 ▶		9
Expenses	10	Grants and similar amounts paid (list in Schedule O)		10
	11	Benefits paid to or for members		11
	12	Salaries, other compensation, and employee benefits		12
	13	Professional fees and other payments to independent contractors		13
	14	Occupancy, rent, utilities, and maintenance		14
	15	Printing, publications, postage, and shipping		15
	16	Other expenses (describe in Schedule O)		16
	17	**Total expenses.** Add lines 10 through 16 ▶		17
Net Assets	18	Excess or (deficit) for the year (subtract line 17 from line 9)		18
	19	Net assets or fund balances at beginning of year (from line 27, column (A)) (must agree with end-of-year figure reported on prior year's return)		19
	20	Other changes in net assets or fund balances (explain in Schedule O)		20
	21	Net assets or fund balances at end of year. Combine lines 18 through 20 ▶		21

For Paperwork Reduction Act Notice, see the separate instructions. Cat. No. 10642I Form **990-EZ** (2019)

After you complete the form, come back to this line, and check the box if you need a Schedule O.

Line 1 reflects *all* voluntary contributions, donations, gifts, and grants. This includes the value of noncash contributions at the time of donation (e.g., the gross value of a donated car on the day it was received). It also includes the excess donation over the retail value of a fundraiser (see Line 6 for more details). Do not reduce the total for uncollectible pledges or refunds of service revenues. These are expenses that will be reported on Line 20. Other changes in net assets are explained on Schedule O.

Line 2 totals your program service revenues from your exempt function. Here are some examples of an organization's potential revenues that would be included on this line:

- Tuition if your exempt purpose is a school
- Any grants for a specific product or service that is not to the benefit of the general public[§]
- Registration fees for a convention
- Program-related investment income like interest on scholarship loans or loans to victims of a disaster
- Government fees and contracts that benefit a government agency, not the general public[**]
- Unrelated business activities that generate fees for service
- Money a social club receives from both members and nonmembers for the use of its golf course

Line 3 includes membership dues and assessments if the dues received are reasonably equal to the value of the benefits for the members. This line may include magazines, free or reduced rate admission to events, use of facilities, or discounts on products or services.[††]

Line 4 reflects interest, dividends, and gross rents. It does NOT include capital gains and losses (Line 5) or exempt function rental income (Line 2).

Line 5 includes all sales of securities and other types of investments (real estate, royalty interests, etc.) and capital gain dividends. Do NOT include any unrealized gains or losses.

Line 5a is the gross amount received.

Line 5b is the related cost. For sales of securities, you can use an average cost basis for the particular security sold.

Line 5c calculates the gain by subtracting 5b from 5a.

[§] If the grant was to carry on your regular programs and activities, it would be considered a contribution and recorded on Line 1.

[**] Contracts from the government that benefit the general public would be reflected in Line 1.

[††] If the dues are primarily to support the organization's activities, they should be reported on Line 1. An example would be a "Friends of the Library" group whose dues go purchasing additional books for the library.

Keep in mind a solicitation campaign by mail to generate only contributions is NOT a fundraising event, and the money received should be recorded on Line 1.

Line 6 covers gaming and fundraising. If you have over $15,000 of revenue from either, you will need to complete *Schedule G Supplemental Information Regarding Fundraising or Gaming Activities* Parts II or III (but not Part I).

Line 6a includes any gambling conducted directly or through a promoter, and it includes sweepstakes, raffles, and lotteries. If a minimum payment required for a raffle entry and the prizes are of only nominal value, the raffle income should be shown as a contribution on Line 1. The gross income should be reported whether or not is regularly carried on.

Line 6b is the gross income received for goods and services sold as a fundraiser MINUS any amount received that exceeded the value.

If a live auction was held and an item sold for $1000 more than the retail price, the $1000 would be reflected in the Line 1 total and notated between the parenthesis on 6b.

Line 6c is the total of the direct expenses for the fundraisers and gambling events. This is only the DIRECT expenses for the event; no overhead should be allocated to it. Fundraising expenses related to contributions (e.g., mailings) are reportable on Lines 12-16.

Line 6d calculates the net income or loss by adding 6a and b and subtracting 6c.

Line 7a reflects sales of inventory unless they have already been reflected in the fundraising numbers on line 6. Inventory items are goods the organization makes to sell to others or that it buys for resale.

Line 7b is the cost of goods sold. Cost of goods sold includes labor, materials, and supplies consumed, freight, and a proportion of overhead expenses. Marketing and distribution costs are NOT included but should be reported on Lines 12-16.

Line 7c calculates the gross profit by subtracting 7b from 7a.

Line 8 is a catch-all for any other revenues not recorded in lines 1-7. An example is interest on loans to officers or employees. If you include anything on this line, explain it on Schedule O (and check the related box at the top of Part I).

Line 9 adds all your revenue to show *total revenue.*

Lines 10-16 reflect your actual expenses for the year.

Line 10 includes grants, scholarships, and fellowships paid to individuals and organizations. If your local charity pays dues to an affiliated state or national organization, this is where you would reflect the cost. This line is not the place to record dues to an unaffiliated group. You must list on Schedule O each grantee organization or individual to whom you go more than $500. On Schedule O, you would list:

- Each class of activity,
- Grantees name and, if an organization, its address,
- The aggregate amount given to each, and
- The relationship of the grantee to any significant donor, trustee, key employee, officer, etc.

Line 11 is primarily for 501(c)(8), (9), (17) organizations.

Line 12 totals all salaries and wages paid to officers and employees as well as payments made to directors and trustees. It also includes all employee benefits and contributions made to pension plans.

Line 13 reflects money paid to outside legal and accounting professionals and all other independent contractors. Do NOT include any penalties or fines that were paid through an attorney or accountant. Expense reimbursements to these individuals should be reflected on Lines 14-16.

Line 14 reflects the cost of your charity's workspace and includes mortgage interest or rent, utilities, janitorial services, property taxes, and insurance. It does NOT include the expenses on any real estate held for investment. Those expenses are included on Line 16.

Line 15 is the publication and mailing costs of your newsletters, leaflets, videos, and other informational materials. Do not include any costs that have previously been recorded as part of fundraising or inventory costs.

Line 16 is for anything not already covered. Common examples include travel, conferences, unrelated business income taxes, penalties or fines, and occupancy costs for real estate held for investment. These expenses will need to be listed on Schedule O.

Line 17 totals Lines 10-16 to calculate *total expenses.*

Lines 18-21 reflect the changes in the net assets of the organization. (These are the equity accounts of a nonprofit).

Line 18 is the excess or deficit for the year, calculated by subtracting Line 17 (total expenses) from Line 9 (total revenue).

Line 19 is the beginning net asset balance and taken from your previous year's tax return. If this is your first year, it will be blank.

Line 20 is a catch-all for other changes in net assets. Uncollectible pledges and refunds of service revenues are recorded here, as are unrealized gains and losses on investments. Details are required on Schedule O.

Line 21 calculates the net assets at the end of the year, by adding Lines 18 and 19 and adjusting them by line 20.

3. Part II (Balance Sheets)

Part II reports on the balance sheets (or statement of financial position for nonprofits) for the beginning and end of the reporting period. If this is your first year, complete column A with $0, so the IRS will not find it incomplete.

Line 22 totals all cash, savings, and investments. The total should include your reconciled checking account and your investment accounts at market value. It should also include any land and buildings held for investment.

Form 990-EZ (2019) Page 2

Part II **Balance Sheets** (see the instructions for Part II)
Check if the organization used Schedule O to respond to any question in this Part II . . . . ☐

		(A) Beginning of year		(B) End of year
22	Cash, savings, and investments		22	
23	Land and buildings		23	
24	Other assets (describe in Schedule O)		24	
25	**Total assets**		25	
26	**Total liabilities** (describe in Schedule O)		26	
27	**Net assets or fund balances** (line 27 of column (B) **must** agree with line 21)		27	

Line 23 is the book value of the land and buildings your charity owns but is not used for investment purposes. Book value is the purchase price less accumulated depreciation.

Line 24 reflects all the other assets of your organization and needs to be listed on Schedule O. Other assets include accounts receivables, inventories, prepaid expenses, and any shares of assets in joint ventures or other partnership entities.

Line 25 is the total assets calculated by adding Lines 22 to 24. This line must equal the sum of lines 26 (total liabilities) and 27 (net assets). If they do not equal, you have an error somewhere. Double-check your beginning balances (if applicable), then make sure there isn't a revenue or an expense entered twice, perhaps in fundraising and expenses.

Line 26 includes accounts payables, grants payable, mortgages due, and any revenue received but not yet earned as part of total liabilities. These also need to be listed on Schedule O.

Line 27 is the total net assets. It must equal line 21 from Part I.

4. Part III (Statement of Program Service Accomplishments)

The first question asks for your primary exempt purpose. It should be similar to the exempt purpose listed on your IRS determination letter.

Lines 28-30 asks for descriptions of the accomplishments of your three largest programs. The IRS refers to the size based on *expenses* of each program, not revenue. You will need to describe the services provided, the number of persons benefitted, and other information you deem relevant. You can use Schedule O for additional space.

Part III Statement of Program Service Accomplishments (see the instructions for Part III)		
Check if the organization used Schedule O to respond to any question in this Part III . . ☐		**Expenses** (Required for section 501(c)(3) and 501(c)(4) organizations; optional for others.)
What is the organization's primary exempt purpose?		
Describe the organization's program service accomplishments for each of its three largest program services, as measured by expenses. In a clear and concise manner, describe the services provided, the number of persons benefited, and other relevant information for each program title.		
28		
(Grants $) If this amount includes foreign grants, check here . . . . ▶ ☐	28a	
29		
(Grants $) If this amount includes foreign grants, check here . . . . ▶ ☐	29a	
30		
(Grants $) If this amount includes foreign grants, check here . . . . ▶ ☐	30a	
31 Other program services (describe in Schedule O)		
(Grants $) If this amount includes foreign grants, check here . . . . ▶ ☐	31a	
32 Total program service expenses (add lines 28a through 31a) . . . . . . ▶	32	

You will also enter the amount of the grants received to support each program and the related expenses if you are a 501(c)(3) or (4).

Line 31 adds the grants and related expenses for the other programs not already detailed.

Line 32 adds all the program service expenses from Part III.

Remember: the 990-EZ is a public record once it is filed. Potential donors often read the descriptions of your programs when deciding if to donate.

5. Part IV (List of Officers, Directors, Trustees, and Key Employees)

This section asks for all officers, directors, trustees, and key employees. Here are the IRS definitions.

An **officer** is a person elected or appointed to manage the organization's daily operations, such as a president, vice president, secretary, or treasurer. The officers of an organization are determined by reference to its organizing document, bylaws, or resolutions of its governing body, but at a minimum include those officers required by applicable state law.

A **director** or **trustee** is a member of the organization's governing body, but only if the member has voting rights.

The **governing body** is the group of persons authorized under state law to make governance decisions on behalf of the organization and its shareholders or members, if applicable. The governing body is, generally speaking, the board of directors (sometimes referred to as the board of trustees) of a corporation or association, or the board of trustees of a trust (sometimes referred to simply as the trustees, or trustee, if only one trustee).

A **key employee** is any person having responsibilities or powers similar to those of officers, directors, or trustees. The term includes the chief management and administrative officials of an organization (such as an executive director or chancellor). A chief financial officer and the officer in charge of the administration or program operations are both key employees if they have the authority to control the organization's activities, its finances, or both.

Part IV **List of Officers, Directors, Trustees, and Key Employees** (list each one even if not compensated—see the instructions for Part IV)
Check if the organization used Schedule O to respond to any question in this Part IV . . . .

(a) Name and title	(b) Average hours per week devoted to position	(c) Reportable compensation (Forms W-2/1099-MISC) (if not paid, enter -0-)	(d) Health benefits, contributions to employee benefit plans, and deferred compensation	(e) Estimated amount c other compensation

Part IV requires that each person's name and title must be listed in **Column a**. The IRS requests you list them in the following order:

1. Individual trustees or directors
2. Institutional trustees
3. Officers
4. Key employees

Column b records the average hours per week devoted to position. You will need to ask each person to give their estimate. Do NOT say "as needed"; you must estimate a number. If the average is less than one hour per week, round to the nearest tenth.

Column c is the reportable compensation found in the W-2, Box 1 or 5 (whichever is greater) or Form 1099-Misc Box 6 or 7. You MUST show a number for each person. If they are not compensated, enter a $0. Otherwise, enter the amount submitted to the IRS. For institutional trustees, list the fees for service paid under contract.

Column d is the total of each person's deferred compensation and health benefits. Reasonable estimates are allowed if precise figures are not available.

Column e reflects both taxable and nontaxable fringe benefits that are not already included in columns c and d. Fringe benefits include the value of personal use of housing, automobiles, or other assets owned by the charity as well as any other fringe benefits not already covered in the previous two columns. An organization whose total for Column e would be less than $10,000 can leave the column blank.

This column should not include expense reimbursements and allowances under an accountable plan or de minimis fringe benefits (e.g., occasional meal when working late, flowers sent on a birthday).

6. Part V (Other Information)

This section consists of a variety of questions regarding your organization. Unless the instructions specifically say you do not need to answer, either the "Yes" or "No" box must be selected.

Line 33 asks about any change in significant activities. If this is your first return, the answer is "No." If you no longer do one of the significant activities you listed the previous year, select "Yes" and detail it on Schedule O.

Line 34 looks at changes to your governing documents. If you have changed your clear mission, governing body composition, or voting rights, you will select "Yes" and detail on Schedule O. If you have had a change in the organization's name, you will need to attach the amended documents.

Lines 35a-b look at unrelated business income. If you have more than $1000 for the year and filed a 990-T, select "Yes."

Line 35c asks about a proxy tax on lobbying expenditures for (c)(4), (5), and (6) organizations. All others should select "No."

Line 36 looks at significant dispositions of net assets. If this was done to terminate the charity, you also need to select the "Final Return" box in Section B on the header area. Other significant dispositions would be transfers of assets for a reorganization and sales of assets or property to further its mission. If you think this may be applicable, find Form 990EZ Schedule N on IRS.gov.

Lines 37a-b relate to political activity, and there are precise regulations around what a charity can and cannot do on both state and federal levels. Please refer to IRS.gov and your state nonprofit association for guidance if applicable. If there were political expenditures, Form 1120-POL might need to be filed.

Lines 38a-b ask if loans were made to officers, directors, or key employees. If so, Schedule L will be required.

Lines 39a-b are only for social clubs exempt under 501(c)7. **Line 39a** is for capital contributions, initiation fees, and unusual amounts of income. **Line 39b** is the gross receipts for any public use of the club facilities. (These amounts are included in the total revenue number on line 9.)

Lines 40a-e relate to additional taxes paid. **Line 40a** asks about excise taxes imposed for excess lobbying, disqualified lobbying, or political expenditures. **Lines 40b-d** cover excess benefit transactions disqualified persons. The IRS states that

> *"the vast majority of section 501(c)(3), 501(c)(4), or 501(c)(29) organization employees and independent contractors won't be affected by these rules. Only the few influential persons within these organizations are covered by these rules when they receive benefits, such as compensation, fringe benefits, or contract payments. The IRS calls this class of covered individuals disqualified persons."*

The answer will probably be "No" for your organization. **Line 40e** asks if the organization was a party to a prohibited tax shelter. If so, Form 8886-T is required.

Line 41 requires the list of states to whom you will be filing the return.

Line 42a is for the contact information of the person holding the accounting records.

Lines 42b-c must be completed if you have a foreign bank account (with a combined value of more than $10,000 at any time throughout the year) or a foreign office.

Line 43 is for nonexempt charitable trusts only.

Lines 44a-b is a checklist to be sure you are filing the correct return.

Lines 44c-d relate to indoor tanning services as there is a federal excise tax on such services.

Lines 45a-b asks about controlled entities. The controlling organization must file a full Form 990 (not 990EZ) and Schedule R.

A controlled entity within the meaning of section 512(b)(13) may be a stock or nonstock corporation, association, partnership, LLC, or trust of which the controlling organization owns more than 50% of:

The stock of a corporation (measured by voting power or value),

The profits or capital interest in a partnership, or

The beneficial interest in a trust or other entity.

(ref: Exempt Organizations Annual Reporting Requirements - Form 990, Schedule R: "Related Organization" and "Controlled Entity" Reporting Differences, IRS*)*

Select "No" to both a and b if you are not a controlled entity.

Line 46 asks if you engaged directly or indirectly on behalf of, or in opposition to, a political candidate, including publishing statements made by the candidates. If "Yes," you will need to complete Schedule C, Part I.

7. Part VI (Section 501(c)(3) Organizations Only)

All 501(c)(3)s need to answer each question and complete these tables. Write "None" in the tables if appropriate. Use Schedule O to offer more detail for the public record.

Part VI **Section 501(c)(3) Organizations Only**
All section 501(c)(3) organizations must answer questions 47–49b and 52, and complete the tables for lines 50 and 51.
Check if the organization used Schedule O to respond to any question in this Part VI . . . . ☐

			Yes	No
47	Did the organization engage in lobbying activities or have a section 501(h) election in effect during the tax year? If "Yes," complete Schedule C, Part II	47		
48	Is the organization a school as described in section 170(b)(1)(A)(ii)? If "Yes," complete Schedule E	48		
49a	Did the organization make any transfers to an exempt non-charitable related organization?	49a		
b	If "Yes," was the related organization a section 527 organization?	49b		

50 Complete this table for the organization's five highest compensated employees (other than officers, directors, trustees, and key employees) who each received more than $100,000 of compensation from the organization. If there is none, enter "None."

(a) Name and title of each employee	(b) Average hours per week devoted to position	(c) Reportable compensation (Forms W-2/1099-MISC)	(d) Health benefits, contributions to employee benefit plans, and deferred compensation	(e) Estimated amount of other compensation

f Total number of other employees paid over $100,000 . . . . ▶

51 Complete this table for the organization's five highest compensated independent contractors who each received more than $100,000 of compensation from the organization. If there is none, enter "None."

(a) Name and business address of each independent contractor	(b) Type of service	(c) Compensation

d Total number of other independent contractors each receiving over $100,000 . . ▶

52 Did the organization complete Schedule A? **Note:** All section 501(c)(3) organizations must attach a completed Schedule A . . . . ▶ ☐ Yes ☐ No

Line 47 asks about lobbying activities. If the answer is "Yes," Schedule C Part II is required.

Line 48 is to designate if the organization is a school or not.

Lines 49a-b covers transfers to exempt non-charitable *related* organizations.

> *For example, if your charity sister organization that is used to lobby for the election of a specific candidate and you give them cash, free rent in your offices, or some other asset, you will need to record "Yes" on line 49a and b. If the related organization is not exempt under section 527, you would select "No" to line 49b.*

Line 50 lists the five highest-paid employees, for each one with total compensation of at least $100,000. Columns a through e are defined the same as in Part IV.

Line 50f totals the number of people on the table.

Line 51 asks for the five highest-paid independent contractors who received more than $100,000 and a description of their services. **Line 51d** is the total number of persons listed on this table.

Line 52 asks if the Schedule A Public Charity Status and Public Support has been completed. It must be attached if you are a 501(c)(3). We'll go over it in the next section.

Once you have completed and reviewed the form, you will need the signature of an officer and the date. Check IRS.gov for the mailing address or to see how to file electronically.

E. Schedule A (Public Charity Status & Public Support)

If substantially all your funding comes from a single private source, your organization may be treated as a private foundation, which requires different filings and more complex laws. Therefore, every 501(c)(3) organization filing Form 990 or 990EZ must complete **Schedule A** to explain the reason it is a public charity and where it receives its support.

The form is eight pages long, but you will not be required to fill in every section. I'm going to step you through the basics of the form. If you have unusual items or it is not clear how your organization would fill out this form, I strongly recommend hiring a knowledgeable accountant to help.

With that caveat, let's get started. At the top, enter the name of your organization and the employer identification number.

1. Part I (Reason for Public Charity Status)

EVERY organization has to fill out Part 1. Your organization is NOT a private foundation because it is one of the 12 options on this page. Read through them carefully and choose only one. It probably will be the one described in your IRS determination letter, but it does not have to be.

If you do not see an obvious fit, your organization probably falls under **Line 10**. This category requires at least 33 1/3% of a 501(c)3 organization's revenues come from a variety of donors and exempt-related revenues and no more than 33 1/3% to come from investment income and unrelated business income.

SCHEDULE A (Form 990 or 990-EZ)
Department of the Treasury Internal Revenue Service

Public Charity Status and Public Support

Complete if the organization is a section 501(c)(3) organization or a section 4947(a)(1) nonexempt charitable trust.
▶ Attach to Form 990 or Form 990-EZ.
▶ Go to *www.irs.gov/Form990* for instructions and the latest information.

OMB No. 1545-0047
2019
Open to Public Inspection

Name of the organization | Employer identification number

Part I Reason for Public Charity Status (All organizations must complete this part.) See instructions.

The organization is not a private foundation because it is: (For lines 1 through 12, check only one box.)

1 ☐ A church, convention of churches, or association of churches described in **section 170(b)(1)(A)(i).**
2 ☐ A school described in **section 170(b)(1)(A)(ii).** (Attach Schedule E (Form 990 or 990-EZ).)
3 ☐ A hospital or a cooperative hospital service organization described in **section 170(b)(1)(A)(iii).**
4 ☐ A medical research organization operated in conjunction with a hospital described in **section 170(b)(1)(A)(iii).** Enter the hospital's name, city, and state:
5 ☐ An organization operated for the benefit of a college or university owned or operated by a governmental unit described in **section 170(b)(1)(A)(iv).** (Complete Part II.)
6 ☐ A federal, state, or local government or governmental unit described in **section 170(b)(1)(A)(v).**
7 ☐ An organization that normally receives a substantial part of its support from a governmental unit or from the general public described in **section 170(b)(1)(A)(vi).** (Complete Part II.)
8 ☐ A community trust described in **section 170(b)(1)(A)(vi).** (Complete Part II.)
9 ☐ An agricultural research organization described in **section 170(b)(1)(A)(ix)** operated in conjunction with a land-grant college or university or a non-land-grant college of agriculture (see instructions). Enter the name, city, and state of the college or university:
10 ☐ An organization that normally receives: (1) more than 33 1/3% of its support from contributions, membership fees, and gross receipts from activities related to its exempt functions—subject to certain exceptions, and (2) no more than 33 1/3% of its support from gross investment income and unrelated business taxable income (less section 511 tax) from businesses acquired by the organization after June 30, 1975. See **section 509(a)(2).** (Complete Part III.)
11 ☐ An organization organized and operated exclusively to test for public safety. See **section 509(a)(4).**
12 ☐ An organization organized and operated exclusively for the benefit of, to perform the functions of, or to carry out the purposes of one or more publicly supported organizations described in **section 509(a)(1)** or **section 509(a)(2).** See **section 509(a)(3).** Check the box in lines 12a through 12d that describes the type of supporting organization and complete lines 12e, 12f, and 12g.

a ☐ **Type I.** A supporting organization operated, supervised, or controlled by its supported organization(s), typically by giving the supported organization(s) the power to regularly appoint or elect a majority of the directors or trustees of the supporting organization. **You must complete Part IV, Sections A and B.**

b ☐ **Type II.** A supporting organization supervised or controlled in connection with its supported organization(s), by having control or management of the supporting organization vested in the same persons that control or manage the supported organization(s). **You must complete Part IV, Sections A and C.**

c ☐ **Type III functionally integrated.** A supporting organization operated in connection with, and functionally integrated with, its supported organization(s) (see instructions). **You must complete Part IV, Sections A, D, and E.**

d ☐ **Type III non-functionally integrated.** A supporting organization operated in connection with its supported organization(s) that is not functionally integrated. The organization generally must satisfy a distribution requirement and an attentiveness requirement (see instructions). **You must complete Part IV, Sections A and D, and Part V.**

e ☐ Check this box if the organization received a written determination from the IRS that it is a Type I, Type II, Type III functionally integrated, or Type III non-functionally integrated supporting organization.

f Enter the number of supported organizations . . . .

g Provide the following information about the supported organization(s).

(i) Name of supported organization	(ii) EIN	(iii) Type of organization (described on lines 1–10 above (see instructions))	(iv) Is the organization listed in your governing document?		(v) Amount of monetary support (see instructions)	(vi) Amount of other support (see instructions)
			Yes	No		
(A)						

The line you choose may direct you to fill out an additional schedule or one of the other parts of this form. If you are a supporting organization and mark the box on Line 12, you will need to choose between Lines 12 a, b, c, and d; answer questions on Lines e and f, and fill out the table on line g.

2. **Part II (Support Schedule Described in Sections 170(b)(1)(A)(vi))**

This part is only completed if you checked a box on line 5, 7, or 8 or if your organization failed to qualify after completing Part III. Lines 5, 7, and 8 are for universities, government units, and community trusts, so I'm going to skip over this part and go into the detail of how to fill out Part III.

3. **Part III (Support Schedule Described in Section 509(a)(2))**

If you marked the box on Line 10, you are required to fill out Part III. These numbers may differ from the dollars on the 990-EZ, as additional information is requested.

Schedule A (Form 990 or 990-EZ) 2019 Page 3

Part III **Support Schedule for Organizations Described in Section 509(a)(2)**
(Complete only if you checked the box on line 10 of Part I or if the organization failed to qualify under Part II. If the organization fails to qualify under the tests listed below, please complete Part II.)

Section A. Public Support

Calendar year (or fiscal year beginning in) ▶	**(a)** 2015	**(b)** 2016	**(c)** 2017	**(d)** 2018	**(e)** 2019	**(f)** Total
1 Gifts, grants, contributions, and membership fees received. (Do not include any "unusual grants.")						
2 Gross receipts from admissions, merchandise sold or services performed, or facilities furnished in any activity that is related to the organization's tax-exempt purpose . . .						
3 Gross receipts from activities that are not an unrelated trade or business under section 513						
4 Tax revenues levied for the organization's benefit and either paid to or expended on its behalf						
5 The value of services or facilities furnished by a governmental unit to the organization without charge						
6 **Total.** Add lines 1 through 5						
7a Amounts included on lines 1, 2, and 3 received from disqualified persons .						
b Amounts included on lines 2 and 3 received from other than disqualified persons that exceed the greater of $5,000 or 1% of the amount on line 13 for the year						
c Add lines 7a and 7b						
8 **Public support.** (Subtract line 7c from line 6.)						

The first section is **Section A**, the table of public support. This schedule tracks five years' worth of data. If this is your first year, you will show the values under column (e) and column (f).

Line 1 is the annual amounts of your usual donations, grants, membership fees[‡‡], etc. Noncash contributions (except donated services) are included here at fair market value.

[‡‡] Membership fees that do not support the organization, but are used to purchase admission or use of facilities (e.g., access to tennis courts) should be recorded on Line 2.

If you have an uncollectible pledge expense from a prior year, deduct it from the prior year's number, not the current year total.

If you receive a large one-time or unusual grant, this is considered "an unusual grant" and is NOT included. Otherwise, a large grant from a donor could disqualify you from the 33 1/3% rule.

Line 2 reflects your revenues for admissions, merchandise, services, or facilities, which are related to your tax-exempt purpose.

An example may be the sales of art books by a museum.

Line 3 is for gross receipts from activities that are not an unrelated business income.

These activities may include a book fair where substantially all the work is performed by volunteers or thrift store where all of the product is donated.

Line 4 records any tax revenue levied for the organization's behalf. An example is a sales tax percentage that goes to an art council or an association to assist the libraries. The amount must be recorded whether or not it includes the revenue on Form 990-EZ.

Line 5 shows support from governmental units that do not bill your organization.

For example, if your county allows you to set up an office in one of their buildings free of charge, you should record the fair market value of the space. If you are allowed to use a public county park for free, you would not include an amount. (The fair market value of park use is $0, as anyone can use it for free.)

Line 6 adds up Lines 1 through 5.

Lines 7a-c ask about disqualified persons. Disqualified persons include:

- substantial contributors (someone who donates over $5000 or more than 2% of total contributions, whichever is greater),
- managers of the organization,
- owners of more than 20% of the voting power of a corporation, profits of a partnership, or beneficial interest in a trust that is a substantial contributor to the foundation, and
- members of the families of the previous three definitions.

A list of these persons and their annual contributions should be maintained by the nonprofit but not filed with the 990-EZ as it is public record. **Line 7a** is the annual totals of contributions from disqualified persons. **Line 7b** totals the gross receipts from donors other than disqualified persons giving greater than $5000 or 1% of the amount on Line 13 that was included in Lines 2 and 3. An example is a donation from an unrelated corporation. **Line 7c** is the sum of Lines 7a and b.

Line 8 calculates public support by subtracting Line 7c (disqualified donations) from Line 6 (total donations).

Section B is the table of total support.

Section B. Total Support

Calendar year (or fiscal year beginning in) ▶	(a) 2015	(b) 2016	(c) 2017	(d) 2018	(e) 2019	(f) Total
9 Amounts from line 6						
10a Gross income from interest, dividends, payments received on securities loans, rents, royalties, and income from similar sources						
b Unrelated business taxable income (less section 511 taxes) from businesses acquired after June 30, 1975						
c Add lines 10a and 10b						
11 Net income from unrelated business activities not included in line 10b, whether or not the business is regularly carried on						
12 Other income. Do not include gain or loss from the sale of capital assets (Explain in Part VI.)						
13 **Total support.** (Add lines 9, 10c, 11, and 12.)						

14 **First five years.** If the Form 990 is for the organization's first, second, third, fourth, or fifth tax year as a section 501(c)(3) organization, check this box and **stop here** ▶ ☐

Section C. Computation of Public Support Percentage

15	Public support percentage for 2019 (line 8, column (f), divided by line 13, column (f))	15	%
16	Public support percentage from 2018 Schedule A, Part III, line 15	16	%

Section D. Computation of Investment Income Percentage

17	Investment income percentage for **2019** (line 10c, column (f), divided by line 13, column (f))	17	%
18	Investment income percentage from **2018** Schedule A, Part III, line 17	18	%

19a **33⅓% support tests—2019.** If the organization did not check the box on line 14, and line 15 is more than 33⅓%, and line 17 is not more than 33⅓%, check this box and **stop here.** The organization qualifies as a publicly supported organization ▶ ☐

b **33⅓% support tests—2018.** If the organization did not check a box on line 14 or line 19a, and line 16 is more than 33⅓%, and line 18 is not more than 33⅓%, check this box and **stop here.** The organization qualifies as a publicly supported organization ▶ ☐

20 **Private foundation.** If the organization did not check a box on line 14, 19a, or 19b, check this box and see instructions ▶ ☐

Schedule A (Form 990 or 990-EZ) 2019

Line 9 carries forward the total support from Line 6.

Lines 10a-c reflect the other income received by the organization. **Line 10a** totals money received for interest, dividends, rents, and royalties that did not further the exempt purpose. (Those amounts are included in Line 2). **Line 10b** is the net of your unrelated business taxable income after taxes paid. **Line 10c** totals lines 10a and b.
Line 11 records any unrelated business activities not included in line 10b.

Line 12 includes all support that isn't included elsewhere in Part III. Any values here must be explained in Part VI as to the nature and source of the amount. Do not include gain or loss from the sale of capitalized assets (buildings, large equipment, etc.)

Line 13 adds lines 10c, 11, and 12 to get *total support.*

Line 14 asks if your organization is in its first five years. If so, check the box, and you have finished this form. If not, leave it blank and continue.

Section C, Line 15 calculates your public support percentage by taking the Public Support amount from Line 8, Column (f) and dividing it by the "Total Support" amount on Line 13, Column (f).

Line 16 asks for the previous year's line 15 (public support percentage).

Section D, Line 17 is the percentage of investment income to total support (Line 10c divided by Line 13, Column (f)).

Line 18 is the previous year's investment income percentage.

Line 19a has a box to check if line 15 (public support percentage) was more than 33 1/3%, and line 17 (investment income percentage) was not more than 33 1/3%. If so, you have met the 33 1/3% test and are considered a publicly supported organization. The form is now complete. If not, go on to line 19b.

Line 19b is to check the percentages from the previous year. If Line 16 (previous public support percentage) was more than 33 1/3% and line 18 (previous investment income percentage) was not more than 33 1/3%, you have met the 33 1/3% test. The form is now complete. If not, go on to line 20.

Line 20 is only checked if you could not check line 14, 19a, or 19b. If you do not qualify as a public charity, you may be considered a private foundation.

If your organization is in its *sixth tax year*, it should compute the public support percentage and the investment income percentage on its Form 990 for its first five tax years. If its public support percentage for those first five years is more than 331/3% and the investment income percentage for those years isn't more than 331/3%, it WILL qualify as a public charity for its sixth tax year. You will need to document that on Part VI.

If that still doesn't allow you to qualify as a public charity, complete Part II of Schedule A to see if you qualify as a publicly supported organization under section 170(b)(1)(A)(vi) which covers churches, schools, hospitals, and governmental units.

If neither of those help, the IRS allows you to qualify as a public charity under the Facts and Circumstances Test.

> *If your organization receives more than 10 percent but less than 33-1/3 percent of its support from the general public or a governmental unit, it can qualify as a public charity if it can establish that, under all the facts and circumstances, it normally receives a substantial part of its support from governmental units or the general public.*
>
> *To establish this support, your organization should describe on Part VI of Schedule A the facts and circumstances which establish that the organization is in the nature of an organization that is publicly supported.*

https://www.irs.gov/charities-non-profits/exempt-organizations-annual-reporting-requirements-form-990-schedules-a-and-b-facts-and-circumstances-public-support-test

If you have determined you will be deemed a private foundation, you will need to file a Form 990-PF and check the *Initial return of a former public charity* box at the top of page 1.

4. Parts IV and V (for Supporting Organizations)

These parts are only completed only for supporting organizations. Per the IRS, "a supporting organization is a charity that carries out its exempt purposes by supporting other exempt organizations, usually other public charities."

Pages 4 and 5 of the 990-EZ lists questions for supporting organizations to answer. Pages 6 and 7 cover the income, assets, and distributions of non-functionally integrated organizations. To keep this book from becoming too complicated, I will not go through all the questions and steps. If you are filing for a supporting organization, go through the list.

5. Part VI (Supplemental Information)

Part VI covers supplemental information. If you filled it out as you went through the form, it should now be complete. If not, read through the instruction at the top of the page and double-check the listed lines. Part VI can be duplicated if you need more space.

Schedule A (Form 990 or 990-EZ) 2019 Page 8

Part VI **Supplemental Information.** Provide the explanations required by Part II, line 10; Part II, line 17a or 17b; Part III, line 12; Part IV, Section A, lines 1, 2, 3b, 3c, 4b, 4c, 5a, 6, 9a, 9b, 9c, 11a, 11b, and 11c; Part IV, Section B, lines 1 and 2; Part IV, Section C, line 1; Part IV, Section D, lines 2 and 3; Part IV, Section E, lines 1c, 2a, 2b, 3a, and 3b; Part V, line 1; Part V, Section B, line 1e; Part V, Section D, lines 5, 6, and 8; and Part V, Section E, lines 2, 5, and 6. Also complete this part for any additional information. (See instructions.)

Remember: everything on Part VI (and this return) will be public information. Do not include names of donors, grantors, or contributors.

F. Schedule B (Schedule of Contributors)

If you had donors who gave over $5000, you need to complete **Schedule B (Schedule of Contributors)**. It is a four-page form. The first page asks for the type of organization and if it is covered by the "general rule" or "special rules."

Schedule B
(Form 990, 990-EZ, or 990-PF)
Department of the Treasury
Internal Revenue Service

Schedule of Contributors

▶ Attach to Form 990, Form 990-EZ, or Form 990-PF.
▶ Go to *www.irs.gov/Form990* for the latest information.

OMB No. 1545-0047

2019

Name of the organization	**Employer identification number**

Organization type (check one):

Filers of:	**Section:**
Form 990 or 990-EZ	☐ 501(c)( ) (enter number) organization
	☐ 4947(a)(1) nonexempt charitable trust **not** treated as a private foundation
	☐ 527 political organization
Form 990-PF	☐ 501(c)(3) exempt private foundation
	☐ 4947(a)(1) nonexempt charitable trust treated as a private foundation
	☐ 501(c)(3) taxable private foundation

Check if your organization is covered by the **General Rule** or a **Special Rule.**

Note: Only a section 501(c)(7), (8), or (10) organization can check boxes for both the General Rule and a Special Rule. See instructions.

General Rule

☐ For an organization filing Form 990, 990-EZ, or 990-PF that received, during the year, contributions totaling $5,000 or more (in money or property) from any one contributor. Complete Parts I and II. See instructions for determining a contributor's total contributions.

Special Rules

☐ For an organization described in section 501(c)(3) filing Form 990 or 990-EZ that met the 33 1/3% support test of the regulations under sections 509(a)(1) and 170(b)(1)(A)(vi), that checked Schedule A (Form 990 or 990-EZ), Part II, line 13, 16a, or 16b, and that received from any one contributor, during the year, total contributions of the greater of **(1)** $5,000; or **(2)** 2% of the amount on (i) Form 990, Part VIII, line 1h; or (ii) Form 990-EZ, line 1. Complete Parts I and II.

☐ For an organization described in section 501(c)(7), (8), or (10) filing Form 990 or 990-EZ that received from any one contributor, during the year, total contributions of more than $1,000 *exclusively* for religious, charitable, scientific, literary, or educational purposes, or for the prevention of cruelty to children or animals. Complete Parts I, II, and III.

☐ For an organization described in section 501(c)(7), (8), or (10) filing Form 990 or 990-EZ that received from any one contributor, during the year, contributions *exclusively* for religious, charitable, etc., purposes, but no such contributions totaled more than $1,000. If this box is checked, enter here the total contributions that were received during the year for an *exclusively* religious, charitable, etc., purpose. Don't complete any of the parts unless the **General Rule** applies to this organization because it received *nonexclusively* religious, charitable, etc., contributions totaling $5,000 or more during the year . . . . ▶ $ ____________

Caution: An organization that isn't covered by the General Rule and/or the Special Rules doesn't file Schedule B (Form 990, 990-EZ, or 990-PF), but it **must** answer "No" on Part IV, line 2, of its Form 990; or check the box on line H of its Form 990-EZ or on its Form 990-PF, Part I, line 2, to certify that it doesn't meet the filing requirements of Schedule B (Form 990, 990-EZ, or 990-PF).

If you need to file this form as a 501(c)(3), you will probably select "General Rule" as it covers an organization that has contributions totaling $5000 or more from any one contributor. Contributions include cash and noncash items but do not include payments for services given.

The Special Rules come into play for 501(c)(3) organizations that had to report Part II (instead of III) of Schedule A and for 501(c)(7), (8), and (10) organizations.

Part I lists contributors on page 2 of the schedule.

Schedule B (Form 990, 990-EZ, or 990-PF) (2019) Page 2

Name of organization	Employer identification number

Part I **Contributors** (see instructions). Use duplicate copies of Part I if additional space is needed.

(a) No.	(b) Name, address, and ZIP + 4	(c) Total contributions	(d) Type of contribution
		$	Person ☐ Payroll ☐ Noncash ☐ (Complete Part II for noncash contributions.)

(a) No.	(b) Name, address, and ZIP + 4	(c) Total contributions	(d) Type of contribution
		$	Person ☐ Payroll ☐ Noncash ☐ (Complete Part II for noncash contributions.)

Column (a) is used to number each donor. This same number will be used for that donor on the following pages.

Column (b) lists the name and addresses, though "N/A" can be used for the addresses if the donor wishes. Only use "anonymous" if the organization does not know the donor.

Column (c) is the total contributions for the tax year, including noncash contributions. It does not include payments for services (e.g., tuition).

Column (d) asks for the type of contribution. Select all that apply. Cash, credit card, and wire transfers are considered "Person." Use "Payroll" for any payroll deductions. "Noncash" is used for securities and in-kind contributions.

Part II covers noncash property on page 3.

Column (a)'s number must tie to the donor number on page 2.

Column (b) is the description of the property donated.

Column (c) is the fair market value (FMV) or best estimate. Even if securities received through a broker or agent are immediately sold, the amount listed should be the net proceeds plus the broker fees and expenses. If the securities are not immediately sold, use the average selling price on the contribution date.

Column (d) is the date the contribution was received.

Schedule B (Form 990, 990-EZ, or 990-PF) (2019) Page 3

Name of organization	Employer identification number

Part II **Noncash Property** (see instructions). Use duplicate copies of Part II if additional space is needed.

(a) No. from Part I	(b) Description of noncash property given	(c) FMV (or estimate) (See instructions.)	(d) Date received
		$	

(a) No. from Part I	(b) Description of noncash property given	(c) FMV (or estimate) (See instructions.)	(d) Date received
		$	

Part III covers "exclusively religious, charitable, etc. contributions" for section 501(c)(7), (8), or (10) organizations.

Column (a) uses the same donor number as in Part I.

Column (b) asks for a brief description of the purpose of the gift.

Column (c) describes how the gift was to be used.

Column (d) asks how the gift is held. Here they want to know if the funds are co-mingled with the general fund or held in a separate account.

Schedule B (Form 990, 990-EZ, or 990-PF) (2019) Page 4

Name of organization	Employer identification number

Part III *Exclusively* **religious, charitable, etc., contributions to organizations described in section 501(c)(7), (8), or (10) that total more than $1,000 for the year from any one contributor.** Complete columns **(a)** through **(e)** and the following line entry. For organizations completing Part III, enter the total of *exclusively* religious, charitable, etc., contributions of **$1,000 or less** for the year. (Enter this information once. See instructions.) ▶ $

Use duplicate copies of Part III if additional space is needed.

(a) No. from Part I	(b) Purpose of gift	(c) Use of gift	(d) Description of how gift is held

(e) Transfer of gift	
Transferee's name, address, and ZIP + 4	Relationship of transferor to transferee

(a) No.

If the organization transferred the gift to another organization, use section 3 to show the transferee's name and address and the relationship between the two organizations.

Several other schedules may be required.

As you well know, U.S. tax regulations are very complex, and there is no way I could cover them in detail, so if there are any areas you are not sure about, please contact a local accountant or lawyer who specializes in not-for-profit work.

G. Summary

Wow, there was so much to cover! In this chapter, you learned:

- What different annual forms are nonprofits required to file,
- How to determine which form your organization needs to file,
- How to file the 990-N (e-Postcard),
- How to complete the 990-EZ,
- How to fill out Schedule A-Public Charity Status and Public Support, and
- How to fill out Schedule B-Schedule of Contributors.

Handling the bookkeeping for a small nonprofit can be challenging. I hope this book has reduced your stress and made your job easier!

For helpful videos and discussions, please check out my blog at AccountantBesideYou.com.

18. Appendix

A. **Month-End Check List**

B. **Simplified UCOA (Unified Chart of Accounts)**

A. Month-End Check List

Non-Profit Month & *Year-End Checklist	
Duties	**Completed**
Enter all bills (remember to check email)	
Move emailed invoices/receipts to appropriate files	
Enter any vendor credits	
Pay all bills	
Enter any manual checks	
Enter/download all online banking payments	
Enter/download all bank drafts	
Enter/download payroll	
Pay any payroll liabilities	
Review expenses for any chargeable to grants	
Enter any invoices required to donors	
Enter all donations	
Download/enter any other receipts	
Count inventory and adjust COGS (if applicable)	
Download/enter credit card charges	
Reconcile credit card bill	
Reconcile bank account to statement	
Charge prepaid expenses	
Review *Receivable Aging* Report	
Review *Payable Aging* Report	
Review *Statement of Financial Position* (Balance Sheet)	
Review *Statement of Activities by Class* (Income Statement)	
Review *Income Statement Comparison to Budget*	
*Allocate fund balances	
*Set year-end closing date	
*Mail 1099s and 1096	
*Mail W-2s and W-3	
*Prepare and file 990N or EZ (if applicable)	
*Prepare and enter next year's budget	

www.accountantbesideyou.com

B. Simplified UCOA (Unified Chart of Accounts)

Account Number	Account Name	Account Type
10000	Cash & Invest	Bank
10100	Checking Account	Bank
10200	Investment Accounts	Bank
10900	Petty Cash	Bank
11000	Accounts Receivable	Accounts Receivable (A/R)
11100	Dues Receivable	Accounts Receivable (A/R)
11200	Pledges Receivable	Accounts Receivable (A/R)
11400	Grants Receivable	Accounts Receivable (A/R)
11500	Other Accounts Receivable	Accounts Receivable (A/R)
11900	Allowance for Doubtful Accounts	Accounts Receivable (A/R)
12000	Undeposited Funds	Other Current Assets
13000	Prepaid Expenses	Other Current Assets
13500	Inventory Held for Sale	Other Current Assets
15000	Furniture and Equipment	Fixed Assets
15100	Buildings - Operating	Fixed Assets
15500	Facility Construction	Fixed Assets
15700	Land – Operating	Fixed Assets
15900	Leasehold Improvements	Fixed Assets
16400	Vehicles	Fixed Assets
17100	Accum Depr - Furn and Equip	Fixed Assets
17200	Accum Depr – Building	Fixed Assets
17300	Accum Depr - Leasehold Imps	Fixed Assets
17400	Accum Depr – Vehicles	Fixed Assets
18000	Other Assets	Other Assets
18700	Security Deposits Asset	Other Assets
18900	Other Asset Suspense	Other Assets
20000	Accounts Payable	Accounts Payable
20200	Grants Payable	Accounts Payable
20300	Credit Card	Credit Card
24000	Payroll Liabilities	Other Current Liabilities
24100	Accrued Leave and Payroll	Other Current Liabilities
24200	Accrued Expenses	Other Current Liabilities
25000	Current Portion of Loans	Other Current Liabilities
25400	Loans from Officers, Directors	Other Current Liabilities
25600	Short-term Notes - Credit Line	Other Current Liabilities
25800	Unearned or Deferred Revenue	Other Current Liabilities
27100	Notes, Mortgages, and Leases	Long Term Liabilities
27200	Other Liabilities	Long Term Liabilities
27300	Refundable Deposits Payable	Long Term Liabilities

Account Number	Account Name	Account Type
30000	Opening Balance Equity	Equity
31300	Perm. Restricted Net Assets	Equity
31500	Temp. Restricted Net Assets	Equity
32000	Unrestricted Net Assets	Equity
43300	Direct Public Grants	Revenue
43310	Corporate and Business Grants	Revenue
43330	Foundation and Trust Grants	Revenue
43340	Nonprofit Organization Grants	Revenue
43400	Direct Public Support	Revenue
43410	Corporate Contributions	Revenue
43430	Donated Prof Fees, Facilities	Revenue
43440	Gifts In-kind - Goods	Revenue
43450	Individ. & Busin. Contributions	Revenue
43460	Legacies and Bequests	Revenue
43480	Volunteer Services - Non-GAAP	Revenue
44400	Government Contracts	Revenue
44500	Government Grants	Revenue
44800	Indirect Public Support	Revenue
44810	Affiliated Org. Contributions	Revenue
44820	United Way, CFC Contributions	Revenue
45000	Investments	Revenue
45020	Dividend, Interest (Securities)	Revenue
45030	Interest-Savings, Short-term CD	Revenue
45050	Other Investment Revenue	Revenue
46400	Other Types of Income	Revenue
46410	Advertising Sales	Revenue
46420	Inventory Sales	Revenue
46430	Miscellaneous Revenue	Revenue
47200	Program Income	Revenue
47220	Member Assessments	Revenue
47230	Membership Dues	Revenue
47240	Program Service Fees	Revenue
47500	Rental Income	Revenue
47700	Rev Released from Restrictions	Revenue
48400	Securities	Revenue
49000	Special Events	Revenue
49010	Special Event #1	Revenue
49011	Special Event #1 Revenue	Revenue
49012	Special Event #1 Retail Value	Revenue
49013	Special Event #1 Cost of Event	Revenue
49020	Special Events # 2	Revenue

Account Number	Account Name	Account Type
49021	Special Event #2 Revenue	Revenue
49022	Special Event # 2 Retail Value	Revenue
50700	Cost of Sales - Inventory Sales	Cost of Goods Sold
60300	Awards and Grants	Expenditures
60900	Business Expenses	Expenditures
60920	Business Registration Fees	Expenditures
60930	Fines, Penalties, Judgments	Expenditures
60940	Taxes - Not UBIT	Expenditures
60950	UBIT	Expenditures
62100	Contract Services	Expenditures
62110	Accounting Fees	Expenditures
62120	Donated Prof Fees – GAAP	Expenditures
62130	Fundraising Fees	Expenditures
62140	Legal Fees	Expenditures
62150	Outside Contract Services	Expenditures
62160	Volunteer Services Non-GAAP	Expenditures
62800	Facilities and Equipment	Expenditures
62810	Depreciation and Amortization	Expenditures
62820	Depr and Amort - Non-allowable	Expenditures
62830	Donated Facilities	Expenditures
62840	Equip Rental and Maintenance	Expenditures
62850	Janitorial Services	Expenditures
62860	Mortgage Interest	Expenditures
62870	Property Insurance	Expenditures
62880	Real Estate, Personal Prop Tax	Expenditures
62890	Rent, Parking, Utilities	Expenditures
65000	Operations	Expenditures
65010	Books, Subscriptions, Reference	Expenditures
65020	Postage, Mailing Service	Expenditures
65030	Printing and Copying	Expenditures
65040	Supplies	Expenditures
65050	Telephone, Telecommunications	Expenditures
65060	Website/Technology Costs	Expenditures
65100	Other Types of Expenses	Expenditures
65110	Advertising Expenses	Expenditures
65120	Insurance - Liability, D and O	Expenditures
65130	Interest Expense – General	Expenditures
65140	List Rental	Expenditures
65150	Memberships and Dues	Expenditures
65160	Other Costs	Expenditures
65170	Staff Development	Expenditures

Account Number	Account Name	Account Type
66000	Payroll Expenses	Expenditures
66100	Salaries & Wages	Expenditures
66300	Medical Benefits	Expenditures
66400	Other Benefits	Expenditures
68300	Travel and Meetings	Expenditures
68310	Conference, Convention, Meeting	Expenditures
80300	Additions to Reserves	Expenditures
70100	Reserve Transfer Deposit	Other Revenue
70400	Other Changes in Net Assets	Other Revenue
70600	Unrealized Gains and Losses	Other Revenue
80000	Ask My Accountant!	Other Expenditure
80100	Capital Purchases	Other Expenditure
80110	Grant Capital Purchase – Land	Other Expenditure
80120	Grant Capital Purchase – Bldg	Other Expenditure
80130	Grant Capital Purchase – Equip	Other Expenditure
80140	Grant Capital Purchase- Vehicle	Other Expenditure
80200	Payments to Affiliates	Other Expenditure
80400	Program Admin Allocations	Other Expenditure

Index

A

accounting controls *See* internal controls
accounting programs, 33, 36
accounting system
  double-entry, 27
  selecting, 33
accounts, 26–28, 34
  accrued liability, 165
  balance sheet asset, 25
  chart of, 25–26, 226
  discretionary benevolence, 80
  in-kind donation, 60
  operating income, 153
accrual basis, 153, 164, 182
acknowledgments, 9, 54, 62, 69, 72, 75, 162
  as an accounting control, 10
  alternative forms, 64
  example, 59
  fraudulent, 72
  required information, 53
  sending, 55
  using form 1098-C, 68–69
advertising, 174
aging report, payable, 165
airplanes, 65, 68
allocation, 84, 89
assets, 21–23, 27, 165
  defined, 23
  list, 165
auction, 62–63, 70
audit
  preparation, 164–66
  record retention, 42–43, 72
  year-end, 163
automobiles, 65, 97, 208

B

balance sheet, 30, 32, 153–54, 204
benefits, intangible, 62
benevolence, for employees, 80
benevolence funds, 77, 79, 81–82
  benevolence policy, 77–78
    example, 82
  discretionary, 80
bills, 13, 16, 90, 92
  approval, 13, 92
  auto drafted, 90
  controls, 13
  electronic, 14, 43
  paying, 12, 84
  scams, 85–86
bingo, 172
board minimum standards, 3
boats, 65, 68
budget, 139
budgeting, monthly, 142

C

capital campaign, 19, 141
cash
  contributions, 52–53, 162
  controls, 5–7
  method, 32, 141, 143, 147
  petty, 14
charitable mileage rate (2020), 97
charity, foreign & tax eligibility, 75
chart of accounts, 25–26, 226
checklist, month-end, 225
contractors, independent, 104
contractors vs employees, 109
contributions, 48, 81
  credit card, 49
  discounts, 75
  earmarked, 74, 77, 81
  in-kind, 221
  non-cash, 56, 177
  recording, 48
  statements, 75
  stock, 55

D

daycare, UBI, 177–78
debits, 27
de minimis value, 69
disclosure statements, 62, 69
discretionary benevolence, 80
donated labor/services, 60
donations, 19, 52–53, 71, 75, 77, 81
  acknowledgement, 52, 53, 162
  budgeting, 139
  discounts, 75
  fees & discounts, 50
  grouping/ stacking, 61
  honorariums, 176
  hurricane relief fund, 74
  labor/services, 60
  local merchants, 64

by mail solicitation, 202
online, 150
pass- thru, 77
recording, 48
required information, 53
donor-restricted fund, 22
double-entry system, 27
dual-use of facilities, 172
dues, 5

E

EFTPS, Electronic Federal Tax Payment System, 105, 128
EIN. *See* employer identification number
employees, 104
key, 206–7
new, 112, 115
Payroll Check, 124
reimbursement, 97
employee's withholding allowance certificate, 113
employer identification number, 104
e-Postcard, *See* Form 990-N
estimate, good faith, 71
exemptions, 105
expenses
accountable, 102
employee's, 101
pass-through, 176
personal, 16, 95, 97
prepaid, 164
unreimbursed, 61, 103

F

facilities
Dual-Use, 172
laundry, 172
fair market value, 64, 71
FASB, Federal Accounting Standards Board, 20
Federal Insurance Contributions Act, 105, 123
FICA. *See* Federal Insurance Contributions Act
financial accounting standards, 20
financial accounting standards board, 20
financial position, statement of, *See* income statement
financial statements for nonprofits, 28
fixed assets, 154
FMV. *See* fair market value
forecasts, 144–47
vs budget, 145
development, 146
forms
941-Employer, 128
990-EZ, 163, 188, 190, 192, 198–99, 215
990-N, 191
990-T, 163, 179
I-9, 112
W-2, 133, 158
W-3, 135
W-4, 113
W-9, 110, 191
fringe benefits, nontaxable, 208
fund accounting, 21,22
fundraisers, 10
auctions, 70
carnival-style, 11
event admissions, 70
Quid Pro Rules, 70
funds, 21
discretionary, 81
general, 21
memorial, 176

G

GAAP Generally Accepted Accounting Principles, 20
gas, mileage rates, 97
general fund, 21
general ledger, 23
gift cards, 16, 152
gifts
acknowledgement, 63
benevolence policy, 77
budgeting for, 142, 145
earmarked, 73, 81
gifts-in-kind, 177
noncash, 56
over $75, 62
service fees, 50
to specific individuals, 73
vehicles, 65, 66
without donor restrictions, 21
giveaways, small, 69

GL. *See* general ledger
grants, 89
  budgeting, 139, 145
  in QuickBooks, 30
gross income, 178
gross pay, def, 104

H
hourly workers, 112
hybrid approach, budgeting, 139

I
imprest fund, 14, 91
improper reimbursement items, 96
income statement, 30, 153
independent contractor, 109
in-kind work, 60
insurance & contracts, 87
interest and dividends, 153
internal controls, 2
  audits, 163
  disbursement procedures, 81
  fundraisers, 10–11
  invoicing, 11, 14
  money received in person, 7
  recording donations, 45-49
  separation of duties, 4
  written policies, 45
investment accounts, 153
  for donations, 55
  reconciliations, 153–54

L
labor
  donated, 52, 60–61
  volunteer workforce, 174
letters
  acknowledgement, 60
  from IRS, 17
liabilities, 21, 23–24
  accrued, 165
  payroll tax, 131, 165
logos
  advertising, 174
  sold merchandise, 176
low-cost items, distributed, 173

M
materials, donated from in kind work, 60
meals
  federal per diem rate, 101–2
  value, 63
medical bill, benevolence paid for an employee, 80
Medicare taxes, 123
meetings
  bylaws, 41
  donations collected during, 6, 46
  monthly board, 149
membership, bylaws, 41
method
  accrual. *See* accrual accounting method
  percentage, 120
  wage bracket, 117–18
  wage rate. *See* percentage
mileage rate
  employee, 99
  volunteer, 100
miscellaneous excluded revenues, 178
missionaries, 74
month-end
  check list, 225
  financial requirements, 149
mortgages, 176

N
naming protocol, chart of accounts, 26
net assets, 21, 153–54
  combined funds, 21
  def, 21, 23–24
  with donor restrictions, 21
  without donor restrictions, 21
net income, 167
net operating losses (NOL), 184
net pay, 125
  def, 104
net payroll check, 137
noncash contributions, 56, 58
  contribution receipt, 61
non-employees, 158–59
non-exempt sources, 163
nonprofit accounting terminology, 20, 32
nonprofit reporting differences, 28

O
officers, 206
ordering IRS forms, 136
other income/loss, 153

outreach program, 19
  restricted donations, 19
overhead, 89, 140

P
PayPal, 8–9
pay period
  def, 105
  determining, 112
payroll, 17, 104
  basic steps, 104
  calculating and filing, 117
  employee's, 137
  methods, 117-120
  tax filings, 128
  terms, 104
payroll tax deposits, 127
per diem rates, federal, 101
permanently restricted net assets, 21
personal commuting, 96
pledges, 26, 142
  uncollectible, 200
the postcard. *See* form, 990-N
percentage method, 137
private foundations, 188
private source, single, 212
profit & loss statement, 30, 155
property
  contributed, 58
  debt-financed, 178
  donated. *See* noncash contributions

Q
qualified sponsorship activities, 173
QuickBooks 30, 36, 88-89, 100, 143, 154-157
quid pro quo
  contributions, 62, 64, 71
  gift, 53
  receipt, 62–63, 71
  rules, 70
  value, 63

R
raffles, 10
receipts, 6, 60, 62–63, 90
  issued, 53
  written, 56
receivables, 26, 156
receiving cash & donations, 5
reconciliations, 151–52
recording credit card donations, 49
recording donors' contributions, 48
recording errors, 10
record retention, 39, 42
reimbursement policies, 93-94
remote imaging device (for checks), 7–8, 47
rent income, 176
request, employee reimbursement, 100
resources, lack of, 78–79
revenue, excluded from UBIT, 178
RID scanner. *See* remote imaging device

S
salaried workers, 112
sales
  of art, 177
  bake, 70
sales tax, 40, 163
scams, 85–86
schedules
  A, 181, 218
  aging, 164
  B Schedule of Contributions, 219
  J, 182
  O, 200, 203
self-employment taxes, 105
selling, donated merchandise, 174
selling products, of exempt functions, 171
services
  determining value, 63
  discounts, 75
  fair market value, 71
  paid, 70
  receipts for, 62
SFAS. *See* Statement of Financial Accounting Standards
signers, 12–15
social security withholding, 105, 123
standard deduction amount, 61
standard mileage rate (2020), 97
state and local identification numbers, 109

state filings, 115, 123, 132
statement of activity, *See* income statement
Statement of Financial Accounting Standards, 20
statement of financial position *See* balance sheet
stock, 52, 55
  Donations, 55
  over $5000, 57
  sale of, 153
subscriptions, 94
substantially related, 170

T

taxable income, 80, 102
taxable wages, 105
taxes, employer, 105
TCJA, Tax Cuts and Jobs Act, 61
temporarily restricted, 21
thrift stores, 174, 177
tickets
  admission, 10, 64
  airline expenses, 102
  banquet, 72
  donor purchases, 72
  food/game, 11
  raffle, 10
timesheets, 17
trade, 168–69, 172–74
  excluded, 175
transactions
  arm's length, 67
  conduit, 73
  pass-through, 73
  recording monetary, 27
transmittal of wage and tax statements, 135
transposition, 152
tuition, as a provided good, 70

U

UBI, unrelated business income, 168-178
  advertising, 174
  daycare, 177–78
  donated merchandise, 177
  educational materials, 177
  excluded trade/business activities, 172
  IRS pub 598, 168
  logos and candy, 176
  mortgages, 176
  parking lots, 177
  pass through, 176
  pet rescue organizations, 169
  rent income, 176
  selling products, 171, 175
UBIT, unrelated business income taxes, 163, 167
  IRS form. *See* form 990-T
  requirements, 175
UCOA, unified chart of accounts, 26
unemployment taxes, 105, 126
unrealized gain/loss, 153
unreimbursed expenses 60, 103
unrestricted net assets, 21
unusual grant, 215
upkeep, reimbursement for, 96

V

value
  gross, 200
  market, 153
  stock's, 55
vehicles, 65–68
volunteers
  conflict of interest policy, 3
  deduction claims, 61
  mileage rate, 97
  professional help, 60
  reimbursement, 103
  volunteer workforce, 174

W

wage and tax statements, 133
wage bracket table, 119
web-based accounting packages, 36
website, charity's, 174
withholding, 17, 105, 117
  payroll tax, 117
withholding-estimator, 115
workers' compensation, 105, 127

Y

year-end
  audit, prep, 163–65
  donations, IRS rules, 48
  donor acknowledgements, 162
  filings, 133
  requirements, 158

Made in United States
Troutdale, OR
11/18/2024

25024089R00137